D1508533

SEARCHING

FOR

THE

CARAVAN

A Reconciliation with Love, Science and Divinity

Germaine Avila

SEARCHING

FOR

THE

CARAVAN

A Reconciliation with Love, Science and Divinity

Parradigm Solutions, LLC
Vienna, Virginia

Published and Manufactured in the United States of America.

Library of Congress Cataloging-in-Publication Data is available from
the publisher.

ISBN-9780-9895630-0-0

Parradigm Solutions, LLC
P.O. Box 405
Dunn Loring, VA 22027-9998

www.searchingforthecaravan.com

First Printing

For My Mother

Acknowledgements

Many thanks to those who blessed me with their compassion and understanding while I found my own.

I am especially appreciative to my parents and brothers and sisters who let me cut my teeth on them before being released into the world. Thank you, Mom, for teaching me "to do the right thing," and for having the strength and courage to be the example of what that means.

Sincerest thanks and blessings to my husband and most influential teacher. There is no one other than you to have captured my interest, imagination, love, and confidence to lead our family on a most unique journey. Thank you for your optimism during those years, and for believing in yourself.

Heartfelt gratitude, admiration and deepest love to my two miracle daughters, my darlings who gave me the privilege of raising them. I have learned much more from you than you have from me. Thank you for your courage, trust and permission to write about the intimate details of your lives. You are so brave.

Thanks to Barbara Dills for her patience and oceans of "Ren" Water to nourish me while I peeled back layers of memory that exposed more detail. Thanks to Robin Dorfman for polishing those details and helping crystallize that extra dimension, and to Rosemary Delderfield for her Divine Light in the process.

Many thanks to my dear friends Linda Vandenberg, Jennifer McCann, Glen Surles and Sally and Leigh Buckner; my niece, Molly Murray; and my wonderful book group friends, Suzanne Zeinfeld, Sonja Killie, Victoria Schaefer, Linda Thorpe, Sara Lauritzen, Sara Ray, Marjorie James and Tamera Wolverton who gave their time, patience, personal skills, professionalism, kindness, sensitivity and consideration in handling the review of my manuscript and for providing their encouragement and suggestions on how to make it better. Thank you for your love and support.

Brittany Miller, your pleasant disposition and patience while helping me create charts, floor plans and pictures made you a pleasure to work with. Thank you.

Thanks to my favorite artist and talented niece, Hope, who gave her creative input for the cover of this book, and to Diane Olson for her professional design, experience and organizational skills to move this work forward to publication.

Finally, deepest and heartfelt thanks and appreciation to Master Joey Yap. It is an honour and privilege to have Master Yap write the Foreword to *Searching for the Caravan*. Thank you, Joey, for sharing your brilliant understanding of Feng Shui, BaZi and I-Ching, the metaphysical tools that helped me to reflect on the questions surrounding my experiences from a deeper perspective. Your knowledge of these ancient concepts, and providing access to them, has helped me to change my life.

Foreword

I still remember hearing about Germaine's autobiographical book and spiritual chronicle, *Searching for the Caravan*, in London.

The subtitle of the book, "A Reconciliation with Love, Science and Divinity", promises a lot. I'm happy to say that achieving such reconciliation is indeed possible as Germaine proves. This is a story of self-discovery, personal growth and understanding, written by a woman who walked many paths in life, embraced both science and God, and fulfilled many roles. Germaine demonstrates her most profound lesson: that science and faith aren't mutually exclusive. Balance is the real truth—a balance which Feng Shui can help restore.

Early on, Germaine recalls the spiritual and emotional low point in her life: a heart attack at age forty-two. This experience led her to seek out Feng Shui, among other things, and begin an ascent towards a state of understanding. I am so glad she embarked on this journey of self-discovery, and that Feng Shui and BaZi helped her to do so.

As a Feng Shui practitioner and consultant, I have long known that the application and study of Feng Shui can bring missing harmony, focus and energy back to life. Germaine shows how she found these things again—once considered lost—during her time as a mother, wife and woman. From the moment Germaine first read a flyer describing the potential of Feng Shui, she felt a magnetic attraction to the subject. This compulsion to study the topic eventually brought her to study with me, where she combined her previous knowledge with my own teachings to great effect. I believe that this book will help encourage others to embark upon a similar journey to hers.

Feng Shui is a vast subject which involves many forms, formulae and theories. It is also extremely flexible and can be applied alongside other systems and Chinese Metaphysical concepts as Germaine explains.

The application of Feng Shui in Germaine's own living spaces gave her newfound strength from the beginning. Improved energy flow allowed her to take everyday life, conflict and negativity in her stride. It gives me great pleasure to hear of the positive impact that Feng Shui has had on the lives of my students, and this book is a particularly compelling case study on its effectiveness.

Searching for the Caravan is a fascinating, entertaining autobiography by a woman who has led an extraordinary life. Stories about the benefits of Feng Shui in practice are extremely powerful. I hope readers take this opportunity to learn from Germaine's experiences and see how Feng Shui can work for them, too.

On a personal level, I'd like to congratulate Germaine on penning this book and wish you, the reader, the best of luck in your own efforts to reconcile *Love, Science and Divinity!* While the book deals with big themes, it does so in a straight forward and entertaining way. Reading about Germaine's gains and losses through life is inspiring. I look forward to reading Germaine's next title as I'm sure you will, too!

Warm regards,

Joey Yap
Founder, Mastery Academy of Chinese Metaphysics

June 2013

Preface

I slipped into bed, careful not to awaken my sleeping husband. Within minutes I fell asleep. At some point I woke up freezing, with much pain and too weak to pull up the blankets. My left arm felt as if a horse had kicked it; the crushing pain and weakness overpowered me. I rolled into my husband for warmth. As I did so, I remember whirling off into the blackness, not knowing the destination. Then, I arrived at this place . . . an awful place.

The depressing, lifeless scenery reminded me of my first glimpse of a Pakistani landscape when we drove from the airport to the hotel: dirt encrusted trees dangled black plastic garbage bags from their leafless branches. Desert sand appeared everywhere in Karachi, creating a beige, muted impression which caused me to squint when I went outside. Here, too, I squinted to adjust my eyes to the dimness. Where was I?

Thick, gooey mud was all around me. Then, just as I thought there was no life, I saw people in the distance. "How strange," I thought, "they're not wearing any clothes." Only their backs, not their faces were visible, but I sensed hopelessness in their bent heads and heavy steps. They all walked in the same direction with no apparent destination. In their slow procession to nowhere, they reminded me of scenes from the Holocaust where Jewish prisoners were marched off to the gas chambers.

Unexpectedly, one of the men in the back row turned his head to the side. It was my husband.

"Mike?" I thought. "What are you doing here? What is this place?"

At that moment I became aware of my "guides," the ones who were giving the tour. Although there was one on each side of me, I was not able to see their faces.

Steering my attention away from Mike and without them

saying a word, the guides directed me to look at the densest part of the spongy quagmire. As one of the guides pointed to the mud pool that lay in front of me, the second stooped to pull off a net that was laden with inches of gooey earth and soaked, decayed leaves. As he threw back the net, a cat sprang from the detritus with the power of a gushing geyser. It was as though the cat had been waiting to be released. I caught only a glimpse of it as I heard its frenetic squeal when it raced past me. I marveled that the cat emerged from the slimy mire perfectly clean. How had it survived? How had the cat remained fresh and alive, untouched by this soulless environment? Somehow the cat was determined to live. It didn't belong there.

The guide on my left interrupted my thoughts as he motioned for me to look inside the hole. Without stepping forward, I stooped over to peer inside. How strange. There lay a once beautiful woman, bloated from having been there for so long. "At least ten years," I thought to myself. "Why hadn't the body decayed?" Then, I noticed that the woman was wearing a one-piece denim jumpsuit that zipped up the front. It looked like the one I had worn while living in Switzerland but had abandoned decades earlier. The woman's hairstyle was similar to my own, too. I paused briefly to assemble my thoughts. The reality became clear to me. "Ohhhhh nooooooo . . ." I groaned.

Sensing the guides could read my thoughts, I squeezed my eyes shut and put my hands over my ears in an attempt to stop them, lest I acknowledge the horrible truth.

"Nooooooooooooo! No mooooooore!" I screamed to myself. The fight within me was useless.

I was in Hell, and the woman was me!

* * *

I came to think of my life as a spiral in the shape of a funnel or ice cream cone, where as a child I was at the broadest, most expansive part of the coil, nurtured by caring parents, wide open spaces, clean air and sunshine, healthy food, wholesomeness and Christian principles that were well-grounded in our homogenous community.

I was raised on a farm in Iowa, surrounded by a stable base from where I could dream and live fearlessly.

In my mid-twenties I drifted from this base and slowly began the spiral downward until I had a near death experience that compelled me to reconcile the issues in my life. After having spent years in laboratories and research institutions, I had followed a path that revered science instead of God and I arrogantly abandoned the spiritual richness I had embraced since childhood. Divine communication that came from my heart was subverted by intellectual information that appeased my ego. Science became my new God. Eventually my search for the elusive caravan led me to the tip of the spiral—the bottommost part of my being.

My life experiences had whittled me down, and now there was nowhere else to go. I had hit rock-bottom—fear, anger, victimization, impotence, i.e. Hell. The healing process could begin only after I had taken responsibility for the choices I had made and let go of the beliefs that kept me a victim. In the same way that it had taken years to reach the bottom of the spiral, it would also take years of persistence and hard work to undo the thoughts and habits that brought me to that point. The climb back is the spiral upward.

I had lived in France and Switzerland as a single, professional woman, and my husband's career led us to Pakistan, the Philippines, Bangladesh, Thailand and Indonesia. Seventeen years of living overseas provided an opportunity to explore a multitude of cultures, religions and other-worldly experiences that would ultimately clarify my own truth.

Ironically, science was an important part of my journey back to grace. I began studying metaphysical sciences while living in Manila and continue my studies today, forever fascinated that the wisdom used to analyze balance and harmony thousands of years ago remains applicable in a modern world.

My experiences—as a single woman and as a wife and mother—were not traditional in any way. They were considered taboo. No clear path to understanding how and why such events could have happened was available. My life—our lives—didn't make sense to me until I reviewed my past from the prism of Feng Shui and BaZi, ancient metaphysical sciences. With these tools I could emotionally distance myself from the experiences, and examine the past pragmatically. Only then was it possible for me to rediscover balance, recreate the spiritual stability and nurturing I assumed as a child, re-define myself and regain control of my life.

When I began writing my story I thought that it was about the connection between all things—especially the connection between science and God—and that balance was the answer to every question that asked "why" or "how". Little did I know that this knowledge was the foundation of this story, and that studying a science that balanced energies was just the beginning.

The real story is about seeking understanding, not answers. My story did not end with discovering a science that explains the nuances of balance, and understanding that balance affects our destiny. The real story was about discovering divinity—Love—in all its representations, and that Love is the connection between science and God.

The path to divinity and the journey getting there is as personal as the nose on our faces. This is my story. It is a true story* about my personal reconciliation with Love, Science, God and returning my life to balance.

* * *

Since this is the story of my life, not another's, I've changed the names of the characters out of consideration for them, their families and their spiritual process.

Part One

LOVE

CHAPTER 1

I removed the pieces of paper from the manila envelope and spread them out in front of me, not sure where to begin. During the past six years I had written down details from events that occurred while living with my husband and children in Pakistan and the Philippines. We had just returned to the States. I didn't want to forget what had happened before I could make sense out of it. The notes I kept helped me to reaffirm that I wasn't crazy. They also helped me to piece the details together so that I could examine them for explanation. There were so many questions. Part of my dilemma was not knowing if I had both a scientific problem and a spiritual one, or if it was possible to correct a spiritual problem with a scientific solution. What was the relationship between science and spirituality?

What I did know was that my children had been victims of a heinous crime and I had almost died of a heart attack at the age of forty-two. The heart attack—which I obviously survived—wasn't nearly as troubling to me as the near death experience that accompanied it. I was deeply disturbed that I visited Hell instead of Heaven; the experience that compelled me to review my life critically. Now that we were back in the familiar, safe surroundings of our country, it was time to begin that process.

I had a background in science and economics and my husband had a background in math, economics and engineering. Certainly I was more open to studying metaphysical sciences than he was. But, I was not so open to them that I would drift from a logical base without logical explanations that would keep me from logical conclusions. I needed to reconcile the connection between science and God. Metaphysical sciences appealed to my scientific orientation and grounded me while looking at events from a different perspective.

After my near death experience I was introduced to Feng Shui. It resonated with me, both before I applied simple Feng Shui steps to improve our living space, and after. Feng Shui is a dynamic science that has been developed from thousands of years of empirical evidence, and contains layers and layers of wisdom. Feelings and observations formed the foundation for the first science. Some of our experiences couldn't be explained logically, but I could not deny my *feelings* about them any longer. What happened was real, whether conventional science could prove it or not, whether society was ready to accept it or not. Feng Shui was exactly the tool I needed to help me understand how and why our lives had gotten so seriously off track, and the tool to change that.

BaZi, another metaphysical science also known as Chinese astrology, is the complement to Feng Shui. Both sciences are based on elemental theory, meaning that the five elements of Fire, Earth, Metal, Water and Wood have a relationship based on whether they are nurturing, controlling, conflicting, destroying, or mitigating to one another.

Feng Shui is the science that communes the polarity (Yin and Yang, or positive and negative) of our DNA with the polarity of our environment. BaZi and Feng Shui are interrelated. Everyone and everything is connected to everyone and everything else. Our relationship with other people and our environment is related to our elemental composition, formulated from the four pillars of our birth date—the year, month, day and hour that we were born.

By the time we arrived home from Manila in 1996, we had already lived in five homes during our ten years of marriage. My home had always been special to me, but now that I understood something about Feng Shui, I saw it as a sacred space. At the time I was a novice at understanding the mechanics of how Feng Shui and BaZi worked together, but I knew that it impacted the happiness and well-being of our lives. This enjoyment had nothing to do with the size or expense of our home. It had to do with elemental relationships.

I examined the scattered notes in front of me for elemental linkages to years, people and events. The connections did not come together when I began with our overseas experiences. I needed to start from the beginning.

* * *

I was born May 30, 1950, around dinnertime. It was *the Year of the Tiger, the Month of the Snake, the day of the Ox and* "the same hour the cows come home," as my mother would blandly recall it. She had eleven children and I was number four, so the details of each birth became less and less memorable over time.

Something about Mom's recollection of events didn't resonate with me. I believed that I was adopted. Actually, the story I imagined from early on was that I was traveling across country when, as an infant, I fell off the back end of the royal caravan wagon, unnoticed by my servants, and was taken in by the family who now claimed me as one of their own. My idea of the caravan was a group of covered wagons headed cross-country, presumably to California. My world-view during early childhood, the fifties, was limited to television shows that were predominantly westerns, depicting exciting tales involving cowboys and Indians. Perhaps it was the prairie landscape that I related to? I can't say for sure, but for some reason this was the tale and the backdrop for imaginative distraction. It was more intriguing to imagine myself as a lost princess finding her way back to the caravan, than living on a farm in Iowa with parents and all those siblings who simply didn't understand me.

There I was on a hundred acre farm, located midway between several small towns that didn't appear on most maps. We claimed Dyersville as our hometown because it was where we attended Catholic Church and school. In this town of four thousand residents, only Doc Theissen, the local veterinarian, considered the smartest guy around, was a self-proclaimed agnostic. Other than Doc, there were only Catholics in the local and neighboring communities, and no other churches existed. Doc did not normally attend church on Sundays. Regardless, his equally brilliant children were raised Catholic and attended Catholic school, and when Doc died, he was given a Catholic burial, which dispelled any notion that he may not have been a believer.

 Dyersville is especially proud of its church which is one of only seventy-one designated basilicas in the United States. The Gothic architecture and towering twin steeples stand as moral beacons to the residents of Dyersville and to the entire surrounding community. Our church, built by German immigrants in 1800, is impressive by anyone's standards. Exquisite stained glass windows, life-size statues, three altars and mosaic tile floors portray an imposing, dignified presence that reflects the proud backbone of our upstanding, close-knit community. My siblings and I, like all the local children, attended the Catholic elementary school and high school, which was run by Franciscan nuns and Jesuit priests. Mom and Dad had little money to spare, but Catholic education was considered a necessity for any respectable Catholic family, not a luxury.

 Our community was homogenous. Most families were not perceived to have more or less or be different. There was an equal playing field where the rules were the same and everyone knew what they were. Honesty, humility, chastity, "Love thy neighbor as thyself," "Honor thy father and thy mother," and so on. We looked to the Catholic Church and the Ten Commandments for guidance in most things, and could count on one another to help us uphold these fundamental principles.

 Mom and Dad barely missed a year without having a new baby. By the time they were finished, we were six girls and five boys. I was preceded by two sisters, Maggie and Sue Ann, and a brother, Dale. After me came Linda, Ted, Lawrence, Thayne, Leona, Fred and Joanne. Sometimes we entertained ourselves to see who could say all the names the fastest: MaggieSueAnnDaleMaryLindaTed-LawrenceThayneLeonaFredJoanne. All thirteen of us shared a three bedroom farmhouse that judiciously allotted just enough space to sleep the girls in one room, the boys in another and my parents in the third.

CHAPTER 2

My mother bore her lot as a farm wife with grace and dignity. She helped my father with barn chores in the morning before making breakfast and getting us off to school, and grew a huge vegetable garden in the summer from which she canned everything she could for winter use. Mom baked all of our bread from scratch, and had fresh, homemade cookies or cake waiting for us when we returned from school each afternoon. For the first twelve to thirteen years of my life, she did the laundry in an old-fashioned wringer washer with only a clothesline for drying. Carefully hung outside to insure freshness, a never-ending cycle of diapers and clothes of all sizes flapped out back in the prairie winds year-round. During the winter months her fingers would be frozen after hanging out a load of laundry, but she was undeterred in her efforts to "do the right thing." She followed the example of her parents by doing her best for her husband and family and contributing her efforts in the best way she could to live wholesomely within a frugal budget. She learned a host of other "right things" growing up on a farm herself, and considered it her responsibility as a good mother to have us learn them, too.

During my entire childhood, I can remember my mother owning only three "Sunday" dresses. They came out of the closet for trips to church and town during those rare periods when she was not draping her figure with loosely-fit maternity clothes. She was always neatly groomed when she went anywhere with my father and took great care to present herself nicely while at home. I enjoyed watching Mom at the dressing table with the big mirror, applying lipstick and combing her hair before my father arrived home in the evening. The table was stained from where I spilled her perfume, but she had covered it neatly with a starched, hand-crocheted doily and her cherished black comb and brush set, accented elegantly with a huge rhinestone. She never used the rhinestone brush set, but used instead the brush with a broken handle so that the black set could be there to look pretty. How my mother managed to juggle all her responsibilities while continuing to look beautiful, maintain a nice home and be pleasant with a baby on one hip and so many kids underfoot is beyond earthly comprehension.

Both Mom and Dad had only eighth-grade educations. Unfortunately, further studies were not an option for them. Once they finished school it was expected that they contribute to the family income, or at a minimum pay for themselves. At an early age my mother worked as a housekeeper and nanny. When she was old enough to be on her own, she moved to Dyersville and stayed in a rooming house while working as a waitress at Link's Café, which is where she met my dad. They used to joke that their date nights included trips to the city dump to shoot rats. This may have been courtship in Iowa farm country in the 1940s, but such stories—funny as they were—only cemented my determination to get out of Dyersville to find the truly romantic world I was confident awaited me.

Mom's natural beauty was mirrored by my father's own good looks. He was also a farm boy. Whereas she had started life in other parts of the Midwest—in Minnesota before moving to Iowa—he was from a well-established and somewhat prominent local farming family. They both came from good German backgrounds and had been raised devout Catholics. Dad's farm heritage stretched back generations to the old country, where there was also a sprinkling of notable priests and nuns among the ancestors, as we were reminded with much pride. Grandpa used to cajole me with his finger pointed at my face, "Yup, Mary's going to be the nun in the family."

"Oh sure, why me?" I grieved to myself sadly. "Why shouldn't Sue Ann or Maggie or Linda have to be the nun?"

True, my first name was Mary, but every girl in my family had Mary tucked someplace into her name as either a first, middle or Confirmation name. So why me?

Farmers, priests and nuns. Nowhere in this bloodline was there any mention of royalty, which only reinforced the caravan tale I believed to be true.

CHAPTER 3

I never got the impression that Dad liked being a farmer.
Fortunately he was able to get a job with the Iowa State Highway
Commission, as the farm was not sufficiently viable to support our
large family. He worked there during most of my childhood and
until his retirement. Dad was home every night, but not until he
had visited his after-work buddies at one of the thirteen taverns
stretched along Main Street. He would get off work at five o'clock,
call the house to see if Mom needed groceries, then go to the bar
before heading home. Normally he ate separately from the rest of
us before falling asleep on the sofa in front of the TV. Many nights,
especially during the snowy winters, he was called at all hours of the
night to put down sand on the icy roads or to plow snow from the
highways.

My father was an intelligent, affable man who was very well
liked by all who knew him. It's hard to say what his possibilities
for success in life could have been at a different time and under
different circumstances. The fact remains that he chose to be a
farmer, a profession that didn't suit him personally. He wanted to
enlist in the Army like his brother, maybe to have an adventure, too,
but was turned down for having flat feet. With no encouragement
from his parents or imagination of his own, he accepted the only
role he knew, which was to follow in his father's footsteps.

Dad found solace in alcohol early on, diminishing any chances
he might have had to advance or do better financially, and certainly
limiting any possibility for my mother or brothers and sisters and
me to have a real relationship with him. We were mostly afraid of
Dad since his assigned household task was to punish us if Mom
couldn't manage it. We rarely interacted individually with him. It
wasn't until my late twenties that I realized I'd never had a personal,
one-on-one conversation with my father. When finally given the
opportunity to do so, I didn't know how.

I'd like to make excuses for Dad's drinking. I think he
started as a young man, like many men in Dyersville. Main Street's

thirteen taverns serviced a town of only four thousand people, a ratio indicating that the community enjoyed its brew. Other than the taverns, there wasn't much for recreation. Certainly there were reasons for Dad to want to escape, just like my mother may have had plenty of reasons to want to escape. The difference is that Mom accepted her responsibility and did not turn to alcohol.

Dad was a Yin Xin Metal Day Master represented as a piece of jewelry. Xin Metal Day Masters like the limelight and enjoy being noticed, but they can't handle pressure. Just like a piece of jewelry, Xin Metal Day Masters cannot be subjected to too much stress. Mom was a Yang Geng Metal. An ax. Geng Metal Day Masters are resolute, determined and fiercely loyal. A refined Geng Metal is more like a sword. Mom was a much stronger Metal than Dad; she was a stronger person.

As a child I never considered the reasons for my father's evenings uptown, nor the burden he must have felt with his enormous brood. I only noticed how it affected our mother, who compensated for all our strengths and weaknesses in one way or another. Besides the stress of raising a very large family, Mom had the additional burden of worrying about our father and his ability to make ends meet. She did her best to stretch the homemade chili with noodles, and skimped and saved wherever it was possible. She occasionally complained to us about him as she lamented her woes out loud, but she never made a public spectacle of her husband's failings. She was the epitome of the good wife, the classic stoic who raised her children and supported her husband with an unwavering strength that came from her Christian upbringing.

Mom never learned to drive. Since we never had more than one car, it was not expected that she would learn how, nor did anyone assume that she *wanted* to learn. She was just there for us, secluded on the farm with her "eleven mouths to feed," as we were referred to, a husband who tested her patience more than her eleven mouths combined, and occasional interactions with neighbors who mostly took her for granted. Always home, she was the logical choice as gratis babysitter when the other mothers planned shopping trips or organized their day care. Even the lifetime service of complimentary fresh milk she provided to two neighboring families went unnoticed without so much as an annual Christmas present. Unheralded though Mom was, she was the genuine altruist, a role model of moral decency to all those who knew her, especially her children. There was never a moment when she sacrificed her standards of "doing the right thing" for personal desires. She was a giver in the true sense of the word, extending her generosity beyond her exceptionally large family to the surrounding community in a steady stream of uncounted ways.

The precariousness of our financial situation coupled with her deep commitment to protect and provide for her children fueled my mother through her daily survival routines. That and her deep devotion to God, Catholicism and goodness, which she struggled mightily to instill in us. I guess it was a combination of fear, faith and selflessness that carried her through the laundry, bread baking, gardening, food preservation and other chores, not to mention the endless scolding and coercing of my siblings and me.

One of my earliest memories of Mom was at breakfast on a freezing winter morning. I must have been about five and in kindergarten. She had just come in from outside after helping my father milk the cows and feed the chickens, and now she was getting us ready for school. There was little heat in our drafty old home, so Mom turned on the gas stove to warm our shoes in the oven before we stepped out into the frozen morning. She thought of caring things like that. She gave us her life's breath: wholehearted and unselfish devotion.

For all her stoicism and goodness she had little patience with ambitions she didn't understand. She knew one kind of life and felt we should be satisfied with what that life had to offer. Mom was particularly hard on me, convinced she needed to keep me in line, lest my expectations got out of hand. She believed that everything had to be earned and that we "know your place," a belief system that manifested in all sorts of strange ways.

Because we were farmers and didn't pay city taxes, she felt that the townspeople wouldn't want us swimming in the community pool, nor would they want us using the public library or any other facilities that were funded with town taxes. Our resource for research papers was a set of encyclopedias that were kept on one of the two shelves of a small bookrack known as the library. On Halloween, she and my dad refused to let us participate in trick-or-treat, reasoning that since the town kids didn't come to the farm, we couldn't go to town.

Because we were farm kids and because we came from such a large family and because, because, because and blah, blah, blah . . . we were not to expect much from life.

CHAPTER 4

Compared to my parents and siblings, I did expect much. My differences with my mother on this fundamental point would be the source of a lifetime of conflict between us, one more trial in her already difficult life. We simply didn't understand one another. Strangely, her protests and spankings did not dishearten me. On the contrary, the harder she tried to redirect my aspirations, the more resolute I became. *I am a Yin Yi Wood, as opposed to a Yang Jia Wood. Yi Wood Day Masters are represented as a vine, flower or a blade of grass. Yi Wood Day Masters are flexible and adaptive. Creeping plants and flowering bushes find a way to reach sunlight. They're survivors. Mom's Geng Metal ax is too big to chop a vine. Even if it did, the vine would just sprout up somewhere else.* I can only imagine how frustrating I must have been to my mother.

Visualizing the caravan provided solace and encouragement. Despite my frustration I always felt blessed. I felt a spiritual connection in a friendly sort of way, praying for everything and speaking to the invisible friends who shared my excitement and beliefs. They weren't imaginary kids like many children invent, but more like a collective angelic presence, a higher, wiser voice that comforted, guided and encouraged me. I trusted these divine beings who were always nearby and ready to help. I felt great love from their energy, and developed confidence from their support.

My relationship with this private, unseen world provided nurturing beyond my family. I spoke to my angels, to God, to Jesus, to anyone up there who would listen, knowing that my prayers were always heard and usually answered. We had a relationship, He and I. It wasn't something I questioned, just something I assumed.

In sixth grade I wanted to be chosen for the lead in the Christmas play. The part required singing six solos, and to my amazement and everyone else's I got it. I had put my whole heart and soul into connecting with my angels, who responded favorably to my requests time and time again, who helped me get what I wanted.

I don't think I developed this spiritual connection or sense of the divine from going to church six days a week. Don't get me wrong, I valued the Catholic Church, at least aspects of it, but as a child the ritualistic tedium was hard to accept. In fact, most days I resented attending those long church services.

Sunday morning Mass in our family was dealt with in shifts in order to accommodate babysitting and driver and car requirements. There was no way we could all be ready on time to attend the same six a.m. service. Mom and Dad always went together early to get the day organized, and more often than not I got assigned the early shift along with them. This meant getting up before dawn in sub-zero temperatures, which did not make Sunday church a happy event for me. The only consolation was that Mom and Dad would stop at the bakery to pick up cinnamon rolls and liverwurst before returning home. My favorite kind was the package with six to eight buns baked together in one tin. These were better than the individual Danish variety because they held more frosting in the crevices where the buns had merged together after baking. Sometimes when I pulled the rolls apart I could claim a little bit more of the gooey sweet stuff next to mine without being noticed by my siblings, and the thick icing that separated the two would magically fall onto my bun.

When I went to church early, I'd get first dibs on the cinnamon rolls. After scouting the one with the thickest layer of icing soaked into the dough, I'd then pile cold creamery butter on top of it and liverwurst on top of the butter. Sometimes I'd add potato chips (another Sunday treat!) for a touch of crunch. This weekly extravaganza provided just enough incentive to keep me satisfied most Sunday mornings, and the anticipation helped me forget how cold the five mile car ride was to town before the heater warmed up.

As I got older, I rebelled against gender distinctions and the tight control I thought they represented, citing the chapel veil as an example and refusing to wear it. During biblical days the act of a woman covering her head with a veil was a sign of modesty or chastity, and women were expected to wear the veil while praying. In modern times the chapel veil replaced the traditional veil as a symbolic gesture of respect while inside of a church. Its use was one of those Catholic prescriptions for women that I didn't understand, and for whatever reason it made me angry. I was too recalcitrant to wear the veil out of respect for an ancient tradition, and came off as a defiant young woman who needed to learn a lesson or two. I was not a bad kid. I wasn't even particularly difficult. I was, however, an independently minded individual who challenged the status quo.

Out of the ten possible elements one can have in their BaZi chart, I have nine. Some analysts would say that so many elements lead to confusion. Sometimes maybe, but I'd say that a chart with many elements adds an extra dimension of curiosity and understanding. I viewed situations from many different perspectives. I assumed nothing, and gave the benefit of the doubt. Very few things were black and white. In defense of my chart, I'd say that I was misunderstood while I analyzed all the possibilities. I was not confused, but needed time to reach my own conclusions.

I didn't question the legitimacy of the Catholic Church as a religious institution, and I generally appreciated the historical framework from which I developed my own spiritual thoughts; it helped me to understand the spiritual relationships that I had developed. But, as a "headstrong young lady" I rejected many of the strident Christian beliefs that did not measure up to the personal relationship I had developed with God while catching lightening bugs or running through corn stalks. At the time, I couldn't understand how daily rituals helped me to understand God better, just like I didn't understand my parents' admonishments to be satisfied with our life in Dyersville, a perspective, I assumed, that had sprung from the rigid Christian principles with which they had grown up. Neither the Church nor my parents' counsel jibed with what my rich inner life was telling me.

CHAPTER 5

Our farm presented a neat, tidy image to the world. The house was painted a pale green that stood out in an area where every other farmhouse was classic Midwestern white. Well-kept outbuildings—a barn, corncrib, hog house and chicken coop—stood like friendly sentinels near the house. The land was flat and mostly treeless, except for my favorite box elder tree that shaded the outdoor pump. The apple orchard and the long windbreak of evergreens behind the house, which my parents had planted when they first moved to the farm, completed the landscape. Some years, in addition to our large garden, we planted an acre of sweet corn in one of the fields. When the stalks grew tall enough, the field, too, became a destination point for exploration.

Summers on the farm were a strange mix of duty and discovery. We were assigned constant chores, but oftentimes we goofed off and didn't finish them. Besides the routine dishwashing that only the girls were expected to do, my main job was to clean the upstairs and the basement on Saturdays with Linda. During the summer we pulled weeds in the garden and clipped the grass along the sidewalk edges. As the fourth child, on most days I was lucky to get outdoor assignments, where I learned how to steal my freedom when I could. Maggie and Sue Ann, being the eldest girls, were usually the ones trapped into helping with the indoor chores.

Since we were rarely allowed to go swimming during our summer school vacation, we made our own fun. There were few organized sports and activities available to Iowa farm kids in the fifties, so we set up our own games, occasionally pulling in neighbor kids when we could. I was always in the middle of things, out there with a baseball bat slugging away, until I became more concerned with painting my fingernails than batting home runs.

In my younger years I trapped gophers and ground squirrels, rode pigs, jumped from trees and, with the help of brother Dale, converted my doll buggy into a go-kart. Ever the opportunist, I once pulled railroad ties out of a pile we'd found on the backside of the farm, made a seesaw out of them, and charged the other kids admission to ride! We were constantly active, making fun with whatever was available.

Linda and I were usually seen together, finding a way to turn our chores into a playful adventure. We cleaned out the abandoned brooder house—the place where baby chicks were hatched and raised—and turned it into a playhouse, a whole new retreat for ourselves that was away from the watchful eye of our mother. Intense summer heat and poor circulation made this a difficult feat. We choked on years' worth of desiccated chicken poop and inches of accumulated dust before we could call it our summer home, an activity that bewildered and exhausted our parents. They couldn't understand how we enjoyed working in chicken filth and summer heat but begrudged cleaning the upstairs bedrooms of our home.

Sometimes we packed a lunch and headed out across the fields with a can of fresh worms and fishing rod in hand, destination Demmer's Creek, a small stream that ran across our neighbors' farm. *My Yi Wood was drawn to whatever water was available. Water nurtures Wood. I thrilled with walking through the cool water, enjoying the minnows swimming around my ankles.* We never caught anything, but the trek and anticipation of *possibly* catching a fish was greater than bringing one home for dinner. I loved these precious summer days and the outdoors, which provided the gentle space needed for an active imagination.

Sometimes during the summer I could sneak away unnoticed. This wasn't possible, however, during the long winters when I strained under the confines of our close living quarters. I resented the prolonged, frigid winters that gobbled up the spring and fall months and encroached on summer's claim to at least three full months of glorious, beaming sunshine.

Indeed, my fantasy life was nurtured by the acres and acres of nature and farm life that surrounded us. Summer mornings beckoned me to the magic of what waited beyond our three-bedroom house. I would often rise before everyone else so I could be free and alone (a stealth feat, given that I shared a room with four sisters and at any time a bed with at least one of them). I'd sneak down to the kitchen, grab a jar of my mom's homemade rhubarb jam from the pantry and slap generous amounts onto fresh homemade bread before taking it outside to inhale. Mmmmm . . . I can still taste it. For some reason, rhubarb jam and bread always tasted different—and better— when early morning air embraced the sweetened rhubarb.

I loved the barn, too. After having my fill of jam I headed out there to jump from the hay bales. During a summer when we were raising pigs, a hog we'd named Pal became my special friend. As soon as he noticed me crossing the cement barnyard floor on my way to play in the barn, he'd lie down and roll over, inviting me to knead his belly. I happily knelt down in front of him, punching and rolling his hairy pink flesh with my small hands like I'd seen my mother do hundreds of times with bread dough. Pal grunted and laughed with satisfaction until he fell asleep and I continued on to the barn loft. In the fall, Pal went to slaughter just like all the other farm animals we had named. Sadly, no matter how many times this happened, it never became easier to let them go.

As soon as the weather turned cold and we were herded back to school, everything changed. I went from being a free spirit whose imagination could roam to the far horizon and beyond, to feeling like a bird with its wings clipped.

Two bedrooms were upstairs—one for the boys, one for the girls—and a third bedroom was located on the main floor. My parents shared this bedroom with the latest newborn who occupied the crib close to their bed. There was one bathroom on each of the three floors and a ground floor utility room that housed my mother's prized, modern washer and dryer that eventually replaced the wringer washer and clothesline. The utility room, located next to my parents' bedroom, also housed the sewing machine and had a closet for storage. An eat-in kitchen and living room completed the picture. The mostly unfinished basement had a shower and third toilet (that no one wanted to use because the cement floor and walls made it too cold), and a storage room with a freezer and shelves for Mom's canned fruits and vegetables.

The girls' bedroom was the larger of the children's rooms and contained two double beds. Our occupancy maxed out at five, three in one double bed and two in the other. By the time my youngest sister, Joanne, was old enough to move out of my parents' room to join us upstairs, Maggie, the eldest, had left home to attend nursing school. The five boys shared a set of bunk beds and one double bed. All this closeness was not such a problem when we were little, but the lack of privacy took a greater toll as we approached our teens. The only place to be alone in the winter was the coveted upstairs bathroom with the perpetually broken door lock. This was my favorite space in the whole house because of the heating vent on the floor. I loved the smallness of the space, the warmth from the vent during the winter and the privacy that only a toilet could offer. Whether the toilet was being used or not we would shout out "bathroom" in response to anxious knocks in order to signal that it was indeed occupied and wouldn't be available anytime soon. Too bad for whoever had to go in a hurry, particularly for the person who got stuck sitting on the cold porcelain of the basement commode.

As early as five I plotted my escape from this family who didn't understand me. My plan was to walk to Dyersville and hop on the Land O' Corn, a train which passed through town a few times a week on its way to Chicago. Somehow I thought I would find my way to the Waldorf Astoria Hotel, sing and dance in the lobby, and be discovered. These plans surfaced more frequently during the long, freezing winters, when I decided quite practically to wait until summer to carry them out. Fortunately, I was happier during the warmer weather and never had to learn the hard way that the Waldorf Astoria was in New York City and not Chicago.

With some frequency, however, I did challenge my mother with very real attempts at running away. I must have been about seven when, feeling sad, misunderstood and unloved, I confronted her in the utility room after a nasty scolding. Through some terrible miscalculation I choked out, "Maybe you should get Maggie's suitcase down for me," indicating my intention to leave and hoping for some comfort.

A small, brown, alligator-embossed, cardboard overnight bag known as "Maggie's suitcase," was stored on the top shelf of the utility closet. Presumably it had been given to her, even though we were all allowed to use it.

"Huh? The brown suitcase?" Mom queried without skipping a beat. "If you want to go, you can just get yourself a brown paper bag!"

I stood there, not knowing what to say next. As Mom walked away, she turned to look back over her shoulder to end this nonsense with a dismissive "harrumph" saying, "Who do you think you are anyway? Maggie's suitcase!"

Naturally, in a family of eleven children, there wasn't nearly enough attention to go around. Not for me, not for my siblings and certainly not for my parents. The attention that I did get individually from both parents was mostly negative, which led me to think that I probably wouldn't be missed if I disappeared anyway. How crazy of me to test this theory.

It was a winter weekend morning. I got up before everyone else and went downstairs to hide behind the large green sofa in the living room. Would anyone notice? I waited, curled up like a fern frond so nobody would see me. My parents came out of their room and as my sisters wandered down the stairs without me, a surprising group hysteria set in. My mother ran around the house franticly shouting, "Where's Mary? Where's Mary?" My brothers and sisters joined in, and before long everyone was scurrying about searching for me.

When the excitement had reached epic proportion and I was delightedly surprised to see that I would be missed after all, I stepped out from behind the sofa, and threw up my arms dramatically with a merry "Here I am!" assuming they'd be happy to see me.

Really, what world was I from and did I not know anything at all about what to expect? All the excitement turned immediately into another seriously miscalculated moment when I received a stinging spanking from my mother whose mood had shifted with lightning speed from worry to fury.

Although my father was mostly absent from our everyday lives, my childhood fancies did not escape him. I'll never forget the day he was driving us to school in our old, white Ford station wagon. I was probably six at the time, so in the car there would have been my three older siblings, Linda (who was in kindergarten), me, and the six Kramer kids who rode to school with us. Eleven kids and Dad in one car. Since I was one of the smallest, I was able to stand up without hitting my head on the ceiling of the car. I tried to position myself behind my father to smell him, taking in his scent of bleach mixed with daily grind, wanting to be as close to him as I possibly could. I hung on to the seat behind his shoulders, listening intently to the rapid conversation. Donald, the oldest Kramer boy, was talking about an actor he had seen on TV the night before claiming to be a millionaire. Donnie was impressed and didn't believe that anyone could have such a large amount of money. Without hesitation I confidently interjected, "So what, we're millionaires too!"

Letting up on the gas, my dad threw back his big, prematurely white head and looked at me eyeball-to-eyeball exclaiming, "Judsas Proost!!!! Don't you ever repeat that. People will think you're crazy!"

Judsas Proost, his rendition of Judas Priest, was one of Dad's favorite expressions reserved for the outrageous. Even my father, who thought he'd heard it all, couldn't believe his ears.

Until that moment I thought that we were millionaires. Mom and Dad may have doled out their form of disciplinary action and had a limited vision for us, but we always had food in our stomachs, a warm home and clean school uniforms. We were well cared for despite financial and personal circumstances. In the eyes of a little girl, this care had translated into millions of dollars.

CHAPTER 6

Mom and Dad weren't the only ones who questioned my defiant attitude and, to them, farfetched notions. Maggie, Sue Ann and Dale, the three older siblings, and Linda, who was thirteen months younger than I, also found me baffling and annoying much of the time.

Maggie was pretty, smart and the high school homecoming queen. She had plans for gaiety and fun just like me, but she never felt for an instant that we were sisters from the caravan. She accepted that she was a farmer's daughter who wasn't allowed to swim in the city pool. She lacked self-confidence, even though she was a gifted student and very popular. Maggie claimed life was more difficult for her because, as the eldest, she had to fight for all the rights and privileges of adolescence that we took for granted. She may have had grounds to complain since her summers were not spent in the barn, cornfields and apple orchard like mine. She was seldom allowed to play and spent many summer hours listening to the radio in a hot room with her face in front of a fan, stooping over the ironing for thirteen people. For at least one month each summer until my grandfather passed away, she was sent to help my maternal grandparents on their farm a distant hour away. For some reason Maggie continued these expeditions even after Grandpa died, expected to give up one of her precious summer months to spend on an isolated farm with our Grandma and Uncle Tony. Uncle Tony was my Godfather and Mom's only brother, who remained at home to work the farm and take care of Grandma until she died.

The summer I turned twelve, my parents sent me off with Maggie, but after two weeks I'd had enough. Grandma was plagued by a chronic lung infection that caused incessant hacking and spitting. This infirmity, along with the isolated location of their farm, was more than I could bear. I called home and demanded that someone come to get us. Maggie—who had endured the loneliness at my grandparents' farm in silence for all those years—was stunned that her little sister would assert herself so forcefully . . . *and* get her way. *Maggie was a Yang Jia Wood. A giant oak tree. Jia Wood Day Masters are nurtured by Water, but Maggie lacked Water in her chart. Not a drop. It would have been difficult for her to stand up for herself without Water for support.*

Sue Ann, the second in line after Maggie, was different. Sue Ann had a beautiful figure and gorgeous face but hid herself under a hairstyle that didn't quite work for her. She was a bit of a mama's baby, perceived to be "fragile" since childhood because of an asthmatic condition. Sue Ann rarely showed any interest in our outside activities and spent most of her time baking. She had no interest in baseball, gophers or riding pigs. Consequently, we had a hard time relating to one another. We were at constant odds with one another for a multitude of reasons, but usually because she tattled on me whenever she could. I resented being caught during those stolen moments when I wasn't doing my chores, or for eating the caramel swirl from the ice cream or picking the chocolate chips from the cookies.

Dale, the eldest boy and child number three, was my buddy. He assumed my adoration, but didn't reciprocate it. Little did he know that I set my standards for ruggedness against his, competing to be tougher, braver and stronger. I could jump further, climb trees higher, and run across cornstalk stumps with my shoes off. I was so much into my own world that I didn't realize what a pain I was, proving only to myself that I was better at being a boy than he was. *Yi Wood people appear to be competitive and have a tendency towards one-upmanship. However, Yi Wood people are not as competitive as much as they are insecure. Consequently, they outdo themselves looking for approval.* My siblings certainly resented this competitive behavior. I insensitively assumed we were all having fun, especially when I was winning.

Linda and I were very close as children. On the Saturday mornings when we were supposed to be cleaning the upstairs, we shared secrets, compared breast development, and imagined what it would be like to wear lipstick when we grew up. She was a grumpy child who was always crying about one thing or another. To her death she believed that her disposition resulted from the times I stole her full baby bottle from her crib and replaced it with my empty one. Forty years later, she still got upset with the laughter that ensued when my parents retold that story.

Linda was an empath who felt everyone's pain as well as her own. *She was a Yin Ding Fire. A candle, who had a tendency to put others' needs before her own, and burned herself out in the process. Ding Fire Day Masters need constant nurturing in order to keep the flame alive and to be noticed.* Sadly, there was little to no patience available for understanding her tears. She was a giver whose feelings were easily hurt, especially when her generosity went unnoticed.

CHAPTER 7

I tried to explain to Linda my inner yearnings to break away from Dyersville, eager to convince her of all the reasons a college degree was valuable and important to me. I believed whole-heartedly that higher education was a personal enrichment that no one could take away and that a degree would propel us into a different station in life.

In the end, I realized that a college degree was my dream. It was something I needed to feel better about myself, and assumed she did too. No doubt I also wanted to prove something to my parents. I needed to experience a new environment away from them. Somewhere inside of me I believed that the sort of man I'd want to marry would only be interested in a girl with a college degree. It was a mixed bag of reasons for pursuing dreams that seemed so far out of reach. I attributed the unidentifiable feelings of inferiority that I had accumulated along the way to education. Perhaps I wished that my parents had finished high school, or had a college degree, attaching my personal insecurities to them. However it happened, I came to revere academic credentials, and firmly believed that an education was key to paving my future.

I needed to end our inherited belief system that portrayed desire and ambition as character flaws, a vain display of self-aggrandizement. "Humility is a virtue," we were constantly reminded, and setting oneself apart was not humble. Linda didn't see how an education would make me a better person or provide a happier life, and therefore she didn't aspire to go to college, despite my persuasion. Nonetheless, she did the best she could to accept my perspective and support my dream.

Three years after Linda's birth, three boys were born a year apart from one another and were referred to as "the little boys." Then there was another three-year gap before three more children were born. The last threesome was referred to as "the little darlings." Sometimes it was easier to discuss family tales by referring to the "set" or "family" of children we were born into. Since I was one of the "big kids," neither "the little boys" nor "the little darlings" were part of my childhood schemes and they had completely different childhood experiences from mine. Many lessons were learned and behaviors modified by the time the little boys and little darlings graduated from high school, including the value of a higher education, which they all pursued.

CHAPTER 8

My imaginary friends were a relentless, reassuring source of encouragement. "Indeed," they insisted, "you are destined for college." They provided the continuous reinforcement I needed to organize my next steps. To that end, I threw myself into all sorts of activities and enjoyed the benefits of being popular. When I told my mother that I had been nominated for homecoming queen, which I hoped would be good news, she said, "Oh, God no! I guess that means we have to buy you a new dress." Of course her reaction was disheartening, but intuitively I understood that financial worries blocked any pride she might have shown me otherwise. I had come to expect and accept those reactions.

College was beyond my parents' realm of possibility for us. They told me on many occasions, "It's a waste of time since you don't even know what you want to study."

Their opposition was more about managing financial expectations than it was about not wanting us to further ourselves. There was no way they could have afforded any amount of college tuition for any of us. I never expected their financial support, but only hoped for their blessing. When it was obvious that would not be forthcoming, I tucked my dreams into the fertile loam of my imagination until it was safe for them to be realized.

What did please my parents was my landing a summer job at the local toy factory. Initially, I worked side by side with the mentally disabled female adults who were hired through social services. Our job was to remove the raw metal riding tractors from the hangers before they were placed on the conveyor belt for painting. The tractors were too big and cumbersome for any of us to lift; the job was better suited for a strong man who was properly protected against the raw metal. I truly resented the assignment for myself as well as for the other women, and felt disrespected and underestimated mentally, physically and emotionally. To our employers we were bodies, paid the bare minimum to get the job done. To myself, however, I believed that I could and would do better, and mentioned to the foreman that the job was best suited for a man. We were all assigned to something different almost immediately. As a result, I ended up as one of the decal girls, a coveted assembly-line position. It was my job to decal the toy tractor with its respective brand name as it came down the conveyor belt.

My parents were comfortable with my position at the toy factory. They thought I should do this until I turned twenty-one when I would miraculously know what I wanted to be when I grew up. Only then should I leave home to pursue college, a notion that they expected me to abandon long before that magic age ever arrived. "For now," they advised, "be satisfied to work on the assembly-line where you could be elevated to something superior. If you're lucky," they reassured me, "maybe you'll get promoted to an office job."

Maggie, my oldest sister, did break away from home after high school. She won a scholarship to a Franciscan nursing school in Dubuque, a city of sixty thousand people located about thirty miles away. There was no argument from my parents that she should attend: her tuition and expenses were covered, nursing was a respectable occupation, the school was run by nuns and located close to home, and there was a ten o'clock curfew in the evenings. Although I cheered her accomplishment, it wasn't at all what I dreamt of for myself. After graduation, she and a nursing school friend found jobs in Peoria, Illinois, where Maggie met her husband and married at twenty-three.

Sue Ann was less academically interested and didn't start thinking about her future until her senior year of high school. Although she was pretty and bright with every attribute needed to do whatever she wanted, I don't think she really wanted to leave Dyersville. *Sue Ann was a Yin Ji Earth. A paddy field. Ji Earth Day Masters are resourceful, productive and extremely capable, the most talented of all the elements. Ji Earth is a combination of Earth, Metal, Water and Wood. Ji Earth doesn't "need" the other elements, but it does enjoy Fire, sunshine, to remove the chill in the early morning. Fire is also the nurturing element for Earth. Although Earth may not "need" Fire, it was necessary for Sue Ann to have some Fire to dry up the overabundance of Water she has in her chart. Too much Water floods the otherwise rich paddy field.* It came as no surprise to me that our parents convinced her to stay at home and work at a local bank rather than attend an airline stewardess school that she had expressed interest in pursuing.

Dale had planned to attend a technical school in Chicago after high school graduation, but in 1967 boys his age were being drafted for the Vietnam War. A recruiter called our house, asking him to enlist, a move that was promised to guarantee an early out after two years. My parents encouraged him to take this offer, believing it somehow was safer to enlist than to be drafted. Dale joined the army, relinquishing his deposit at the trade school he had planned to attend in Chicago, and went off to Vietnam for two years. Technical school never happened. Instead, he returned to Dyersville after Vietnam, where he happily started work at the rock quarry.

I was heartbroken at the limits my older siblings accepted, and suffered the frustration for all of us by mistakenly assuming they wanted to escape as badly as I did. I resented my parents' anxieties that I felt held us back. Dreams that I had for myself didn't align with their fears of the unknown and our potential failures. They fretted about their inability to help us if we needed it. I mistook their concerns for not caring, but I recognize now that they were just being practical. If we ventured far away and got into trouble, there were no resources to come to our rescue; there was no possibility of help physically or financially. So, we were expected to stay in Dyersville and be safe and satisfied. Any mention of wanting a life beyond their comfort boundaries branded us as "too good" or "better than everyone else," labels intended to guilt us into falling in line.

When it was my time to graduate I kept my plans hidden. I focused on school and read books on travel and potential careers.

My longtime childhood girlfriends, Rose Mary (aka Rosie), Mary Pat and Mary Jill (aka Jill), were my co-conspirators during high school. Mary Pat and Mary Jill worked with me at the toy factory after graduation where I hatched the first step to our futures. I could never be satisfied to stay in Dyersville until I was twenty-one. Even now I get claustrophobic anxiety by recalling thoughts of dying from sheer boredom before getting my chance to experience the world that had my name on it. I had to leave and at least take that single first step towards getting a college degree and liberation. I convinced Mary Pat and Mary Jill to take off for Iowa City with me in order to look for jobs and housing. Without telling anyone, we skipped work and drove the seventy-five miles in Mary Pat's old Oldsmobile. It was a great old cruiser her parents had given her, which we eventually all shared. Influenced by the times, we decorated it with big, cheerful, vinyl flower stickers.

For three small town girls who had never lived anywhere except the town where we grew up, seventy-five miles was a lifetime away. We were undaunted in our determination to explore life beyond the confines of a small town, and threw ourselves into finding work. I took a job as a bill collector and Mary Pat and Mary Jill landed work as keypunch operators. We were to start work in a few weeks.

Rose Mary relinquished her intent to escape Dyersville with us when she took a job as a cashier at a local grocery store while waiting for her sweetheart to return from Viet Nam.

I worked my weekly shift at the toy factory until our agreed upon departure date. As a treat to ourselves, Mary Pat, Mary Jill and I decided to spend our last weekend at a lake beach before saying good-bye to Dyersville. It's painful for me to recall the day I dramatically left my parent's home. As usual, Mary Pat and Mary Jill drove me home from the beach when I asked them to wait for me in the car while I went inside to collect the things I had packed. Without notice, I announced to my mother that I was leaving. I chose a moment when my father was at work, fearing he would stop me. My mother and siblings were crying, especially my little sister Joanne, who was about five years old and couldn't understand what all the commotion was about. She didn't know what "leaving" meant. Would she never see me again? Was our mother crying because she was sad, angry or afraid? Even I couldn't tell, but I didn't stay long enough to find out.

I had already packed my thirty five dollars—money saved from the toy factory job—and my working wardrobe in a brown paper bag as my mother had suggested many years before: two culotte skirts with matching jackets and a culotte jumper that were sewn for me by Linda and two friends of mine in their home economics classes. There were three shirts from K-Mart to go with the culotte outfits, a pair of shoes, and a yellow, two-piece nightie from my godmother, Aunt Germaine. She had given the grown-up nightie to me as a gift for my First Holy Communion when I was about ten, and I had decided to save for a special occasion. This was that special occasion. There was also a house robe with a missing button that I had sewn for 4-H club. I had received an honorable mention ribbon at the Dubuque County Fair for the stitching on this robe, but I hadn't really earned it. Mom was afraid that I'd break her sewing machine, so Maggie did most of the sewing for me.

"I left my address in Iowa City on the kitchen counter, in case you need me for anything," I said to my tearful mother with a tinge of scorn as I headed out the door. It's only now, as a mother myself, that I can appreciate the pain I must have caused her. My intent was only to be determined. I didn't want to hurt her, but I didn't want to be held back either. I was suffocating and couldn't see any other way out. "They'll regret it one day," I told myself. "I'm going to make something of myself and become someone great. They'll regret that they think so little of me."

I felt like Jimmy Stewart in *It's a Wonderful Life*, whose character, George, was going to "shake the dirt from this dusty little town from my feet and never come back."

CHAPTER 9

Mary Pat, Mary Jill and I embarked on our new adventure together, landing housing in a two-bedroom apartment in Iowa City. They had both been much wilder in high school than I, so, unlike my mom and dad, their parents were relieved that their daughters had found some direction. They were happy, too, that their daughters were moving on with their more serious friend-me-at their side.

It didn't take long to unpack our few things in our furnished apartment. Mary Pat took the single bedroom and Mary Jill and I shared the double room. While unpacking my paper bag, I took out the homemade clothes one by one to hang them up, and noticed that my house robe with the missing button had been repaired. My mother must have replaced the button while I was away for the weekend, and I didn't even thank her. She had seen my bag and expected that I would be leaving. Regretfully, we had no way to understand one another and no skills that could have helped us make this transition a positive one.

During our time in Iowa City, I was the only one who did not get a turn with the single bedroom. Surprisingly, I was somewhat timid when it came to asserting my desires beyond my family—even with my best friends—so I acquiesced and let Mary Pat and Mary Jill take turns with the single room. Mom was adamant when it came to her lesson on "being nice," which meant that we should usually be the ones to give in. Compared to Mary Pat and Mary Jill, I had little experience in protecting these kinds of personal interests. I was the sheltered one among us, and the least assertive of our group. They had been allowed to travel to Minnesota for the Beatles concert. They had been cheerleaders and traveled with the team. They smoked and partied, had cars, and overpowered their parents. I was nice Mary, the one expected to give in, the good girl who did the right thing like I had been taught. *Yi Wood enjoys being liked and is naturally nice, a characteristic that complemented the way I had been raised.* It was easy to rationalize giving up the private bedroom since I'd never had a room of my own, and I convinced myself that I didn't really care enough to make a fuss.

The "good girl" lessons left an indelible and confusing message that would trail me for the rest of my life. What did it mean? Accept the status quo? Give up? Give in? Is being liked better or more important than being respected?

Since my mission in Iowa City was to save money for college, I took on extra part-time work in addition to my day job at the credit agency. I was a waitress in a pizza place in the evening, a sales clerk at Sears on the weekend, and I babysat and cleaned apartments in scant free time.

Besides free pizza at my night job, I mostly survived on eggs and Velveeta cheese. Every possible penny was saved with an eye on my goal, which was college.

I stayed busy with work in part to avoid the various social scenes that dominated a sixties' college town like Iowa City, home to the University of Iowa. The few times I tried to hang out in a bar to meet people, I felt like a lamb to slaughter, and got no pleasure out of pretending to enjoy myself in places filled with students who were on drugs. I had no experience, life skills or other defenses in places like that where I struggled to fit in. I also didn't smoke dope or think it was okay, which further limited my social options. If this was recreation, then I preferred to work. At least then I felt like I was doing something constructive.

Politically, I was completely naïve as well. In those days, there was a lot of activity out on the streets, most of which I didn't understand. I walked past war protesters thinking they were just lazy rich kids with too much time on their hands.

"If they only knew how lucky they were to be in school," I couldn't help thinking. "Did they really understand the political positions they supported?"

I would have given anything to be in college, and assumed their demonstrations were just another recreational waste of time since many of the students were stoned.

I did make friends with the two guys who lived across the hall from us. They were unthreatening, straight-laced Republicans who referred to us as "the three Mary's." One of them, Terry Branstad, went on to become Iowa's longest-serving governor from 1983-1999. At this writing he is back at the helm, having been re-elected in November of 2010. Terry and his roommate invited me to go with them to a regional Republican Party convention in Minnesota. I didn't understand politics, let alone support one party over another, but the trip offered a chance to get further from Iowa than I'd ever been, so I gladly accepted. On the drive there I saw my first automated tollbooth. The first time Terry tossed the coins in and a sign flashed "Thank You" while the gate magically went up topped everything for me.

My dream of a higher education grew stronger in Iowa City. After one year of independence I had managed to save five hundred dollars in cash for tuition while all of my Sears pay went directly into a new college wardrobe. With my savings and a new suitcase filled to the brim with outfits befitting my new image, I set off with Mary Pat for Ellsworth College in Iowa Falls—located about an hour and a half from Dyersville—to begin a two-year program. Ellsworth College was affordable, close enough to home without being too close, and I knew the college would accept me. By that time our "Mary" threesome ended when Mary Jill headed off in her own direction without us.

It was August of 1969. The war in Vietnam was raging and U.S. astronauts had landed on the moon. I was taking my next big step, too.

CHAPTER 10

Mary Pat and I found a rooming house near the Ellsworth campus. We occupied the bedroom of an in-law suite that we also shared with two other girls. Eager to get started with my studies, I carried twenty-one credit hours per semester, and worked two part-time jobs. One job was as a secretary in the administration office, and the other was as a waitress in a local cafe. I welcomed the hard work, anything that would allow me to stay in college. Somehow I managed to have an active social life while keeping up with my studies. I dated different guys but didn't allow myself to get overly involved for fear that expectations would develop where I would disappoint sexually. My parents had drilled into me back in high school that we shouldn't give anyone anything to gossip about. Somewhere inside of me I agreed with that advice.

Once again I was fortunate to be nominated for homecoming queen, endorsed by the football team, sophomore class, Spanish Club and a list of other groups. This time I didn't tell my mother. When I won, Mary Pat called home to share the news with her mother, who in turn called my Mom and invited her to drive to Iowa Falls for the homecoming festivities, which they did. I was touched by this effort on my mother's part, aware that she still had six young children to care for at home. I believe she was genuinely happy for me, but

I didn't quite know how to receive the gesture. By that point I had stopped counting on any sort of emotional support or encouragement.

My two whirlwind years at Ellsworth ended before I had made any further plans. Still unqualified to do anything in particular, and with only an associate's degree, I was unsure what to do next. Panic set in. I couldn't return to Dyersville. Suffocation from boredom and limited dreams would end my life, but staying in Iowa Falls was out of the question too. I needed to move forward, but where should I go?

I had only four dollars and change left when the school year ended. Feeling quite lost and in need of a miracle, I prayed to my ever-present angels and friends for guidance about what to do next. The help I was looking for showed up almost immediately. Walking across campus, I bumped into three football player friends who were driving home to Peoria, Illinois, where my oldest sister Maggie now lived with her husband and their baby. When my friends heard that I was thinking of visiting family in Peoria, they offered to give me a lift.

I called Maggie to explain my situation and asked how she felt about my staying with her and her family for a while. Of course she graciously extended an invitation. I packed my clothes, plus the books, pictures, and mementos I had acquired at Ellsworth, into cardboard boxes, which my husky friends squeezed into their car. Off to Peoria we went, waving a firm and, I hoped, final goodbye to Iowa.

CHAPTER 11

Maggie and her husband, Jeff, lived in a charming, manicured, suburban neighborhood, upscale for the times. A large yard that included big trees and a running stream perfected the cozy image. In retrospect, I'm sure Maggie and Jeff were taken aback by my ragtag arrival with all the junk I had collected over the past few years, accompanied by my three friends who I introduced as Bruce, David and Big Dog. My black friends undoubtedly felt out of place in this lily-white neighborhood, too. Being basically colorblind myself when it came to race, I hadn't considered that my companions could be uncomfortable with my sister and brother-in-law in the same way that Jeff and Maggie could be uncomfortable with them. Jeff was probably wondering who these guys were to me—was one my boyfriend? Would they be coming back again to see me while I was staying with them? Such questions were left hanging in the hot, humid Illinois air as we said our goodbyes and I watched them drive off to their homes across town.

Growing up, Dyersville had been as racially monotone as it was Catholic, so my exposure to anyone of color was limited until I left for Iowa City. As I ventured out from Dyersville into the wider world on my own, a black person to me was no more or less to be avoided than a non-Catholic. There *was* one black family in Dubuque. The boy was an excellent athlete who attended a Catholic school, so sometimes our Dyersville teams had played against him over the years. Everyone seemed to admire him for his abilities on the field and court, and personally too, diminishing any notion that he could be viewed differently.

My other introduction to racial diversity had been through 4-H, a popular Midwestern youth organization. The four "H"s stand for head, heart, hands and health. 4-H is a leadership development organization, but I joined because meetings were held once a month in someone else's home. It was interesting to see how other people lived, and what their houses looked like, and at the end of every meeting homemade cake and ice cream were served. During one of our meetings our 4-H leaders brought in two young African women they had recruited through a Christian church group in order to teach us about other cultures. The girls spoke no English, wore traditional African dresses and demonstrated for us how they put their yards and yards of skirt on and off. Then they performed tribal dances for us. When they finished, the 4-H leaders instructed us to touch their skin so we could feel that there was no difference between them and ourselves. I couldn't help but wonder what went through the African women's minds as we circled curiously around them. The intention of our 4-H leaders was sincere, no doubt, but I couldn't help but wonder what went through *their* minds as well and how they could have underestimated us to that extent?

After my things were unloaded, Maggie and Jeff welcomed me generously into their home, and provided me with my very first room to myself. Their lovely home on that quiet street would be the launching pad for my next great adventure.

CHAPTER 12

Jeff's father owned several companies in Peoria, one of which was a discount department store where I got a job selling jewelry. Although I was happy to have work, I couldn't help dwelling on what my next steps would be. My two-year associate's degree provided only an academic foundation, without a particular skill. If I were to move forward as I was determined to do, I needed a four-year college degree, but a degree in what? Where? How would I finance my education? I had no answers for myself and no one to ask for advice. Once again I turned to God for help, and prayed for a miracle without knowing what to ask for specifically. I just wanted the heavens to open and provide me with a solution.

The following week Maggie and Jeff introduced me to their neighbor, Dr. Algeron, a pathologist at the local hospital. Dr. Algeron was curious about me, and why I was living with my sister and brother-in-law. What had I studied? What were my plans? He sensed my determination to complete a college education, and he respected the simple, yet difficult steps I had taken to come this far.

"If you could be anything in the world, what would it be?" he asked.

I didn't know exactly. I knew that I *didn't* want to work in a toy factory for the rest of my life, nor behind a counter making minimum wage, but I still didn't know what I *did* want to be. I also knew that I didn't want to live on a secluded farm, but hadn't ventured far enough yet to know where I wanted to land. Whatever, wherever it was, I wanted to be proud of my profession. I also wanted a career that would enable me to travel the world while being needed, valued, and paid a respectable salary.

I hesitantly expressed all of this to Dr. Algeron over the course of a few casual visits, not knowing if he believed my aspirations were reasonable. If I were to be perceived as a silly dreamer, I'd rather keep my thoughts to myself. "Hmmm . . .," he said to me, pondering my interest in something he had obviously given considerable thought. "Have you heard of cytology?"

I didn't catch everything Dr. Algeron said about cytology—he used big words and talked fast—but I was able to boil it down to something about the study of cells. What I did hear most clearly was that his hospital would sponsor two individuals to study at the University of Chicago; tuition and expenses would be covered by the American Cancer Society.

It didn't matter to me that I had never heard of cytology, I trusted my divine insights that led to this magnificent gift. This was it! I knew it with every heartbeat that pulsed through my body. This was *THE* miracle I had been praying for, the scope of which felt huge, even for a lost princess from the caravan.

As I stood in the yard with Dr. Algeron under that maple tree trying to play it cool by disguising my excitement, I heard the negative, insidious voices that trailed my childhood. *You can't swim at the pool. The city people don't want you.* With steeled determination I fought back those nagging taunts as if they were an army of vicious destroyers. One by one I slaughtered the attackers. Fearlessly I beat them into withered, impotent submission. The battle won, I asked Dr. Algeron how to proceed.

After examining my college transcripts, he determined that I needed another science credit to meet the requirements for the university's cytology program. He asked me to sign up for a science course at the local college as soon as possible. The University of Chicago Cytology classes began in January. The deadline for the scholarship application loomed in front of me, so I had to act quickly.

Within a few months I had completed a zoology course,

had my transcripts sent to the university along with letters of recommendation from my favorite Ellsworth teachers, and submitted a personal reference letter from Dr. Algeron, who was my most avid supporter.

Waiting for a response was agony. The University of Chicago accepted only six to eight applicants into the program per year; the slots were highly competitive. Dr. Algeron had done everything he could on my behalf, knowing that I would be competing against graduate students and medical interns and recognized that my application could be considered weak by comparison. We could only wait and see.

My acceptance into the program would require the biggest miracle of my life so far. During the long weeks after I submitted my application, I begged God and my divine helpers to give me this chance. With every ounce of energy I had in my body, I implored their assistance to come to my aid.

The days of waiting seemed endless, but every day I prayed again, determined not to give up; not to stop believing. Finally, on a crisp, late fall day as I stood alone in the silence of Maggie and Jeff's living room, there it was . . . a letter addressed to me from the University of Chicago Lying-in Hospital. I started crying from tension and anticipation, pleading one last time before opening the envelope, "Please, Lord. Please bless me. Please, please, please let this be an acceptance letter."

Hands shaking, I fumbled with the envelope while tearing it open and slipping out its contents.

"Dear Miss Piers," it began. "You have been accepted . . ."

"Thank you, God! Thank You! A thousand times thank you!!"

Overwhelmed with gratitude for the glory of His kindness, I uttered my thanks as tears streamed down my face. With an outpouring of love for the all-powerful, beneficent Him, I felt my entire body tingle His acknowledgement with a physical sensation that I can only describe as a giant body smile.

Yes, I was on my way to becoming a cytologist, my path to the world that I had always dreamed about, and key to my future.

CHAPTER 13

Maggie and Jeff were stunned and excited by my acceptance to this respected, big-city program. I continued to work the jewelry counter through Christmas and then, on a freezing afternoon just after New Year's Day 1972, Maggie and I set off in her car for Chicago. She dropped me off at my dorm, the International House, where we removed my increasing bundle of belongings from the car and said our farewells before she headed back to Peoria, anxious to get home before it got too late.

I was jittery with excitement and utterly impressed by the grand buildings that housed the university and the city that sparkled around us in the dark—I'd never seen anything like it.

The university had sent me housing information before my arrival, offering only one on-campus selection. I hadn't had any expectations of where to live before I was offered the International House, but the name itself was exhilarating, making it the only place I wanted to be. Excitement riddled joyously through my veins that first night at the check-in counter where I giggled stupidly at the sight of my name typed on their registration list.

They were actually expecting me!

I'm not sure what I had thought. Maybe deep inside I believed my dream could not really come true; that I would arrive and be told that there had been a mistake. This was no mistake. They had assigned me a room of my own and it was waiting for me.

I was told that the International House was available only to students in the university's graduate programs, which the Cytology program officially was not. However, the Cytology program was unique because of its collaboration with the medical school. A bachelor's degree was not a requirement to attend, but the students who were typically allowed into the program had either a bachelor's or a master's degree, thereby giving the cytology school and its students a graduate academic presence. This status warranted cytology students graduate program privileges, one being a room at the International House. I found out later that I was the only one in the cytology program without a bachelor's degree, and the only one never to have traveled beyond the Midwest. I was also the youngest person both in the dorm and in my program.

The woman next door moved into her room at the same time I moved into mine. She was unexpectedly friendly, making it easy to become acquainted that first night. Tonya came from a wealthy California family and had traveled all over the world. She was working on a Ph.D. in Linguistics, doing a thesis project on Noam Chomsky and something about the asterisk, making a joke about "nothing to lose but your 'ass to risk,'" a comparison which went over my head. She said this like I was supposed to find it interesting and expected me to engage in some sort of banter with her. At the time I didn't know what the study of linguistics entailed or why anyone would want to study linguistics, let alone Chomsky, and I wasn't sure if Noam Chomsky was a person or a thing.

Everyone around me seemed so smart, so articulate. They were brilliant, talented, accomplished and well read. They understood politics, knew presidents of various countries personally, and came from important, influential families. Their fathers and mothers were doctors, lawyers, academicians, presidents of companies and heads of state. They expected to become significant leaders in one form or other themselves, and were encouraged to do great things. Self-esteem and confidence were assumed and treated as a good thing. None of them had fallen off the caravan wagon. They knew their royal heritage.

I decided very quickly that the safest posture for me, so nobody would discover how out of place I felt, was to say very little. Despite my lack of conversation, I was welcomed into social circles by my new friends, who could not have been nicer. Regardless, feelings of inferiority plagued me.

One of my best friends was a girl from Connecticut who lived down the hall from me. Julia was a wealthy physician's daughter who had traveled extensively, and seemed to enjoy my quainter background and worldly innocence. Because she was so kind, it was easy to relax around her. She took the time to engage me in discussions that would stretch my worldview and perceptions of myself and others.

Julia and I were talking about Prada one day, or I should say Julia was talking about Prada, proceeding as if I understood. Once again I had to admit my ignorance and tell her that I had no idea who or what Prada was. It was frustrating. Neither I nor anyone else I knew had access to this kind of finery. Consequently, fashion designers were not part of my knowledge base. Julia remained patient and non-judgmental while listening to the anxiety that bubbled up within me. She advised me to start reading magazines like *Time* and *Newsweek* to get more "up" on the world, which I did from that time on. My goal was to participate intelligently in evening conversations when sitting around the table with friends from England, the Middle East, France, Germany, the United States or wherever. At some level I considered this kind of socialization just as important to my education as the degree itself.

My first day of classes required me to use every scrap of knowledge I had managed to collect over the years. Even high school Latin came in handy as I familiarized myself with the medical terminology. In my wildest dreams I had not anticipated that I'd use Latin for anything other than singing the requiem hymns at funerals. It was amazing to be in an environment where one's academic studies were actually used on a daily basis. What a place! History, geography, economics and algebra were all useful— and interesting! How could I have known that these subjects had any practical value? Of course I knew where South America was, but had a hard time remembering that Chile was the long skinny coastal country located in southern South America. There was no reason to learn the details until I met the handsome Chilean who attended the business school. He spoke passionately about their communist president, General Salvador Allende, who had nationalized his family's company. Suddenly geography, history, economics and international politics became important in one fell swoop. There was the alluring Brit who was raised in Ethiopia and destined to work for the British Foreign Service and the handsome Greek fellow who said he loved my green eyes. Vasilli was expected to take over his father's business one day. Exciting people were attached to more exciting places and the world became relevant in a way I had never realized it could.

Walking back to the dorm from classes that first week, I mused about my new life while being distracted by the various languages of passersby. I enjoyed eavesdropping on those who were speaking English, hoping that one day someone would find me interesting enough to eavesdrop on.

It wasn't long before I started dating. Sometimes I accepted offers to early dinners and late parties in the same evening, fearing that I'd miss out on something. Good heavens, these men invited me to the opera, theatre, ethnic restaurants, house parties and dancing. I grabbed at life with both hands, trying to get as much as possible as quickly as possible, not knowing how long this fantasy would last.

CHAPTER 14

I loved cytology. Reflecting upon the conversation I'd shared with Dr. Algeron just one year earlier, I was awed once again by the magnitude of the miracle that had blessed my life. Cytology was everything I had ever dreamed. Not only was it a fascinating subject, but it was valued, and there were employment opportunities all over the world. I was confident I could work while traveling. The fact that I was able to study at the exciting and renowned University of Chicago was an extra special bonus.

We were only a few weeks from finishing our intense academic training before starting the clinical portion of the program when Ms. Kilroy, our head instructor, asked me to take a phone call in her office. It was the hospital in Peoria wanting to make plans for my return.

Return? How could I go back? There was still so much to learn and so much to do. I couldn't possibly go back. I vaguely remembered Dr. Algeron explaining why his hospital would sponsor me to study cytology. It was so I would return to Peoria to work for a few years. At the time it had seemed like a hundred years away and I had intended to do precisely that, but now? My objections must have sounded ungrateful, but I couldn't go back. With heartfelt apologies, I sputtered my regrets.

The lab manager did not insist that I return to Peoria. She graciously accepted my refusal, wished me well, and informed me that the expenses for the second half of the program would not be paid.

Financial panic resonated through every fiber of my being while those same old negative taunts emerged inside me, predicting inevitable failure. Where would I get the money to complete the program?

As they had so many times in the past, my spiritual defenses prevailed, offering protection and guidance against the negativity, stomping it, beating it, defeating it . . .

Quickly I found part-time work managing the café at the International House to cover my room and board, and Dale and his wife lent me money to help cover my expenses. Panic dissipated when I focused on the privilege and unlikelihood of being at the University of Chicago. Hard work became a pleasure and the challenges gratifying when I accepted that if it were easy, everyone would be doing it and my opportunities would be fewer. Perhaps I didn't have the academic pedigree that landed my colleagues their seats at the laboratory, but I was there just the same and I worked just as hard, maybe harder than they.

The end of the program came all too quickly. We had trained continuously for twelve months without a break. I didn't mind since there was nowhere else I'd rather be. But what was I to do now?

Travel to the ends of the earth had been a lifelong dream. After twelve intense months working at the university and living in an international environment, I had developed friendships and experiences that further fed my compulsion to live and work overseas. I desperately wanted to become part of the world-wise community that I enjoyed so much, but that wouldn't be possible unless I, too, had my own international experiences. The longing I felt to live abroad was as determined as the urgency to leave Iowa to attend college had been a few years before. I had gotten out of Dyersville, and trusted that soon I would find a way—any way—to travel and work overseas too.

CHAPTER 15

In January 1974, I successfully completed the cytology program with the highest final exam score in my graduating class. *It was a Jia Wood (tree) year filled with lots of Wood energy for my Yi Wood vine to climb up and reach the sunshine.* Now I had to take the next step to find employment. My approach was guided by a vision for the future, the ever-present discernment of my divine beings and practical steps to examine my approach. First, I needed to find the laboratories that were hiring highly trained but inexperienced cytologists. I searched trade publications for ads, but didn't come up with anything. Ms. Kilroy knew of a position in Paris, but I was reluctant to apply. Relying on my inner guidance, I believed that I needed more practical work experience in cytology before going overseas. I also had no money to pay for the travel expenses to Paris and wanted to return the money that I had borrowed from my brother before incurring further debt.

Although it was difficult to postpone my dream of living in Europe, I had faith that one day soon I would be able to work abroad. The question then became, where should I go in the meantime? I felt like Goldilocks as I contemplated the options available to me. California seemed too far from Europe, plus it would be expensive to fly there so I ruled it out for practical reasons. New York was too large and cold, but Washington, D.C. seemed just right. The nation's capital was in a good location relative to Europe, the winters weren't too harsh, and I heard that it was beautiful. I considered that the Federal Government might be looking for cytologists on military bases, of which there are several in the general D.C. area. The winds were blowing me in that direction.

As it turned out, a fellow classmate named Barbara was traveling east to visit relatives who lived in the D.C. area. She was looking for a driving companion and offered her car trunk to carry my belongings as an exchange. Barbara had already found a job in California, so her trip to D.C. was a side jaunt before driving cross-country to settle on the West Coast. Together we weaved our way along the East Coast, ready to embark on the first chapter of our professional lives.

My father was not in a financial position to offer a monetary gift, but with a very touching and quiet show of support and pride he co-signed a thousand dollar loan for me through the local Dyersville bank. The loan was intended to help me get started with my career. He used the farm as collateral, entrusting me with the responsibility to repay the loan without a lecture or admonishment to do so. By Dad's actions I accepted that he wanted to be part of my life's adventure. This was his way of offering his blessing.

The next day I returned to the bank to take out an insurance policy on the loan in the event something unexpected should happen to me. I felt much better.

One thousand dollars was a lot of money to me, even though I understood that the funds could run out quickly. Dad didn't offer much in the way of advice, presumably saddened by his absence from my life, but cautioned against staying in expensive hotels that could cost as much as fifty dollars per night. I heeded his advice and sought to find employment and an apartment as soon as possible.

Barbara and I had planned to stay at the YWCA in D.C. while I looked for a job and a more permanent place to live. Unfortunately, we failed to make reservations at the "Y" in advance of our arrival, neglecting a rather obvious detail. Imagine our surprise when we arrived in D.C. only to discover that the building had been torn down.

Barbara's relatives eagerly came to our rescue, inviting us to stay in their home until we could sort things out. Not having had children of their own, they looked forward to doting on us. Harold and Evelyn were long-time residents of the D.C. area, familiar with the city and anxious to share their favorite sites, including a variety of authentic, quaint, Greek restaurants located between Baltimore Harbor, D.C. and Virginia. Most evenings we dined at restaurants where they knew the owners by first name and introduced us with the same pride a parent would their children. For hours we listened to the passionate singing of minstrels while sailors danced tales of loneliness before snapping into happier tunes and livelier dance steps.

Harold and Evelyn invited me to stay with them longer, but I refused. Without a car and no plans to get one, it would have been a logistical nightmare to search for a job while living in Maryland when most of the military installations and hospitals were located in D.C. or Virginia.

CHAPTER 16

Dale had given me the name of his friend, Belinda, who lived in the D.C. area, just in case I wanted to look her up. I accepted the contact information, without expecting to need it. Belinda was a farm girl from Dyersville just like me. We were familiar with one another in the same way we knew all our classmates, their parents, siblings and cousins, but we didn't know one another well. Our families attended the same Catholic schools and Belinda was in Linda's class, just a year behind me. We did, however, share the same value system that assumed an unspoken camaraderie. Even though I didn't "know" Belinda, the unexpected likelihood that we were meeting in Washington, D.C., where I sought her help, created an immediate bond.

Belinda had recently begun working for the U.S. Government as an accountant, and was living in a small, one-bedroom apartment in Arlington, Virginia, which I soon discovered was a suburb of Washington, D.C. She didn't hesitate to invite me to share her apartment until we could find something larger together.

Things were falling into place. Now that I had a place to live, it seemed only natural to look for employment nearby. Without a car I'd be commuting on foot or by bus, so I quite practically decided to make Arlington Hospital the first stop in my job search. There was no ad in the paper, nor any reason to believe Arlington Hospital was looking for an additional cytologist, but I set up a meeting with the head of the Pathology Department, Dr. Nolan, who was responsible for hiring lab personnel. Fortunately, Dr. Nolan was a personal friend of the Cytology Program Director at the University of Chicago.

Arlington Hospital wasn't in need of a cytologist in the near term, but there were plans to build a new laboratory and expand the hospital. Dr. Nolan's decision to offer me a job was in anticipation of the expected increase in the workload when it opened.

My first job in my new career, and it was the first place I had applied. Best of all, I could walk to work, which began the following week. Until then, anxiety had been difficult to separate from excitement, but now that I had a job, I could see my life coming together and I felt exhilarated. The world had beckoned and I answered the call. To be in control of my life was an invigorating experience. One that I had not known before. I felt invincible.

CHAPTER 17

My more seasoned laboratory mate, Nancy, was also a small town escapee, but satisfied with the excitement the nation's capital offered. Somewhat charmed by my enthusiasm and by all the plans I had for myself, she indulged my dreams. She wasn't taken aback when on my first day at the lab I announced that I was staying at Arlington Hospital only as long as it took me to organize employment overseas.

On and off during the entire day, the cytology laboratory received batches of Pap smear slides, which we stained and covered with little glass slips. One slide after another was screened in a steady parade, hour after hour. Nancy and I entertained ourselves with friendly chitchat while sharing the staining and other preparatory work that was done before the slides could be read. I suppose that the repetitive work could have been considered boring, but my thoughts were fueled with excitement, and I approached every day with wonder for the future. If I'd had no dreams for myself, it would have been easy to slip back into the same frustration I felt on the farm before I escaped. Instead, optimism energized every morning, and got channeled into handling the practical steps needed to fulfill the next dream.

Laboratory work tended to attract people who liked predictability, i.e., those who found comfort from a daily routine. These types may have had imaginations but were not risk takers. Many of my laboratory mates would have loved to throw caution to the wind if there had been a safety net underneath them, but they lacked the faith in themselves to take this chance.

Nancy was the exception. She was an enigmatic woman, careful to wear her emotions close to her chest. She was quiet, discreet, kindly and patient, a pretty young woman from Youngstown, Ohio, who had settled into her job as a means to support her life in the Capital. Her big leap to freedom came when she left Ohio, but now she was content to explore the many interesting diversions and attractions of the D.C. area from her vantage point at Arlington Hospital. Outside of work, she was as interested in pursuing excitement as I, scoping out operas, ballets and art exhibits. Nancy kept her ear to the ground in search of affordable entertainment and somehow always knew what was playing at the Kennedy Center, Wolf Trap or on the lawn near the Washington Monument. She introduced me to her favorite features of life in D.C., including her friend, George, who knew every ethnic restaurant, landmark and museum in the entire metropolitan area. He gladly accompanied us wherever we wanted to go.

George insisted on calling Nancy "Natasha," a name he thought suited her far better than ordinary "Nancy." She loved it, and so did I. From then on, Nancy became the glorious, mysterious Natasha.

Natasha may have projected a demure image, but her assertive side was not to be underestimated. She questioned our pay as cytologists after fastidiously analyzing the costs of preparing specimens against the revenue that was generated as a result of our work. In 1974, the customary charge for a Pap smear was sixty dollars. It cost twenty-five cents to prepare the specimen from one patient, which included the slides, dyes, and other materials *and* the wages of the cytologist who screened it. Cytologists were barely making a living wage. For the first time it dawned on me that cytology might not be the best career choice after all. How could all these intelligent, educated and well-qualified people accept such a small piece of the pie? I had no patience for that. Cytology would still be my ticket to travel and I was determined to follow it as far as it would take me, but beyond that point, I knew that I could make no further commitment to the profession.

As I became exposed to the variety of experiences and cultures available in Washington, D.C. through Natasha, George, Belinda, Harold and Evelyn and others, I was no longer solely focused on living in Europe. In fact, I wasn't particular about where I'd end up as long as I crossed an ocean. The Atlantic had the advantage of being cheaper.

Within my first week at Arlington Hospital I began searching trade publications and military hospital ads for any available oversees jobs. I contacted Ms. Kilroy, my instructor from Chicago who connected me to her friend and colleague, Dr. Nuovo. Dr. Nuovo had had a position available in her Paris laboratory the previous year. She was familiar with the reputation of the Chicago program and would have hired anyone who was referred by Ms. Kilroy. She owned two laboratories, one in Paris and a second in Monaco, and was now looking for two cytologists. Without further scrutiny, Dr. Nuovo offered me the option of where I would prefer to work, Paris or Monaco.

Wow!! What choices!

Deciding between the two wasn't all that difficult in the end. Paris offered a wider cultural experience, and I could go to Monaco for vacations. Paris it was. With my next job now firmly secured, I finished out the remainder of my year at Arlington Hospital, which allowed time for all the arrangements to be made for my departure.

In those final few months stateside, I scrambled to learn a bit of French by taking night classes at the Alliance Française, secured my visa and purchased a plane ticket. I packed a suitcase with my somewhat meager wardrobe, but carried with me a treasure trove of well wishes and vicarious thrills from my D.C. friends.

CHAPTER 18

All I knew as I landed in Paris for the first time was that I had a job. There was no one to meet me at the airport, and no friend to call. I took a taxi into the city to find Dr. Nuovo's laboratory, located on Rue Cortambert in the swank sixteenth *arrondissement,* or district, near the Eiffel Tower. The laboratory arranged for temporary housing, which I assumed had belonged to the woman I replaced. Historic beauty and the wide boulevards that I passed on the drive to the apartment took my breath away, and stood in sharp contrast to the harsh reality of the one room apartment I was expected to occupy. Its dreary cement walls were adorned with no more than a picture calendar and accented by a bare light bulb in the middle of the ceiling. The shared bathroom down the hall echoed flushes and body functions of at least six people, and bone-chilling temperatures drew attention to the window that didn't close, inferior space heater and thin blankets. It certainly was not the exotic Paris apartment of my dreams, but I was determined to accept the circumstances if, in fact, this was the way the average Frenchman lived. It didn't take me long to realize, however, that most Frenchmen did *not* live this harshly, a condition that I set out to rectify immediately. Adele, the English-speaking receptionist at the laboratory, helped me to find something more suitable. Within a short time I had relocated to a small studio apartment on Rue de La Pompe. It was clean, light-filled, new, modern, small and a convenient walk to work.

Paris offered boundless opportunities for distractions with new experiences around every corner, and just as many hazards. For the first time since I'd left home, I felt truly vulnerable. Women were openly harassed by men in public. It was confusing, though, because so many women were obliging. At night, both men and women and couples drove around the city with their interior car lights on, signaling that they were available for sexual action. It seemed to be expected that women would disregard sexual offenses as if it was all in good humor, or that both parties were naturally consenting, because not to do so would make one parochial. Regardless, I wasn't prepared for this, or for the stereotypical drab green raincoat that appeared non-threatening until it opened, flashing a lascivious penis. After being manhandled on a crowded metro train I found out that it was useless to approach the police about most sexual crimes. They just laughed it off, making women feel ridiculous. Sadly, a friend was raped when visiting me, and received the same humiliating treatment when she tried to file a report.

Dr. Cornieu, the presiding pathologist at the laboratory, explained that American people have a certain look on their faces. He called it "a look of space." To interpret his meaning, he described it as a wide-eyed, somewhat vacuous openness that conveys innocence and vulnerability, a neon alert system that signals to predators.

This new understanding helped me to become less agreeable or "nice," *a natural tendency for my Yi Wood vine energy*, and hopefully a bit more street smart. I walked with heightened awareness, preferring long walks along the wide avenues and lovely neighborhoods to the Metro, which housed many miscreants.

The charm of the Rive Gauche and Montmartre presented new thrills. Abundant art galleries and street artists satisfied creative yearnings, but the food and wine offered the greatest surprises, appealing to taste buds I didn't know existed. I salivated with anticipation over a simple bowl of lentils for lunch, excited about a little brown bean that sated every possible culinary desire during a sixty-minute break.

Mmmmmm . . . the pastries, too, were out of this world: playful little decadences enticed defenseless passersby. It was impossible to walk past a patisserie without being visually and physically seduced by the sight and smell of cream-filled fantasies.

The extraordinary bounty of delicious food and wine softened the harsher aspects of my time in Paris.

Something I couldn't get used to was the rudeness of the average Parisian. I'd never encountered public disrespect to strangers like this before, certainly not in Iowa, nor anywhere I'd been, including Chicago and D.C. Did I have "a look of space" and could the metro ticket-taker tell I was an American? Was that the reason? I tried not to take these rude affronts personally. As a result and without deliberate awareness, I intuitively donned a more standoffish persona, a survival tactic intended to ward off anyone who thought they were going to mess with me.

Over time my wardrobe changed to accommodate French fashions, and laborious attempts at being understood in English, along with futile attempts at speaking French, taught me to deliver all my words with crisp, snapping diction. It's fair to say that within a few months my vulnerable "look of space" image morphed into a more complex version of itself.

Life became a series of feasts as I traveled across Europe from Portugal to Hungary, relishing the scenic, artistic and culinary delights I fantasized as a child.

Unlike my Arlington job, I was not responsible for the prep work required before screening the slides. My job was only to read them. I didn't see much of Dr. Nuovo, who was rarely in the lab, but Dr. Cornieu, the attending pathologist, discussed cases with me, which made the work more interesting. He also seemed to enjoy hearing about the sights and sounds of his beloved city from a fresh perspective.

About halfway through my first year in Paris I approached Dr. Nuovo regarding my taking the international cytology exam given in Vienna, Austria. To my relief, she was encouraging. Normally, cytologists were not allowed to take this exam without two full years of experience, but this requirement was waived since I was so close to Vienna and only a few months shy of the two-year guideline. Another opportunity. Another blessing.

The exam was given in conjunction with a large conference

that attracted cytologists and pathologists from all over the world.
The atmosphere percolated with excitement, reminding me of
the exhilarating time I'd spent at the University of Chicago. This
time I was the foreigner, however, hoping to sound interesting to
those who would eavesdrop on me. I stayed at a hostel located near
the conference facility, along with several other women who also
attended the conference.

Everything about Vienna reflected centuries of culture, charm
and exquisite beauty. Chocolatiers graced every corner. Statues of
Strauss and Mozart decorated elaborate gardens whose beauty
was only slightly diminished during the winter months. Kiosks
oozed tempting scents, luring tourists to treat themselves to famed
bratwurst sausages. My stay in Vienna was far too short to enjoy even
a sampling of its pleasures, but I did attend the opera at the State
Opera House. Never mind that my ticket only bought me standing
room at the back of the theatre, I was there to witness the layers of
balconies that towered above me and a performance fit for kings.

Several of us from the conference decided to have dinner
together in a lovely winter-garden restaurant, entertained as we ate
by professional Viennese Waltz dancers who performed to Strauss
classics. Included in our small party was a pathologist by the name of
Dr. Bahr, the director of a research laboratory at the Armed Forces
Institute of Pathology (AFIP) in Washington, D.C. Dr. Bahr was
also a friend of Dr. Weid, my professor at the University of Chicago.

I had met Dr. Bahr earlier at the conference and was seated
next to him at our table that evening. A highly revered and brilliant
individual, he was in Vienna to give a lecture at the conference. As
the group shared wine, stories and ambitions, Dr. Bahr asked about
my plans after Paris. At that time, I hadn't decided exactly what to
do but felt that I should return to the States when the year was up.
"Do you have any suggestions?" I asked.

As a matter of fact, he did. He was starting the International
Registry of Cytopathology, a databank of interesting cytology cases
that would be housed at the AFIP, and he needed a cytologist
to help him organize the material. Dr. Bahr asked if I would be

interested.

The thought that this world-renowned scientist wanted me to work for him was truly an honor and a privilege.

"Why me?" I thought. Certainly there were others who were more academic, more worthy and better qualified than I. Allowing a rush of self-importance to swell my ego, I ignored the nagging insecurities that normally prevented me from indulging my ambitions further. By this time egotism prevailed over any doubt. I jumped at his offer, accepting it on the spot.

I was on a natural high. Soaring from the expansive time in Vienna, my return trip to Paris was a long blur. Best of all, I was returning with a plan. A great plan. I would finish out my year in Paris on a high note and head back to America and another opportunity of a lifetime.

CHAPTER 19

January 1975 was the year of the Rabbit. Yi Mao had lots of Wood to reinforce my own. I returned to the States with the international credentials I had coveted since attending the University of Chicago. Before settling again in Washington, D.C., I made a detour through Iowa to visit my family who I was anxious to see and to share the wonders of my time overseas. It had been a year since I left the states, and I had experienced a completely different life. For some reason I assumed that life in Iowa would have changed, too, and optimistically thought that my family would be interested in hearing about my travels. They had a difficult time relating to me, however. Even Maggie, who came home from Peoria to see me, could not connect the young woman she dropped off at the International House two years earlier to this more seasoned version who had returned from Paris.

My brothers and sisters claimed that I had an accent and ate funny because I had adapted the European custom of using the fork in my left hand and the knife in my right. Maggie mocked me by using her thumb to push peas onto her fork, stimulating peals of laughter from the others. I wanted to tell them about my international escapades, the exam, and also my new position at the Armed Forces Institute of Pathology, but they couldn't have been less interested. I longed to describe the art galleries, Rive Gauche, delicious food and yummy chocolates, fashion boutiques, exciting travels across Europe, bidets, squat toilets, restaurants, and international life as a career woman, but I would have come across as a braggart. They considered me affected as it was, and more obnoxious than ever. Besides, they had never heard of the Armed Forces Institute of Pathology.

"She thinks she's so smart. She thinks she's better than everybody else," was the familiar refrain from my siblings, which they did nothing to hide from me.

Maybe they were right. Perhaps I had changed, and maybe even full of myself. Was it really necessary for me to turn up my nose at specially prepared JELL-O salad made with fake whipping cream and canned fruits? Could I not refrain from commenting scornfully on the fat young girl we saw after Mass on Sunday who gave the impression that she was chomping on an entire package of chewing gum? I didn't hesitate to comment that this same young girl made herself deliberately unattractive with her sloppy, oversized clothing and boisterous behavior. I suppose, I did come off as a know-it-all.

There I was, dressed in my most fashionable French clothes—including knee-high maroon boots and matching purse—which looked especially gorgeous when matched with my brown corduroy belted coat. My favorite dress was a simple, figure-flattering chemise, very Parisian. At a slender one hundred fifteen pounds, I looked great. My mother laughed along with the jokes and ridicule at my expense, and couldn't hide her disapproval of me in my presence. I think I was hoping that she would say something nice to me, like she was proud of what I'd accomplished, but it didn't happen. *My Yi Wood suffered from lack of recognition, or any other kind of acknowledgment that bespoke approval and acceptance.*

I recall that my father was silent during this visit. Only years later did I learn that he had commented, upon hearing of the French transportation strike and fearing that I might be stuck in Paris indefinitely, "Oh, you know Mary. She could take a whale across the Atlantic if she needed to." My guess is that this was his way of expressing a little bit of pride in my independence and gumption.

With little fanfare I left Iowa once again for Washington, D.C., this time as a bold pro at life's adventures.

CHAPTER 20

My first day at the Armed Forces Institute of Pathology (AFIP) reminded me of my first day at the University of Chicago, but on a grander scale. Here I was surrounded by brilliant, accomplished scientists and researchers and was considered an equal, one of the professionals.

Every day I went to work curious about what the day would have in store for me. I was trained to use the various electron microscopes and scanners, the microscopic cameras, and how to develop my own film and prints. There were several projects that Dr. Bahr was working on, but I was to help with the chromosome study since my salary was being paid from a grant sponsored by Georgetown University and the National Institutes of Health for this research. I would also be reviewing the cytology of interesting cases before organizing them for the International Registry.

To my surprise and delight, I was the only cytologist at AFIP. Consequently, many of the doctors asked to study cytology with me. These were some of the world's most brilliant pathologists, trained to analyze tissue but not individual cells. Admittedly, I was delighted when asked to lecture to this elite group of doctors. Me. Lecturing to them. Without a four-year college degree.

I was treated with the professional respect and consideration that comes with laudatory academic accomplishment, not just grit. I knew that I lacked the depth of knowledge that comes with the years of training and discipline that would make me one of them, but they granted me my place among their group, and accepted me without questioning my relatively slim credentials.

I admired these doctors tremendously and aspired to be just like them. I bought into what *I thought* they believed in. These were real scientists . . . the best in the world, who could explain everything from a scientific perspective . . . even creation!

The research I was doing involved taking blood samples for culturing so we could reproduce and harvest the chromosomes. By calculating the exact time the cells were in mitotic metaphase, we stopped the chromatin growth and then attempted to smash them by using radiation or chemicals. The threads from the broken chromosomes were examined for vulnerability, which enabled us to identify the weak areas of chromosomal strands. These chromosomal threads were further examined under the electron microscope, magnified 300,000 times. The aim was to discover both what made the chromosomes vulnerable and what might strengthen or protect them.

I examined the connecting threads intently, enthralled by the possibility of seeing something so minute, and I was overwhelmed by the genius of science and the ability of man to procreate from a petri dish and investigate from a microscope. Imagine that one spec of a spec of a spec of chromatin can literally change one's identity. I gazed upon this breathtaking miracle, fascinated with the instrument that examined the DNA as well as the perfection of the threads themselves.

"This is creation," I thought "and science can explain it." Once again my ego swelled, anxious to simulate the brilliant scientists with whom I worked and to share in their discoveries. My entire spiritual life pivoted in that moment as I pondered science's superiority all too briefly before considering the critical issue at the center of all creation.

Where did life begin? Where did the initial spark of life come from? I'm not talking about Big Bang sparks and bacterial life form theories. I'm talking about the life of the spirit within us;

the one we feel, and who feels us. I'm talking about the Parent Life that connects us to something greater than ourselves; the one that speaks to us through intuition and tells us if we are doing the right thing. It's the compassionate Parent Spirit, the one who connects all of us together as humans through our feelings. This same parent speaks all languages, is everywhere at the same time and is privy to all our thoughts. It's the living, loving, breathing Life Force that exists in the wind that blew the trees, the grass that tickled my feet, the minnows that swam around my ankles, my parents, my brothers and sisters, my pets . . . and me. The Life Force that *feels* and connects us to all other life forms. What made me wilt with sadness when I saw my mother cry or delight when lightening bugs lit up the sky? Where did *that* life begin? *Not* where did life *forms* replicate, procreate or duplicate? *Where did the Parent Life of Spirit begin?* I felt this connection to God in my heart. Until that moment I didn't need to calculate His proof. I didn't even need answers. The understanding—the knowledge—of His existence had always lived inside of me.

With great shame, I recall the moment of my arrogance. Somehow, I let myself rationalize the fine lines of distinction between science and God. Arrogance allowed me to accept, "There is no God. Maybe there is only science." In that instant, I displaced God with hubris and self-importance and just as quickly forgot a lifetime of memories and countless blessings. I forsook my ever-present divine friendships as if they had never existed, and forgot the overwhelming body tingles I had experienced when I was accepted by the University of Chicago, the very blessing that led me to my current position in this grand institution.

Yes, in one instant I literally felt God's familiar, inner glow of Light drain from my body. In its place there was an empty, aching void. I was left to peer down at magnified chromosomes alone, having abandoned the only real source of strength and support I had ever known.

God frowns on arrogance. We choose the relationship we want with Him. His absence is felt most profoundly after we have experienced

his presence, and then invite him to leave. He is not to be taken for
granted. Light from His presence protects from negativity, imbalance
and darkness.

CHAPTER 21

After two years at the AFIP, my contract had come to an end.
Dr. Bahr helped me find a job in a Swiss kantonsspital in Luzern.
There weren't many well-trained cytologists available in Europe,
so it was common for hospitals and labs to recruit technologists
from the United States. In terms of international work, I chose the
right profession. Shortly after I started at the kantonsspital, another
American woman and a Swedish woman were also hired.

The American, Simone, had been living in Luxembourg,
and Anna had come directly from Stockholm. Since I was the
established resident American, it was understood that I'd pick up
Simone at the train station. This was a task I looked forward to,
eager to have another American among the group, and anxious to
introduce her to the city I had fallen in love with.

Even though I had a car, I preferred to walk to work and
enjoy Kappelbrucke, a fourteenth century wooden bridge that
crossed the Reuss River. Kappelbrucke was filled with hand painted
scenes from another era; a plethora of details too numerous to
capture and remember. Mythical, visual luxury spread out from
the bridge in every angle, producing panoramic scenes that fed the
senses. Luzern was majestically surrounded by towering Mount
Rigi on one side and Mount Pilatus on the other, the two peaks
standing guard over this sweet paradise like protective giants. Swans
and ducks languished on the water like picturesque props, and
brightly colored flowers overflowed wooden containers that lined
the length of the bridge. The flowers, fresh air, painted buildings,
medieval castles, and cobblestone paths crafted a fairytale setting.
Kappelbrucke was usually crowded with enamored tourists, drinking
in the magnificence of the bridge and the views that surrounded it.

No matter how many admirers there were, no one could have loved Luzern and Kappelbrucke more than I.

The day of Simone's arrival I was thinking about Luzern, the jewel of Switzerland. Preoccupied with the fun plans I had in store for my new American colleague, I forgot to ask for Simone's description, but "Oh well," I figured. "Surely I'll recognize her."

CHAPTER 22

It's difficult to describe the image of the woman who sat on the bench at the train station waiting to be picked up. She had chiseled facial features, long, blonde hair and a ruddy complexion. Her beautiful figure was obvious, even as she sat on the bench. Long, shapely legs crossed carelessly and her tight sweater revealed a full breast and tiny waist. As I walked closer, I got a full-view of her facial expression that caused me to gasp. A chill ran down my spine. The woman sitting on the bench looked dead from the inside out. "If the Devil exists on Earth," I shuddered to myself, "she is sitting in front of me."

I looked around, hoping that there would be another woman waiting, but there was none. Reluctantly, I approached the stranger with the long blonde hair and introduced myself.

"Hi, I'm Mary from the kantonsspital to pick up Simone. Are you she?"

I tried to be pleasant and to dismiss my initial reaction, hoping that this was a case of mistaken identity. There was no such luck. The blonde haired woman with the long legs now stood up and said with an imperious, intimidating air, "Hi, I'm Simone. I've been waiting for you."

Simone was disturbing to look at, particularly her cold eyes that surveyed me suspiciously through narrowed slits. You would think someone with her physical attributes would be attractive, but she wasn't. Her image was surreal, a confusing, paradoxical blend of attractive, physical components unhinged by cold, dead eyes.

Despite my personal reservations to become too friendly with Simone, we were paired because of our common American background. The technicians worked closely at the lab; there was no way to avoid her. Besides, she kept seeking me out.

My reaction to her unwanted attention was to minimize myself in front of her, but Simone was far shrewder than I. With heightened primitive instincts she targeted my fear, which made lunch breaks even more uncomfortable.

After some months of shared lunches and microscope-side conversations, I got to know her a bit better and liked her even less. She showed me a gorgeous photo of herself taken when she was seventeen. At that time, she was beautiful in every way, beaming a perfect smile that reflected the excitement of an eager, young woman ready to explore a life filled with promise.

I wondered what had happened to Simone until the day she spoke quite proudly of a man who introduced her to Devil Worship. "Whenever I want something," she said, "I just make a pact with the Devil by calling on his energy. It always works."

Without my asking for details, she described her use of dolls and pins in rituals to control people. At the time, I wondered why she would divulge such sensitive information about herself but I later understood that she was trying to intimidate me.

After that, I tried harder to ignore her but it was impossible. My lab mates and I often socialized after hours together. Usually we went to cafes as a group so contact with Simone was inevitable. Since I was the only one with a car, Simone usually asked me to give her a ride home.

During a weekend skiing trip together, the expatriate cytologists shared a chalet at the ski resort. We were chatting casually over breakfast one morning, when Simone complained about her struggles with constipation, claiming that she had a bowel movement only once every three months or so. As difficult as it was to feel sorry for her, the extraordinary predicament evoked my sympathy. Was this the reason her complexion was so ruddy, I wondered? Years later I weighed the possibility that this was the price she had paid for her dark practices.

Milan was easily accessible by train from Luzern and became a favored weekend destination among the women at the lab. On one of these excursions I bought a pair of leather boots, but later became unhappy with them because of the way they were stitched. I vented my frustration openly to my lab mates, but resigned myself into accepting their condition because of the effort and expense required to return them. Simone overheard me expressing my dissatisfaction, and proceeded to coerce me into making the trip to Milan to return the purchase.

"I can't believe you'd accept such an inferior product," she said scornfully. "I'd never let them get away with that," she added, dismissing the time and costs associated with another trip to Milan. In the end, I succumbed to her manipulations and coercive tactics, and against my better judgment arranged a trip to Milan to return the boots.

Before I left for Milan, Simone gave me a box of foil wrapped chocolate liquors, my favorite. I accepted the treats, wanting to believe she intended to be generous, since it wasn't customary for her to do something nice for anyone, let alone me. I thanked her for the chocolates, then passed the box to my co-workers, both as a courtesy and as an attempt to spare myself the calories.

Simone became angry, expressing serious offense. "I gave those to you to take on your trip," she fumed, "to eat on the train. I did not give them to you to pass out."

"Yikes, what is she so upset about?" I wondered, mustering a pathetic "all right," before I meekly put them away.

On the train trip to Milan, I ate a chocolate or two, and a few more over the weekend. I became miserably ill with diarrhea that got progressively worse during the weekend. Back at the lab I went to the toilet every three to five minutes until my gut produced a bile green liquid. Of course I should have gone home, but I forced myself to stay at work since I was expecting houseguests from the States and wanted to avoid any suspicion of playing hooky. Absences of any kind were frowned upon.

I looked ghastly, eliciting concern from my laboratory mate, Christa. Simone, on the other hand, asked about my condition with a breathless, falsetto voice that squeaked insincerity. Her hands moved more rapidly than normal over the slides she examined, refusing to let her eyes meet mine.

The interns at the hospital became concerned when they heard of my dilemma, suggesting that I take a concoction of coal crystals, which acted as some sort of filter. Like magic this remedy worked, and I was better in a few days.

At the time of this incident, I was far too naïve and ignorant to suspect Simone of mal-intent, but in retrospect there is no doubt in my mind that she altered the chocolates with one of her toxic voodoo ministrations to make me ill.

CHAPTER 23

Some months later I quit my job at the Luzern Kantonsspital. After six years of work in research and cytology and having accomplished my dream to live and work overseas, I was ready to set this career aside to pursue a bachelor's degree in economics and business. Having lived in France and Switzerland and travelled as far as Morocco, Portugal and England in the West and Turkey and Hungary in the East, I now had the international experience I sought to become more familiar and connected to the world. I had the opportunity to open my small apartment to many friends, my sister, Linda, and brother, Lawrence. Most importantly, my parents came to stay with me too. I had enjoyed many opportunities and memories and now it was time to re-evaluate my career choice and plan for the future. I loved cytology, but the low salaries paid to laboratory technicians would never afford a lifestyle where I could accumulate money to buy a house or save for the future. As a laboratory technologist I felt I would always live hand to mouth, a depressing thought.

I would miss cytology and Switzerland and especially Luzern, an exceptionally charming Swiss German village that I was sorry to leave behind. I would always remember the walk to the laboratory that took me across Kappelbrucke and along the cobblestone path which twisted through the old city; the cafes and bakeries that came alive in the early morning with the scent of freshly brewed coffee and homemade bread. I'd miss how clean the city was, and how colorful. I'd miss the path up the hill and past the castle wall before entering the sterile confines of the Luzern Kantonsspital.

I loved Luzern and its proximity to other beautiful destinations. There were many places to see, but with little time left before my departure for the States, the only place I really wanted to go was Tuscany in Northern Italy to visit a very handsome friend.

CHAPTER 24

Claudio was a tall, dark, sophisticated, charming, gorgeous Italian man who spoke several languages and was the managing director of a textile company. We first met on a train about a year earlier when I was traveling through Lugano, another exquisite Swiss city located near the Italian/Swiss border. By some strange, cosmic determination, my parents and aunt and uncle were with me on that trip.

My brothers and sisters and I all chipped in to buy my parents airline tickets for their Christmas gift, and here they were with my favorite Uncle Art and Aunt Kay. Together we explored mountains by cable car and cities by train. No matter what we did, it was approached with enthusiasm and child-like wonder. It's interesting how a change of scenery can literally transpose people. My parents' struggles and responsibilities were temporarily left behind to enjoy some of the most beautiful parts of the world, with me! We visited the ancestral family farm in Billerbeck, Germany, which is still family owned. This is my happiest memory with my parents. When we were not travelling, I had them mostly to myself in my small apartment located on Sempacherstrasse. Uncle Art and Aunt Kay stayed in a sweet little boutique hotel located about a block from me. From my balcony we delighted in waving to them on their hotel balcony, enjoying the simple pleasures that added to our never-ending amusement.

Claudio and I had kept in contact and got together a few times when he was in Luzern on business. Now that my work was finished, we spent several weeks together at his villa outside Florence before traveling along the Amalfi coast, saying our good-byes at The Villa d'Este, an historic, luxury hotel located on Lake Como. It was the perfect ending to a very interesting chapter of my life.

The likelihood of meeting the rare man I'd actually find attractive while travelling with my parents was zero to none, but since I had, the relationship felt pre-ordained. Any thought of remaining permanently with Claudio would have been precipitous. Even if he had extended the offer, I was ready to return to the States and anxious to pursue a bachelor's degree at long last. Claudio visited me in Washington, D.C., and I returned to Florence to see him, but the distance between us couldn't be reconciled and eventually our relationship ended.

Before leaving for my trip to Italy, I packed the things from my apartment for shipment to the States, and left some clothes in Luzern with friends to be picked up when I returned from Florence. My departure flight to the U.S. was out of Zurich, so I travelled by train back to Luzern alone where I gathered my belongings and visited friends at the laboratory one last time before bidding Switzerland a final farewell.

The other cytologists, like Simone, chose to live in the dormitory near the kantonsspital. It was there that I visited them in Anna's room before catching a taxi to the airport. Since my departure from the lab, a second Swedish woman, Ulrika, had arrived to replace me. Anna introduced me to her new colleague, who asked about my trip to Italy and plans for college.

It was during this conversation that Simone slithered in. She pretended to be interested in my storybook holiday as well, behaving in the artificial style with which I was now familiar. I knew she would be envious. Unfortunately I did not heed my instincts to be careful when she began to ask pointed, peculiar questions. Instead, I flaunted my romantic summer with Claudio, figuring she couldn't hurt me because I was leaving. I was tired of being nice to her when it wasn't reciprocated and I no longer cared to make an effort to get along.

Her questions were strange. "What day did you leave?" "What was the location of the villa?" "What was the man's name?" "How old was he?" "Do you know his birth date?" The questions didn't offer much of an opportunity to speak of the sunset drives along the Amalfi coast, our charming hotel in Portofino, the delicious food and wine, sultry beaches and handsome companion. I was too busy blabbing to be cautious.

Just like that, she got up and left, her questions having been answered. Ulrika, who was older and obviously wiser, looked at me and asked incredulously, "What are you doing? Why did you give her that information? It wasn't necessary."

"I don't know," I answered stupidly. "I couldn't see why I shouldn't give her the answers." I was too embarrassed to tell Ulrika that I had endured Simone's nonsense for over a year and now that I was leaving, I wanted to enjoy making her jealous.

Ulrika continued somewhat aggressively, sounding annoyed with me. "Don't you find it odd that she's asking you unnecessary, strange questions?"

Yes, it was suspicious. Deflated, I slouched to more modest proportions. Really, when was I going to grow up? Totally ill-equipped to participate in feline bravado, I would have been prudent to be cautiously discreet. What could she have wanted? It would be years before these memories of Simone would resurface, and I would have an answer.

I said my last good-byes and left Switzerland feeling more like a vulnerable, foolish child than the confident princess who fell from the caravan wagon.

CHAPTER 25

July 1978. It was a Wu Horse year, which means that there was an
overabundance of Earth and Fire. Wood nurtures Fire. An imbalance
of too much Fire will cause the delicate Yi Wood to become scorched.
I returned to the United States to fulfill the nagging desire to
complete my education. I had been successful in cytology and
enjoyed the analytical and diagnostic aspects, but it was time to
pursue a career in a field that I hoped would offer more personal
interactions and financial reward.

From Switzerland I applied and had been accepted to
Trinity College, a Catholic women's school in Washington, D.C.
At the time, the irony was lost on me. I could have applied to any
number of secular schools, but there was something comforting
and non-threatening about a small, private school run by nuns that
captured my interest. I would be entering my junior year of college
as a twenty-eight-year old woman who had lived and worked
internationally. Both age and experience would set me apart from
my junior counterparts. Not knowing where this new road would
take me, I wanted a smaller, nurturing environment that would
allow me the space to regroup and reinvent myself.

I trusted the safe surroundings, and perhaps on some
unconscious level I also hoped that returning to the familiarity of
the Church would rekindle the divine spark that seemed to have
disappeared from my life.

Science and basic studies credits from Ellsworth and Chicago
transferred easily to Trinity, but two years of business and economics
courses were still required to complete a bachelor's degree in
economics, which was my goal. It became paramount to me to
receive this degree if for no other reason than to say that I had it.

As an independent twenty-eight year old woman I struggled
with living in a college dormitory with girls who were ten years
younger than I, but financially this was the best option. Fortunately
I was able to work as the resident director which paid for room and
board, and student loans helped pay for tuition. Compared to my

first college experiences in Iowa when I was eighteen, many of these girls seemed spoiled, rich and self-centered. It wasn't easy to figure out how to be an authority figure to them when they were from a different generation and a different economic class than I had grown up in. We thought differently, figured out our problems differently, and had a different value system. On the one hand I was their peer, but on the other hand I was their go-to person for adult advice, their confidante. Someone was always in my room, either needing the key because they had been locked out, or wanting to discuss boyfriends, parents, teachers or roommates.

Despite my inner struggles, Trinity College provided a beautiful setting that was enhanced by the warmth and caring of the Franciscan nuns. I lived in "Main" dormitory, the building where our receptions and classes were held. Main was a grand structure built in the 1800s that displayed the exquisite stained glass, high ceilings, crown molding and hardwood floors of that era.

My room was particularly nice because of its private bath, a benefit that came with being the resident director. If one must return to school and live in a dormitory, it didn't get better than that. I tried to make the best of the situation, but I continued to be deeply unhappy at a fundamental level, unable to fill the inner spiritual void that I had created in a laboratory years earlier. Again I tried praying, and even attended campus chapel services to see if I could find my way back into the good graces of God and my angels. I was aware of a presence, not necessarily my childhood angels, but a presence of some sort. This presence watched me handle life's challenges on my own from a distance, without their assistance. I was desperately lonely without their comfort. Many times I asked others, even my mother and sisters, to pray for me, no longer confident that my own prayers were heard or considered worthy.

In May 1980, after two years at Trinity College, I received my degree in Economics. I was thirty years old and faced the formidable task of finding employment in a city full of high achievers. My previous experience and recently earned bachelor's degree seemed paltry next to the impressive credentials of those competing against me for positions in business or government.

Where was the fearlessness I had exuded since I was five years old? What was wrong with me and why did I feel so frightened and helpless? I no longer viewed things through the enchanted lens that pushed me through past struggles. Life's worries and responsibilities came with price tags, loan payments, decisions, and uncertainty. Where was the magic I could create in a morning under a tree eating a rhubarb jam sandwich? Recognizing that I walked in the shadow of my former self, I lamented the misguided assertions and infatuation with science that had brought me to this place, hoping that I would be forgiven for having abandoned God so the darkness could finally be lifted.

I entered Trinity College as Mary and left as Germaine, assuming my middle name at the insistence of friends who had spent their junior year in France. One-third of the students at Trinity were named Mary, they observed, insisting that the name did not suit me. "You look much more like a 'Germaine,'" they insisted—pronouncing my name with an accent on the second syllable as the French would say it—"than a Mary." I agreed with them, and embraced the new identity "Germaine" before stepping into a new career in the business community.

CHAPTER 26

Despite the competition for good jobs, I was offered several positions before accepting employment as an office manager for a defense consulting firm. This company paid $2,000 a year more than the next best offer, so I accepted, convinced that I could work my way into a more professional role. My goal was to carve out a career for myself. I agreed to work hard in return for a longer-term opportunity.

The owner of the company, George Kaddoura, was a military school graduate, president of a national political organization focused on Middle Eastern policies, and a former official at the State Department. He was a prominent individual with an impressive resume by any account. As a political person, he found his way into the limelight, and appeared on television frequently as an advisor to the White House. This was during the early 1980s when Lebanon was requesting support from the United States to help them fight their war against Syria, who they claimed had invaded their country. It was a complicated situation. Because of Lebanon's diverse composition and its history of border disputes, the U.S. took the initial position that this war was civil, not international, and therefore chose to remain uninvolved. It was George's job to convince the White House Administration otherwise, hoping to get U.S. military assistance for Lebanon.

Every day my job presented a new set of demands. There were the political dignitaries, newspaper journalists who clamored about looking for stories, and the international clients who paid for defense consulting work, the main line of business. George had a finger in many things, including every business endeavor that he thought would turn a dime. I researched these opportunities and scheduled appointments with defense vendors and various television networks. The job was exciting, just what I was looking for. The problem was George, who turned out to be a scoundrel with an extraordinary reputation.

Daily he brought women to his office; some days as many as three. As far as George was concerned, the most important part of my job was scheduling these women. They were mostly uneducated, less fortunate black women, posing as self-styled Zulu Queens. George picked them up at the bus stop, the snack kiosk in the basement of our building, or anywhere else he could find them. He handed out his business card with the message "Call me" handwritten on the back. Some of these women were professional prostitutes while others were just victims. George found it amusing to repeat their conversations, mocking their urban English in an attempt to shock and disgust me. He said he liked black women because he could "remain emotionally detached and treat them like animals."

The women were often lured to the office thinking they were applying for my position. Most appeared to be borderline illiterate, so I never feared that my job was in jeopardy, but I resented being put in this position. I had not signed up for this as part of the job and seethed with the indignity. How could anyone impose this unprofessional, debasing, perverse, exploitative and distasteful behavior on another? Perhaps I should not have assumed something negative, as George accused me of doing, and perhaps I should not have taken his behavior personally. It wasn't possible. After all, I am a woman too.

One weekend day, with the sleet coming down on top of the thirty plus inches of snow that had dropped on the city, George called me to come in to work. Most of D.C. had shut down, but I made my way on foot to the office and showed up at the requested time. George arrived hours later with someone who appeared to be a black prostitute in tow.

This was a side of George's life that I didn't want to know about or be a part of. I desperately wanted to leave the firm, but honestly did not know how to extricate myself without retribution. George Kaddoura was well-connected and powerful. He was the kind of person who cultivated favors and fear at the same time. I had worked too hard putting myself through college, trying to make something of my life for him to discredit me. His tactics worked on me like they had on others. Out of fear I imagined the importance of leaving on a high note—taking time to do so—when I should have just left.

There were other complications, too. His wife, Hala, and I had a very warm relationship. She was his first cousin and about twenty-five years his junior. Hala, which means "sweetness," attended a convent in the mountains of Lebanon before she was sent to the United States to be cared for by George and his mother. She was the embodiment of wide-eyed innocence and had a gentle, sweet manner and profound sincerity that made her the loveliest woman I had ever known. Her big, soft eyes reminded me of my own from earlier years. George was in his early fifties and had been single for many years prior to marrying Hala. I heard that he had been married once before to a professional woman who left him for his best friend. The marriage between George and Hala was arranged, but blossomed into an endearing love. It was clear that she adored her husband and he seemed sincere in his love for her, despite his bad habits.

One day Hala came to the office with their young son, Jimmy. Hala stopped to speak to the receptionist while three-year old Jimmy ran to his father's office door. Jimmy reached up for the knob, barely able to turn it shouting "Daddy, Daddy!"

George opened the door a crack. Visibly shaken he said "Just a second, Jimmy. Daddy will be right there."

Hala arrived at that moment, looking first disturbed and then angry, asking me acidly, "Who is in there?"

"A visitor," I answered, trying not to meet her eyes.

At that moment George came out with a be-bopping, short-short clad young woman who looked at Hala and me indignantly before sauntering arrogantly out of the office. George scolded Hala for visiting unannounced, angry that she wouldn't accept his visitor as a business relationship. After she left in tears, he reprimanded me for not being able to handle the situation more "professionally."

I couldn't bear to see the sadness that engulfed Hala's sweet eyes. Certainly there was no woman other than his beautiful wife that he would have preferred. That wasn't it. Whatever George's problem, it was strictly his own. Regardless, the pain that resulted from his blatant, reckless behavior affected the lives of all who were associated with him. *In one way or another, we are all connected. I didn't know what element either George or Hala was, but George's energy affected my own. I was already in a weakened state after abandoning the Light of God's Divinity and became powerless to extricate myself from the negative influence of George Kaddoura.*

In some way I felt complicit with George, an unwilling accomplice to his misogynist behavior but an accomplice just the same. During the two-and-a-half years that I worked for him, I witnessed many scenes such as this one. Every time it happened, my confidence and esteem eroded further as I was dragged through the debasing behavior that tainted what little self-respect I still had for myself. Incapacitating fear and humiliation robbed me of the strength I needed to move on.

At the end of 1981 I decided to look for another job. I had been working sixty to eighty hours a week for the past twenty-four months, without paid overtime and under cruel circumstances, and it showed on me. What possible impression could I make on a prospective employer in my current state of mind? I certainly didn't have the kind of vital energy needed to project an image of "a dynamic individual and self-starter" as described in the ads. An employment agency told me that despite my qualifications, one male interviewer rejected my application outright after our meeting because, "she has a hundred years of sadness in her eyes!"

CHAPTER 27

February 1982. It was a Ren Shu year. Lots of Ocean Water to nurture my Yi Wood, and to give me a boost. February was a Ren Yin month, too. More Ocean Water. George asked me to arrange a luncheon for him, Hala and a man named Michael Avila. I was instructed to make the reservation at Charlie's Crab, a restaurant conveniently located in the building where we worked so I could babysit little Jimmy while they were at lunch.

Michael Avila was a presidential appointee in the Reagan Administration and director for USAID's Bureau for Private Enterprise. He had been with Citibank for seventeen years previously, was an Air Force Academy graduate and was now serving on the Preston Commission, which had been established to examine issues surrounding the Lebanese crisis.

Jimmy was playing under my desk when George, Hala and their guest returned to the office after their lunch, leading George to inquire boldly, "Jimmy, what are you doing? Are you playing with Germaine? Every guy in Washington would love to play with Germaine!"

Mortified, I tried to ignore him, but George came up to my desk with Michael, who he introduced to me as his friend, Mike.

My first impression was that Mike was a nice looking man . . . a solid sort. Hala had told me ahead of their luncheon that he was single, a rare find in Washington, D.C. She seemed excited to introduce him to me, knowing that I didn't date much because of the crazy hours that I worked for her husband.

"Hmmm," I thought. "He's George's friend. What kind of person would have George for a friend?"

A few days later, Mike called to ask me out. Taken off guard, I reluctantly accepted, not knowing if I should hold the personal connection he had with my boss against him. We agreed to meet at Mel Crupin's, a restaurant that had become an institution in downtown D.C., and was located across the street from our office. On our first date I kept Mike waiting for an hour after which he called the office to find out if I was still coming. I sputtered and stammered apologies, regretting my decision to meet him, but said I hoped to get away in a minute or two. George was making me work late again, which heightened the anxiety I was already feeling. Another hour passed and Mike called again, just as I was walking out the door. I arrived at Mel Crupin's tired, frustrated, chilled from the icy weather and in general feeling disgusted with my life.

Mike was waiting for me patiently, smiling. To my surprise, he appeared pleasant and charming, not angry in the least for my tardiness. He went so far as to offer excuses for me, saying that it was unfortunate to have to work so late in this miserable weather. This man appeared to be a gentleman, unlike what I had imagined. He was polite and understanding, and wasn't a friend to George after all. Their relationship was strictly professional. I felt badly for pre-judging him.

We went on several more dates during the following days. Mike offered personal compliments and attention, and shared a broad vision full of optimism. He had grown up in a small border town in the Imperial Valley, a first generation American. Both of his parents were Mexican whose ancestors had emigrated from

the Basque country in Spain. He had Latin blood from Spanish
conquistadors and German, English and Canadian blood from
adventurous Caucasian ancestors, clear blue eyes, thick, tawny
hair and delicious looking skin. He was a child prodigy who had
received a string of accolades for academic, athletic and musical
accomplishments. Mike was raised bi-lingual. He traversed
cultures easily, feeling equally comfortable in both American and
Hispanic settings. He had received scholarships and offers to several
prestigious universities at the same time he was scouted to play
professional baseball. In the end, he chose the Air Force Academy,
after receiving encouragement from teachers and state senators alike.
His voice melted away my apprehensions, breaking down self-
inflicted barriers that disfranchised me. He listened to stories of my
childhood, European escapades, and George, and he did not hold
the debasing parts against me.

Mike had travelled extensively, and had lived in several
European and South American countries. His worldview came
from personal experience, and he exuded confidence and inspired
trust. Mike's calm, resolute behavior sprang from a blend of personal
experience and academic sagacity that was able to separate reality
from daydreams and arrive at rock solid decisions. He was a leader;
presidential material. Mike was the one who reflected my dreams
and aspirations, and shared my sense of adventure and desire
to travel. He appreciated exotic food and fine wine; he enjoyed
exploring art galleries and historic treasures. Yes, this was the man
I could be proud to introduce. This was the man I could finally give
into completely, wholly, entirely.

Mike opened me up in other ways, too. He helped me tap
into parts of myself that were buried beneath layers and layers of
"good girl" Catholic school guilt, low self-esteem, shyness, timidity,
inferiority, and a rigid sense of "decency."

I was thirty-two years old and not a virgin, but I had never
known a man who could so skillfully put me at ease to enjoy
delicious sex. Mike was an experienced lover who made every
encounter fresh and exciting. Even after months of dating, we

rendezvoused in hotel lobbies pretending to meet for the first time, only to enjoy the newness of discovering each other all over again.

Was there anything he couldn't do? He was an accomplished dancer, played college baseball and football, flew airplanes and even took shorthand. I was smitten, bitten, enamored and head over heels in love, falling deeper and deeper for this handsome charmer.

I had been hounded by married men my entire life and had formed opinions about those who cheated on their wives. I was *not* one of those women who blamed other women for their cheating husbands. I blamed the person with the marital contract—usually the man—who in my experience behaved like a dog, chasing down a scent until it was doused with his own. I believed that marital contracts were sacred, and fidelity was the responsibility of the married individual. I loathed married men who cheated on their wives, using them as an excuse for their reckless self-indulgence.

Although previously married, Mike was divorced and had been unmarried for many years. It was safe to love him, and to adorn him liberally with thousands of kisses.

Mike's presence bolstered my confidence and self-esteem, his aspirations and achievements helped me to realign my own. The polarizing experience of working for a lowlife boss while falling in love with a man like Michael Avila made it impossible to continue working for George. The dichotomy of these two men was more than I could reconcile. With Mike in my life, I had an infusion of renewed self-worth that gave me strength to leave my job. *With the help from a Ren Water year and the positive influence from Mike, the energy balance around me had shifted.* It became easier to project a more desirable image and regain the attitude necessary to attract better employment.

CHAPTER 28

About two months after meeting Mike, I left George's firm to work as an independent contract manager. One of my first assignments was for Roger, a political consultant whose firm specialized in fundraising. This project required that the four of us on Roger's team live in Florida for several months to help with the Amendment Nine campaign, a fight between doctors and lawyers over liability ceilings. We would be representing the trial lawyers against the doctors who wanted to limit physician liability for pain and suffering. My new boss invited the entire office out for dinner as a getting-to-know-you event before we left for Florida. On a whim we decided to visit a fortuneteller, who we felt certain would confirm the success of our new assignment.

The electricity generated between us ignited a spirited banter that evening, setting the stage for an exciting three months in Florida together. We approached the new venture with whole-hearted enthusiasm. No one, not even a psychic, could put a damper on our excitement. After our celebratory dinner, we piled into a taxi to visit the psychic whose sign we had seen on our way to the restaurant. I was in the flow and spirit of my new assignment and friends, eager to turn a page for myself.

As the newcomer, I was encouraged to go first.

The rather heavy-set elderly woman led me through beaded curtains into a small, dark, private room, away from the lively chatter of the group. She asked me to be seated in an old velvet armchair and pulled her chair next to mine. Holding my hand, she turned it over, taking time to examine my palm thoroughly while her pained expression created deep furrows between her brows.

Shaking her head dramatically she said, "No. No. I'm so sorry. Someone doesn't like you. Someone did something terribly cruel to you. I am so sorry."

I wasn't quite sure what she was talking about. Someone doesn't like me on the project? I thought she would be telling me about the upcoming Florida trip in our session. She then went on.

"Someone has put a curse on you. I don't know why they did it, but this is very bad. This is not a typical curse. It's the sort of thing that will change your energy. Good things cannot come your way as long as you are surrounded in this darkness. You can work and work, but still you will have nothing unless you remove the curse."

I sat there dumbfounded, too shocked to display expression. What is there to say when you discover that someone has gone out of his or her way to destroy your life in this cowardly, insidious way? "I don't know if I can help you," she said, "but I'll try."

There were three other people in the waiting room eager to hear their good fortune. I no longer felt like joining the party and couldn't bear the thought of facing them. Before leaving the small, dark room to join my colleagues, I collected my thoughts for a moment and promised the woman that I would contact her again.

The most disturbing part of the psychic's reading was that I felt her comments were accurate. There wasn't any way to share this conversation with relative strangers without risk of exposing an extremely private part of my life, one that I didn't understand myself. Utterly confused and deeply concerned, I deflected the interest of my colleagues with a quiet, withdrawn smile, not knowing what to say. They picked up on the shift in my mood and did not persist in asking for details.

One by one my friends had their palms read, and one by one they emerged from behind the beaded curtain with high hopes for a bright, new future. The group's optimism was reinforced by the reading for the fundraising expert on the project who was told that he would be "surrounded by hundreds of lawyers in a deal that involved millions of dollars." Naturally, he was happy to hear that he would become wealthy as a result of this association.

Indeed, he did end up working with hundreds of lawyers, and he made millions of dollars—not for himself, but for the campaign. Roger, too, gained greater prominence as a result of this project, and he went on to work on larger campaigns. The last member of our group, a woman, was told that the problems in her marriage would be resolved quickly, which is exactly what happened. The accuracy of my colleagues' predictions over the coming weeks lent credibility to the psychic's insights, so I kept her phone number, thinking I would pay her another visit when we returned to D.C.

The psychic's reading gnawed at me during the three months

that I was in Florida. I mulled over the possibilities of those who might have wanted to hurt me. Who could it be? It was disturbing to hear that I could have undisclosed enemies who could be so cruel. More than five years had passed since I left Switzerland, but I vividly remembered Simone's voodoo story of dolls and pins and the bizarre questions she asked the last time we saw one another. Could she be the culprit?

After three months, the campaign ended with a vote favoring the trial lawyers. I returned to Washington, D.C., anxious to visit the psychic again. I needed to understand this curse and, I hoped, find a cure for my predicament. I didn't doubt that this woman was speaking the truth according to her own belief system. I knew, too, that something had happened to me, something weird and inexplicable that no doctor would or could address. If only I could reverse those previous, arrogant pronouncements I had made at the microscope while investigating DNA ...

CHAPTER 29

It was sweltering hot the day of our appointment, one of those familiar muggy days in late summer that plagues the nation's capital. I worked downtown, and calculated that it was closer to visit the psychic directly from the office at the end of the day than to go to her place from my home. I remember wearing a white suit to work, perhaps an intentional gesture on my part to present a counterbalance to the dark energy she'd described.

The combination of the anxiety I was feeling, the hot weather and clothing that was geared more to an air-conditioned building than an afternoon sojourn to Alexandria on a crowded train, made me dizzy and exhausted. I felt totally miserable, scared and alone, having decided against discussing the situation with anyone, including Mike. The circumstances were perplexing enough for me to grasp. Until I knew what I was dealing with, and if there was a cure, there was really nothing to say.

It seemed I had no choice but to return to this psychic. What if she couldn't lift the curse? What if nobody could? I approached her building with a multitude of scrambled emotions that vacillated between terror, skepticism and sadness. Again, she ushered me into the room behind the beaded curtain.

"First," she said, "I need to see if it's possible to help you."

Taking an empty jar in one hand, she walked to a sink in the corner, filled the jar with water and then, setting it on the table between us, put some granules in it. The water turned black.

"Now," she said, "I want you to breathe into the jar. If the water turns clear, I can help you. If the water stays black, then I am sorry, there is nothing I can do."

Her eyes looked sincere as she pushed the jar in front of me, motioning for me to breathe into it. I paused briefly, reflecting on her expression. She seemed tired. Was it the cynicism of people who sought her help and then claimed fraud, or was it just age? She didn't appear to be that old, perhaps fifty-five years or so, but she was certainly tired. She smiled slightly, as if understanding that I had my doubts, and perhaps hoping that I wouldn't be another ungrateful customer.

I continued examining her face while breathing into the jar. Her attention shifted from my eyes to what had happened to the water. While putting a hand up to her mouth, she gasped as if she didn't believe her eyes any more than I did mine. The water had turned crystal clear.

"This is wonderful. You can be helped. I will help you," she exuded. "First, bring me nine bottles of whiskey, the same whiskey your friend (referring to Mike) drinks."

"Hmmm . . . ," I thought suspiciously. "Why would I have to bring a certain type of whiskey? What difference does the brand make?" What does Mike have to do with anything?

"I'm going to have a party for the spirits, using the whiskey," she answered, presumably reading my mind.

"Yeah, right! A big party for someone, that's for sure," I thought.

That evening I went to the liquor store to purchase the required alcohol, becoming irritated with the request. The bottles were costly and heavy. "Is this just a ploy to get free booze? I wondered."

The trip to the psychic's home was especially difficult given my load. I lived and worked in Washington, D.C., and she lived in Alexandria, Virginia, a suburb. It meant traveling by Metro and switching stations with two large, heavy bags of glass bottles in the heat of late summer. From the metro station, I still needed to walk about fifteen minutes. Tripping on cracked sidewalks in high heels while laboring under the weight of the bottles was not how I wanted to spend my extended lunch hour. Negative thoughts preoccupied me until I arrived at her door. The lady could see I was tired and annoyed. She tried to be enthusiastic while explaining what she was going to do.

"Fine," I thought. "Just take this curse away from me."

The psychic said she would be working at night and that I would soon begin to feel better. And oh yes, she also needed copper. She asked me to bring her a hundred dollars' worth of quarters so that she could extract the copper from them.

"What? Why couldn't I just get copper tubing . . . or pennies? It would be much less expensive and wouldn't require so much effort on her part," I mused to myself. "Is this for real?"

"My work is done at night in the caves, when I have to go deep in the ground. It gets very cold. I want you to buy a warm bathrobe for me," she said.

"Caves, what caves?" I speculated to myself. "I've never heard that there were caves around D.C. Besides, I would like to have a warm bathrobe for myself."

My confidence was waning. I truly believed a curse had been put on me, but I was becoming less and less convinced that she was the person to remove it. I had agreed to pay her what I considered to be a large sum of money. The other goodies were costly as well, and then there was the inconvenience. All I wanted was for a service to be provided. Beyond that, I didn't really want to be involved. What a bunch of baloney!

I left that day totally discouraged. I did buy her the bathrobe she wanted, returning the next day to deliver it, but after that I never went back to learn if I had been "cured" or not. I certainly did not feel cured. Meanwhile, she had the whiskey, the bathrobe, and a chunk of money. All that, I reasoned, *in classic non-hostile Yi Wood fashion*, should be enough to make her happy for her efforts. I didn't want her to be angry that I had not returned and do something revengeful. I just wanted to be done with her.

Time passed. I just couldn't break this cycle I was in. I still dated Mike, but our relationship was not progressing the way I had hoped. For some reason, there continued to be a disconcerting distance between us.

CHAPTER 30

Devastated over a recent, messy breakup with her husband, my friend, Susan, and I spent the day together in Georgetown. Slowly and painfully Susan shared the details of their problems. Between tears, laughter and the occasional distraction, she spelled out every emotion she had ever felt in their ten-year marriage. An entire vacation was recreated and lived again, only to be scrutinized for signs of fidelity, sincerity and "did he ever love me?" We walked up one street and down the other, looking through windows, but seeing nothing. Susan was mourning a death; the painful end to the life she and Mark had created as husband and wife.

From what I understood, Susan's husband had surprised her with a lovely dinner and beautiful, romantic evening on their recent wedding anniversary. Since they had been emotionally estranged for months, Susan relished this tender and reflective moment, hoping to reconcile their differences and to start anew. It was during this romantic evening that Mark pulled out a sheath of papers. Couched between sentiment and a willingness to forget their problems and start over, he asked Susan to co-sign a $20,000 medical school loan on his behalf. Documents were ready for Susan's signature and a pen was in his hand. She was already listed as the primary borrower and person responsible for repaying the debt. She signed the documents, believing his sincere intent to move forward with their lives together.

Exactly one week after signing the papers, Mark asked Susan for a divorce.

But, that wasn't the end to this already sad tale. Susan's sleuthing uncovered that her husband had been having an affair for quite some time and was living with "the other woman." Something else. A child, about a year old, was also in the picture. It was an open question in Susan's mind whether or not the baby was his.

Susan churned over late night excuses and long weekends away from home that he claimed were spent in laboratories. She regurgitated the loneliness she felt from those years which saddened her even further. Susan worked long hours herself. The responsibility to provide a comfortable home and lifestyle and to pay for her husband's tuition and spending money were on her shoulders.

Her husband's covert relationship and child and his ruthless extortion had broken her heart. Their entire marriage focused on supporting his ambitions—at Susan's expense—and now it had ended with a calculated, devastating blow.

Susan's situation and pain overwhelmed me. I could find no adequate words of comfort nor meaningful experience to share with my brokenhearted friend. As we walked I noticed a sign jutting out from a narrow brick row house on Wisconsin Avenue. The sign read: "Madame Sylvia, Psychic."

Stupidity or serendipity, I suggested that we stop to have our palms read. Selfishly I thought it would be a good distraction, and I wanted to share the weight of our conversation.

Madame Sylvia occupied a small room the size of a hall coat closet at the end of a long, very narrow corridor. The beaded curtain, which seemed to be a customary fixture in a psychic's parlor, separated her current customer from those who were waiting. After my previous visit to the Alexandria psychic, I was curious what this lady would tell me, and whether this reading would concur with the prior reading. However, I was not there so much for myself as I was for Susan, whose emotional needs were out of my depth.

Susan went in first. After about fifteen minutes, she emerged from behind the curtain looking a bit relieved. We didn't have an opportunity to discuss her session before it was my turn.

Madame Sylvia had an interesting appearance. Her dark hair, white, flawless skin, intense expression and gentle, yet firm voice made her mysterious. Whether she was Occidental or Eastern was difficult to say, but she looked like an elegant gypsy. She was younger than the other psychic—perhaps in her early forties—well manicured and nicely dressed; very pretty and appealing.

Careful not to taint her reading, I decided against telling her about my previous experience with the psychic from Alexandria. Madame Sylvia, too, examined my palm in a careful, methodical way, groping for words to express her horror and compassion as she carefully explained the cruelty of someone who was intent on destroying my life. She told me almost verbatim what the older psychic had, with a few additional details: it was a woman who had done this to me, for no other reason than jealousy. My lifelong suffering would give this person nothing more than the satisfaction of knowing that she was destroying me with a slow, agonizing death.

I was despondent. Madame Sylvia went on to say that, "no effort or good deed could affect a change," and unless I was cleared of this curse, I'd end up without hope, and in total despair. The final work of this evil plan would eventually destroy my soul.

Madame Sylvia then added that there wasn't just one woman who had put a curse on me. There was a second one as well. She cautioned me, "you are surrounded by jealous women and need to protect yourself."

There was no reason not to believe her since she was describing exactly how I felt, and her explanation was as good as any other. It was only after she offered to remove the curse that had plagued me for five years that I told her about the psychic in Alexandria who had tried to help, but was unsuccessful. I told her, too, that I had given up on those earlier attempts because the whiskey, quarters and other requests sounded absurd.

"The other lady is too old and weak. This is not an ordinary curse and needs to be removed by a strong person," she said while puffing up her chest just enough to imply superior physical strength. "It will take considerable time and effort, but it can be done," she reassured me.

There were no vessels to blow in, no bottles of whiskey to buy, and her Georgetown location was easily accessible. My psychological and emotional resolve was dwindling, *making my already Yin disposition even more so.* I was easily convinced that I needed this specialized brand of help and agreed to have her perform the rituals she said were necessary to bring my energy back into alignment. She seemed my only hope.

I pondered the women to whom Madame Sylvia referred, and recounted stories of Simone from Switzerland, and Mike's former girlfriend, Lori, asking if it were one of them. It could have been anyone I supposed, but I strongly suspected Lori to be the second woman. Lori and Mike dated before he met me. Despite their break-up, she continued to maintain a relationship with his mother, Josephine, and his twelve-year old daughter from a previous marriage, Victoria.

When Lori's manipulations became too obvious to ignore, Mike put some distance between them. Because he was on to her, I wasn't concerned until he told me that Lori respected his feelings for me and wanted to just be friends.

"She respected his feelings for me?" There was no way I was going to buy *that* nonsense. In lieu of an intimate relationship with Mike, Lori asked to stay close to Victoria and Josephine.

Lori made dates for Victoria and Mike to go horseback riding with her, knowing that Victoria loved horses and that her father would not want to disappoint his daughter. She invited Josephine out for dinner, frequently returning to Mike's home for coffee afterwards.

Josephine found all this female interest in her son entertaining, freely revealing the conversations she and Lori shared about Mike, which I considered far too personal. Josephine received pleasure by describing the "women who chase after him," proud of her son's magnetism as well as his other successes. She spoke glowingly of her son, appointing herself as gatekeeper to his affections. She revealed details of his previous relationships, never tiring of repeating how attractive he was to other women. I felt that Lori should not have been sharing intimacies with the mother of her former lover, and the mother certainly should not be sharing them with me.

I considered Lori to be a stalker, a psycho, a person to avoid. Her persistent and overbearing interest in Mike's daughter and mother seemed unnatural given the circumstances, so I decided it was safest and best to keep my distance.

After my experience with the first psychic I had read a bit about curses and black magic rituals. For a curse to be effective, I read, it is necessary to have either a physical object or something such as a lipstick print from a glass or napkin from the person you want to harm.

There was an occasion when Victoria came to me with a pearl earring she found near her father's bed, asking if it belonged to me. Although it was mine, I denied it. Victoria was an impressionable young girl. We got along well, but I thought it was premature for her to know that her father and I were intimate. She told me later that Lori had claimed the earring as her own. Why, I had wondered, would Lori want my earring?

Madame Sylvia listened intently, quite certain of Lori's and Simone's desires to hurt me and their sinister methods to do so. She asked to meet again at her little alley on Wisconsin Avenue and to bring a bottle of the perfume I normally wore. At least it wasn't two bags of scotch, I remembered with relief. Madame Sylvia emphasized that her work was clean, and that she worked differently than most, which gave me some additional comfort as she and I concluded our session.

Since Susan and I were instructed not to share our readings with each other, we did not discuss the events of that afternoon. I could tell from her face and her lighter step that the experience had been good for her, which was a further relief to me. Once we'd said our goodbyes to Madame Sylvia, we made small talk as we walked together through Georgetown, back the way we had come.

CHAPTER 31

I did as Madame Sylvia had instructed and returned a few days later. She had been so certain of what she needed, that I felt even more assured seeing her enthusiasm as she studied the bottle of perfume I set in front of her.

"I will be working this evening," she informed me. "You should go to bed early because you are apt to become very tired."

She was right. My head hardly hit the pillow before I fell into a deep slumber and had the most amazing dream. I was in a pool with glass on all sides, swimming like a fish or a mermaid. It was easy, flowing, fun and energetic. I could swim up, down, sideways, and every which way. I could swim forever, without tiring and without breathing. As I swam, I kept getting lighter and lighter, not wanting to stop.

When I awoke the next morning, I felt exhilarated. The oppression had lifted and my face had cleared. For years it had appeared puffy and my eyes were constantly tearing, but that seemed to have stopped. Even the rosacea I had been dealing with recently had disappeared. Everything. Gone overnight.

There was also a side effect Madame Sylvia had warned. "Men will be drawn to you," she cautioned.

She had instructed me to get another bottle of my perfume, Molinard de Molinard, and to use it with Halston, a heavier, muskier scent. I did this. From then on wherever I was, on the street or in the elevator, men stopped to ask the name of my perfume. This didn't happen only once or twice, but perhaps fifty or a hundred times. I was stopped on the train going to New York City, and in parking lots, restaurants and supermarkets. I wore the two perfumes together for about a year, during which time life took a turn upward.

I was hired to work as the assistant to the managing partner of a large law firm, became much happier, and after three years of dating, Mike finally proposed.

We had never discussed marriage, mostly because emotional conversations and those that dealt with feelings were kept at a distance. Consequently, it became a bad habit to defer these conversations or not bring them up at all. Privately, I had decided to give Mike until my next birthday in late May to propose. If he hadn't asked me to marry him by then, I had planned to stop seeing him and move on. We had already dated for two years before I moved in with him and now we had been living together for about a year, long enough for two adults to determine if we were well-suited for marriage or not. There was no threat, just an agreement I made with myself to expect a commitment before investing more of my precious love.

Perhaps Mike felt my unstated resolve. Whatever the catalyst, I was delighted by his proposal and accepted it with an open, happy heart.

CHAPTER 32

Shortly after our engagement in February, Mike informed me that he had invited Victoria to come live with us at the end of her current school year. Without allowing me an opportunity to object or even a discussion regarding his decision, he called his daughter to confirm the invitation and to make plans for her arrival.

Naturally I wasn't happy. Victoria and I had always gotten along. She was fun to be with. I was disturbed that Mike had made the decision without discussing it with me first. There were so many concerns associated with this decision that needed to be addressed, but all discussion was thwarted by Mike's heavy-handed dismissal. I tried to share my disappointment and feelings, but as usual he deflected them.

Victoria flew to D.C. from her mother's home in Florida

during spring break. Details to move in with us were flushed out between Mike, Victoria and Victoria's mother. Everything was happening too quickly. I could not properly digest the dynamic that was unfolding in front of me. All the indicators suggested that this new arrangement was not going to be easy.

I had known Victoria since she was twelve. She was now sixteen years old and accustomed to having things her way. She was a spoiled teenager who spent money lavishly, resented any and all authority, and played her mother and father against one another like a master. Mike was not accustomed to raising children, complicated by his own confusion over the way his first family ended and the affect it had on Victoria. He refused all conversations and family meetings where we could hash things out together, and he outright rejected the suggestion of "ground rules" or anything remotely akin to discipline or structure. My relationship with Mike shifted to a dynamic I had not previously experienced. I wasn't on solid footing and groped uneasily with a way to express my deep concerns about my Midwestern upbringing and how our different set of values could blend harmoniously with our emerging family unit. How would we get along with one another in a family context?

CHAPTER 33

Mike and I were married in June 1986. *It was a Bing Fire, Sunshine year with lots and lots and lots of Fire, Wood and Earth. Wood nurtures Fire, but too much Fire scorches Wood.* Our wedding took place on the same weekend that the United States kicked off the celebration for the bicentennial of the US Constitution. It was a gloriously sunny, D.C. summer day. We kept our guest list short to avoid the expense of a large wedding. Mike's only brother and sister-in-law lived in Switzerland and were not able to make it, so we decided quite practically to have a second reception in Dyersville at a later date when all our siblings could attend.

We did invite our mothers, however. Josephine was already

staying with us that summer, so she didn't need to travel. My mother made the trip with Uncle Tony (my Godfather), and Uncle Art and Aunt Kay, the same aunt and uncle who had visited me in Switzerland with my parents. They all drove from Iowa together.

My father died of a heart attack in 1984, never having had a chance to meet Mike. I wished that I could have learned his thoughts about the man I hoped to marry, but it wasn't meant to be. Fortunately, Uncle Tony was there to take my deceased father's place. I should have asked him to escort me down the aisle myself, but this decision was made quite informally during a discussion with my mother over the phone when I was told that he was coming. The plan went slightly awry when Mom forgot to ask him for me. Uncle Tony showed up unprepared with a beige suit, which wasn't ideal for the role. I made the mistake of commenting on it to her.

Out of sheer habit, my mother gave her predictable response: "There you go again. You think you're so good. You think you are better than everyone else. What's wrong with his suit?"

I felt her response was unnecessary, especially since it was *my* wedding, but I was anxious not to allow anything spoil the occasion. "Never mind, Mom," I said. "The beige suit is fine. It's okay."

The truth is that it was okay with me.

Both the service and reception were held in a lovely, oval ballroom that was part of the apartment complex where we lived. It was a beautiful, intimate room with fireplaces, crown molding, hardwood floors and antique paintings.

I wore a white suit with a wide brimmed hat, suggestive of the style worn on that popular TV show, *Dallas*. Mike looked very handsome in a dark navy dress suit and pink tie that matched Victoria's dress. We were going for a relaxed look, more befitting the groom's second marriage and the bride's *no-longer-a-young-maiden* age bracket. I was not one of those women who'd spent a lifetime planning her wedding, and I had no real sense of correct protocol or prescribed way the wedding was "supposed to be." Before deciding on my suit, which was the first one I tried on, I had never given a wedding gown a second thought. If Uncle Tony was dressed in a beige suit, so be it. If Victoria wore a funny pink dress and put a goofy bow in her hair, fine. I just wanted everyone to get along and have a good time. I wanted the wedding to come from the right place, and I was determined to start the marriage off in the best possible way.

Victoria was my maid-of-honor and the only bridesmaid I had in the wedding party. In hindsight I do regret not having my brothers and sisters with me, especially Linda, who I had always promised would be my maid-of-honor. There was no reason not to have two bridesmaids, except that that single detail would have triggered invitations to approximately fifty members of my immediate family which would set off a series of expensive decisions for all involved. The gesture to include Victoria in the wedding as my bridesmaid was to reassure her as much as possible that I had embraced her as my own. I was sensitive to Victoria's feelings, cognizant that our marriage could make her feel insecure. It seemed like the right thing to do at the time, but came at the expense of omitting Linda.

Mike's friends, the Kaufmanns, had offered us their New York City apartment for a short honeymoon. We had had a busy summer so far. Now it was time to have a few days with my new husband alone before assuming undefined parental responsibilities. But as we were about to leave, Josephine started crying. She asked Mike if she and Victoria could join us in New York. I was taken aback by the request, which clearly put Mike on the spot, but he agreed to send them up on the train the following day. I should have objected, but I didn't. I was taken off guard by the confusing scene that played out in front of me, expecting Mike to defend our right to a few days to ourselves. Victoria recognized the request as being outrageous and tried to refuse, but her grandmother knew all the right buttons to push to get her way, which she did. *Yi Wood goes out of her way to avoid stress on anyone. Being adaptable and agreeable is her nature, a trait that is often misunderstood and perceived as weakness. The Yi Wood personality should be more assertive to avoid being taken advantage of by those who don't respect this quality.*

Mike and I had one enjoyable evening together before Victoria

and Josephine arrived the next day. After that, our foursome visited
the Empire State Building together, we strolled through Manhattan
together, and had dinner together at an Indian restaurant. Soon it was
time to pack up and return to our new life in D.C. Josephine settled
into our marriage more quickly than I by assuming an authoritative
role. She ordered me to "clean" the Kaufmann's apartment. It goes
without saying that I fully intended to leave the apartment the way
we found it, but the heavy cleaning hadn't been tended to in quite
some time. Once again I expected Mike to intervene with a simple,
lighthearted comment to dismiss such a ridiculous demand, but it
didn't happen. We were on our honeymoon, for crying out loud, but
I spent the last morning on the floor with a bucket and scrub brush,
making sure that I got all the corners.

Back home in D.C., the triangular relationship between Mike,
Victoria and me became increasingly stressful. Shortly after our
wedding I returned home late from a long day of work to find a
sink full of dishes left behind by Victoria and her friends. The condo
kitchen was small. Before I could make dinner, the dishes needed
to be washed so there was room for me to work. I called Victoria to
help me clean up. Instead, Mike appeared in the kitchen doorway
with his arm around Victoria saying that she wasn't required to do
dishes or clean up after herself because "she has her studies to focus
on." Resentment sliced through me. I couldn't help but become
angry by the double standard that was fast developing.

After three years of dating Mike, I thought I knew the man
I was marrying. Something inexplicable happened to make our
relationship change overnight. There was no discussion of things
that really mattered, no negotiation or attempt to see things eye-to-
eye. There was no room for compromise on his part. I was dictated
to and bullied into accepting circumstances that seemed insane.

There was a time when our merged bodies could dissolve pain
or disagreement into a faded memory. Now the lack of tenderness
between us made it difficult to heal our anger. The time we spent
together quickly diminished into details related to the daily grind.
I was crushed with disappointment as the love of my life dismissed

me, relegating me to what felt like maid status.

The three-way relationship became more and more confusing and stressful. I couldn't win for losing. No matter what I did or said it was filtered first from the perception of an angry sixteen-year old before receiving an approval rating. I struggled to sort out my relationships, values and self-worth. How misguided could I be with my sense of right and wrong? Values? Ethics? Standards? It felt sometimes like everything I had ever learned or believed was pulverized into meaningless tripe.

I didn't blame Victoria for acting out so miserably. Her father and mother divorced when she was five. I was no therapist, but could imagine that she had plenty of mixed emotions that hadn't been processed. What I couldn't understand was Mike's behavior. He was the father, with responsibilities to guide this child. Surely he knew that his daughter needed to be corrected when doing foolish things, like stowing a bag full of whiskies in her closet "for a friend," or faking the need to go to the emergency room to garner sympathy instead of a scolding. Whatever was going on I simply didn't understand. I only knew that I was in the middle of an impossible situation.

There is always a way to make the most of bad circumstances, and at age thirty-six, I suppose I should have known how, but I was at a loss for knowing how to make things better. I began to crave emotional intimacy. The more I needed to be close to Mike, the more he pushed me away. There was always some diversion, some other priority that prevented him from being available to pursue a relationship that shared thoughts, feelings and a mutual respect for one another's ideas.

Mike traveled extensively overseas, gone about seven months of the first year we were married. During his absences, Victoria and I got along surprisingly well. Most importantly, we talked. If something bothered either one of us, we discussed it. She was much more agreeable when it was just the two of us. If there was a situation I didn't know how to manage, I called her mother and stepfather for advice. Victoria made it a point to be more helpful around the house until her father returned from a trip and the nonsense started all over again.

I wondered why this was so, assuming emotional shortcomings in my husband and old fashioned spoiled behavior in Victoria.

Their BaZi elemental analysis revealed another picture. Mike is a Yang Bing Fire, an omniscient Sun, and Victoria is a Yang Wu Earth, an unyielding Mountain. Fire nurtures Earth. Both Bing Fire and Wu Mountain are domineering elements that have always been and always will be. I am a Yi Wood, a Vine or Flower nurtured by Water. Wood nurtures Fire, and controls Earth. At the same time, Wood needs Bing Fire, Sunshine, and Earth to grow. An overwhelming presence of both, especially in the absence of Water for nurturing, leaves the Yi Wood vine scorched and unable to take root in the hardened Wu Earth Mountain.

CHAPTER 34

Mike and I were married for a little more than a year when we took an Asian business-cum-vacation trip. It was August of 1987. Victoria was with her mother and stepfather in Florida for her summer vacation where she stayed until we returned. Mike and I first went to the Philippines then to Thailand, Hong Kong, Indonesia, and the island of Bali. The longer we were away from home, the more our relationship returned to its pre-marital normal. Mike became more attentive, anxious to see me at the end of the day and to hold me in his arms. When it was just the two of us, we became lovers again.

Mike and I stayed at the Nailert Park Hilton Hotel while in Bangkok, an unexpected oasis in the middle of a bustling metropolis. Eight lush acres of tropical paradise embraced this piece of heaven that existed only for me and the man I adored. The grounds were magnificent. A luxurious pool rested invitingly amidst palm trees. Hanging vines, waterfalls, and orchids that grew from the trunks of trees perfected this exotic utopia. It was just what Mike and I needed to release any problems between us into the gentle night breezes.

Unfortunately, I became very ill, having picked up some bug in

Manila. The luscious paradise that beckoned from the balcony had to wait. The bug hit me hard in Bangkok, forcing me to stay in bed. Believe it or not, this, too, was a treat! Though I was in a fair amount of discomfort, it was the very first time in my adult life that I was nursed while being sick and I loved it. Always before I had pushed myself to go to work, attend class or whatever, no matter how badly I felt. Giving into sickness was a luxury I couldn't afford. Now I was on vacation with my husband where there was room service for everything. I had no immediate worries except the persistent high fever and weight loss.

Tharee, the Executive Housekeeper at the hotel, heard of my affliction and checked on me regularly. She arrived at my room with beautiful flower arrangements and fresh fruits and a smile bursting with sweetness. She plumped my pillows and ordered hot tea for me, and shared tales of the time she spent in the States. Coincidentally, Tharee had gone to Trinity College in Washington, D.C. as I had, and was a personal friend to the one and only couple we knew in Bangkok.

After a few days of this special care, I started to feel a bit better. The hotel physician prescribed some medication, which I could have had delivered, but I was anxious to leave the room. Despite feeling weak, I got dressed and headed out to the pharmacy behind the hotel. I didn't really know where I was going, which must have been apparent by the expression on my face when Mike spotted me from the car he was riding in and shouted, "Germaine! What are you doing down here?"

Relieved that he had come along, I got into the car. Casually, we talked about the events of the day as we passed a rather strange looking park behind the hotel. "My God! Mike, did you see that?" I asked.

"See what?"

"You're not going to believe this," I said excitedly and in total disbelief, "but I just saw an enormous penis. It was huge!"

Mike thought I was being playful, "Come on, you're joking," he teased. "You're delirious, it must be your fever." I gave an exasperated sigh, unable to get him to take me seriously.

Our English-speaking driver muffled his laughter but could not contain his amusement.

"Sir, it's true. That's a fertility shrine," he explained. "If you don't want your wife to be pregnant, don't go any closer. My wife visited the goddess, and she is now three months pregnant. The goddess is very powerful!"

Since I was thirty-seven years old and Mike was forty-seven, we needed to think seriously about starting our own family, if we were ever going to have one. I had visited a doctor several times, fearing early menopause. For some reason, my menses had stopped abruptly and I had not had a period for over a year. I was losing my hair, too. The doctor seemed quite certain that my physiology had changed because of the stress from our new family dynamic, not because of my hormone levels.

"Things will get back to normal after you get used to being married," she had reassured me.

Later that afternoon when we returned to the hotel, I asked Tharee about the fertility shrine. She laughed merrily at my fascination with a practice that they take for granted. "You Americans always enjoy our shrine," she said, enjoying my curiosity. But when she saw how serious I was she composed herself slightly and told me what she could about the little house and huge phallus that had captured my imagination.

Tharee explained that Chao Mae Tuptim was the name of the fertility goddess who occupied the shrine I had seen, but she, Tharee, preferred to call her "Ruby," the goddess' nickname. Tharee could not account for the origin of the name nor the nickname but surmised that "Ruby" referred to the "ruby red" color of pomegranate juice. Tuptim (or rather taptim) means pomegranate in Thai, an explanation she offered for the intensely red colored phalluses surrounding the shrine.

"So, you want to visit the shrine? I will take you tomorrow. Be ready by eleven o'clock a.m., but remember, this is serious. If you do not want to get pregnant, you should not go."

"Shall I bring something with me? What does one wear to a fertility shrine? What must I do?"

"Just dress normally and I will get flowers and incense for you. Don't worry," she laughed, "it isn't possible to make a mistake."

That evening Mike and I had dinner at the hotel with an American business associate, Will Neuhold. I related my conversation with Tharee, the story of the fertility shrine and the powerful goddess, Ruby, and said that I had an appointment the next day with Tharee to visit her. Will and Mike were both enthralled, anxious to visit the shrine themselves.

After dinner, we followed the stone footpath past the pool and service area until we spotted the little house tucked away behind the hotel. Tall trees and bushes had mostly hidden the shrine from passing view. Except for the *khlong* waterway that ran adjacent to it, and the garage and parking area where I had met Mike earlier in the afternoon, it would have gone unnoticed. There were no signs or any other kind of marker pointing the way, and the hotel did not advertise its presence.

From the number of offerings, it was clear that many people visited this site with devotion and expectation. As we entered, the peaceful, somber feeling of the place silenced even Mike and Will, who had been engrossed in animated conversation just a moment earlier.

The actual shrine was a humble, house-like structure located on stilts, just tall enough so that I was able to peer inside. Flowers and burning candles of all sizes and colors decorated the platform. It was too dark to see into the little house, but I assumed that a statue of Ruby was enclosed there. Even more interesting than the shrine itself were the hundreds of offerings that surrounded it. These included other six-foot tall penises, festooned with garlands of flowers. Phalluses or *lingams* resembling torpedoes too numerous to count were stacked against one wall of the modest enclosure. There were airplanes hanging from tree limbs with fuselages in the shape of penises. Every conceivable material, from wood to marble, was used in their construction. They varied in size from six inches

to six feet, and most were painted the ruby red color that Tharee
had described. These offerings exuded the gratitude of hundreds of
believers who visited Ruby to ask for her blessing.

The initial awe having worn off, Mike and Will entertained
themselves once again with less than reverent comments that I, too,
thought were funny, but I couldn't help feeling that we had violated
the blanket of peace that prevailed before we disturbed it. I was
anxious for these two fertility shrine cretins to leave and I could
return with Tharee without them.

The next morning Tharee arrived on time, carrying flowers
and incense as she had promised. Outwardly we were both more
reserved than we had been the day before while discussing Ruby, but
inside I could barely contain my excitement to visit her shrine again.

I had a deep respect for the beliefs of others. If hundreds,
perhaps thousands of people claimed to have gotten pregnant as a
result of visiting the shrine and praying to Ruby, who was I to say it
didn't happen?

As we entered the little park together, Tharee stepped aside
to allow me to go down the path first. Trembling, I stepped toward
the little house where I gently laid lotus blossoms on the shrine's
platform. Then, I burned the incense in honor of the goddess before
saying a simple prayer: "If you believe that my husband and I will be
good parents and are worthy of your blessing, then please bless us
with a child."

The prayer finished and offering made, I lingered briefly to
absorb the magnitude of my request. Tharee gave me some time
to myself before we headed back to the hotel where I met up with
Mike for lunch.

CHAPTER 35

That afternoon Mike and I left Bangkok for Hong Kong. Almost
immediately after the visit to the shrine, I had noticed my body
changing. Even before our departure on the plane I felt the familiar

onset of ovulation, marked by small twinges in my abdomen.

That evening, I stood at the window of our hotel suite admiring the Hong Kong Bay spread out before me. The view and the water were magical. Twinkling lights effervesced from across the Bay to illuminate the downtown skyline, and the orange sails of an ancient fishing boat bobbed gently in the water below me. As I contemplated this special day and its mystical experiences, I felt the sensations in my lower abdomen increase. Could I trust the feeling was real? I had not had a menstrual period for at least twelve months, and now my body was unleashing a year's worth of fertility.

It came as no surprise to me when we conceived a child the following morning. Mike was less convinced of my condition only minutes after our lovemaking, but there was no doubt in my mind that what I was experiencing was the beginning of a new life. We stayed in Hong Kong for a few days longer, enjoying every minute before returning to Washington, D.C.

Back at home, the resumption of our triangular relationship with Victoria presented the same difficulties as before. Blessed with the miracle I carried within, I found it hard to be unhappy. I loved being pregnant, and refused to give in to the slights intended to hurt me. My eyes glistened and my cheeks radiated with that unique glow special to pregnant women. I felt stronger and more attractive every day; never once ill. The pregnancy lifted me above the unhappiness at home. I felt good about myself and my life again.

Sonya Celeste Marie was born in May 1988. *Her Day Master is a Yang Jia Wood, a giant Tree with roots planted firmly in the ground. Yi Wood is fortified by Jia Wood.* She was a beautiful baby with big blue eyes, a mass of curly hair and an edible looking, chubby body. Sonya Marie was the name we had originally chosen: "Sonya" because of its distinction among beautiful women, international familiarity, and its meaning of "wisdom;" and Marie because it is my mother's name. However, her breech position and other complications forced a cesarean delivery after twenty-two hours of labor. Despite the drama, Sonya was the perfect outcome. She was born face up "looking at the celestial heavens" as the Kaufmans would blissfully describe it, and so Mike determined that the baby should be named Sonya Celeste Marie, which she was.

My sister, Linda, stayed with me for a few days until I was strong enough to get around comfortably, and Mike's mother followed some time later. Fortunately I had ample maternity leave, which gave me time to get to know our precious darling before returning to work. Eventually I quit my fulltime job at the law firm, but worked on short-term contracts from home. This gave me an opportunity to spend more time with the baby, save on day care, and explore a lifelong interest in real estate.

Sonya's birth rejuvenated my spirit. She was alert, curious, happy and patient. Every afternoon I dressed Sonya in one of her pretty new outfits and proudly tucked her into the baby buggy for our outing. We visited the cookie bakery, the flowers around the National Cathedral, and the houses for sale in the neighborhood, pretending to be homebuyers. Sonya was the perfect home shopper as she gnawed contentedly on a cookie and babbled her approval of one home after another.

Real estate boomed in Washington, D.C. during the late eighties and prices were going through the ceiling. Mike and I had purchased two condominiums in our complex a year earlier when the prices were low. Now it was a seller's market. We sold both the units, made an enormous profit and retired our debt before reinvesting in a new home. By the end of the summer of 1989, we had found the house we wanted to buy. It was still under construction, but our offer was accepted and we prepared for our move in late fall.

In November of 1989, Sonya was about eighteen months old, Victoria was now in her first year of college, and Mike continued traveling. He was in Asia during some of October and the entire month of November. The closing on our new house was scheduled for the snowy, icy Wednesday before Thanksgiving, hours from where we lived and nowhere near the new house itself. I was preoccupied with the details of the closing and move, and traumatized at the thought of driving alone to an unfamiliar place far from Washington, D.C. in treacherous weather. I was upset that our realtor allowed this inconvenient location for the closing, one that was good for the seller, but terrible for me. It was too late now to make a change.

Then there was Sonya. I felt guilty for neglecting her while I did the packing and organizing, concerned about what I would do with her the day of closing. Victoria was not expected to babysit and not reliable enough to consider. Fortunately I found a friend to help me. Feeling overwhelmed, I was lamenting an impossible week when I was notified that Mike's business partner and best friend, Fred Kaufmann, had died.

Fred's funeral was the same day the movers were scheduled. Wilma, Fred's widow, had expected Mike to give the eulogy at the funeral, but he was unable to catch a flight out of Manila because of what he referred to as a "heated" political problem. I had no details, which added to my anxiety. Mike called almost every evening, reassuring me that he would be home in a few days just as soon as things settled down. I tried to believe him when he said there was no need to worry.

It was a beautiful winter day, perfect for both a funeral and a move, but I was feeling sad and lonely as Sonya and I left Fred's family at the funeral home to travel to our new house in Gaithersburg, Maryland without Mike. Together, he and I had made the decision to move to the suburbs, but I couldn't help feeling nostalgic about leaving D.C., friends, and the safe, familiar routines that I enjoyed with Sonya. Maryland was not that far away, but I knew our life was changing dramatically. It was unclear just how much.

It was now early December and icy cold. I missed Mike who had been away for over a month. Sonya was wonderful during this time, despite the stress she must have felt from me, and all the packing. I felt overwhelmed by the demands of moving into a new house alone with a toddler, but her patience and understanding were exemplary as if she knew I needed her good behavior. Without attention from either parent she remained cheerful, seeming to need only my presence for comfort and to affirm that her world was safe.

Sonya and I left the funeral home on a cold afternoon and followed the moving truck to Maryland. The six lane highways and directional signs between D.C. and Gaithersburg intimidated me. Fast driving had not yet become part of my skill set since my driving experience was mainly in the city. We arrived at our new home to a ringing phone. It was Mike, calling from Manila to ask about our day. Fortunately, the phone had been installed and I had already given him the number. I described the funeral and the disappointment Fred's widow had expressed at his absence. Then we discussed the move, the blizzard conditions on the day of the closing, how Sonya was adjusting, and we joked about my driving deficiencies. I looked forward to starting a life in our new home together and ached for Mike's return, unable to hide my loneliness and frustration.

I was feeling hopeful that Mike would soon be with us when he calmly told me that the *coup d'état* in the Philippines was more serious than he had realized, and it would be another few days before he could leave the hotel. The rebels had taken Makati, the business district of Manila, and it would be too dangerous for him to venture out at that point.

My heart sank. My husband was caught up in an Asian coup. Was he safe? I had a vision that it would all fall apart: the husband, the baby, the house. Fear crept over me. What work could I find that afforded our home, and how would I take care of my baby? Since Mike seemed calm, I tried to remain calm too, not only for his sake, but for Sonya's, who was extremely sensitive to my feelings.

The next day I called the State Department to notify them that Mike was stranded in the Nikko Manila Garden hotel. If they were going to organize some sort of escape mission, I wanted them to remember him. The fellow at the Manila Desk asked several questions about Mike's location within the hotel, his vantage point, and whether or not Mike had any other information. I said "No," but offered to keep them informed if I heard anything more.

The next evening Mike called again. This time he could not

hide his concern. He described a tense situation where he had slept on the floor the night before, fearing bullets that passed over the bed. The rebels now occupied the hotel. Hotel management did its best to provide their guests with food and whatever else they needed to be comfortable, but in the end there was only so much that could be done.

I no longer needed to call the State Department—they called me, asking if I had heard from my husband. "Yes" I said, "he calls every night."

"What is the situation in the hotel?" asked the official.

I described what I could of the scene, saying that the rebels had taken Makati and the hotel, but to my knowledge the guests were not in any immediate danger.

"Is the State Department negotiating an evacuation?" I queried, but got no response.

Mike called again the third night saying the rebels had now occupied the first three floors of the hotel and the management ordered the guests to take refuge in the basement, away from stray bullets and fighting.

There was a priest among the group who claimed to know some of the rebels. He had been in contact with them, and thought he could negotiate a safe passage out. He offered Mike an opportunity to escape with him. At that time Mike wasn't sure what he would do, but he didn't think he would be able to call again.

"Will you keep me in your prayers, Germaine?" he asked softly.

Mike never prayed. He would be the first to scoff at religious or gushy sentiments. He must have believed he was in trouble, fearing the worst. My whole being was in knots, no longer able to control the emotion I had been suppressing for months. I hung up the phone and started crying uncontrollably. A carpenter was at the house working on our fireplace that day. He became concerned for Sonya when he saw me crying and took it upon himself to shake my shoulders, forcing me to regain my composure.

"She suffers too. She doesn't need Mommy to be the baby."

I thought he was out of line, but knew he was right. I needed to get a grip for Sonya's sake. How could he possibly understand my tears? I wasn't crying for myself, but for the lost opportunities of happiness and afraid that dreams for the future couldn't be realized. I had envisioned married life with a loving husband by my side, and a happy family to share our life. How could something so simple become so complicated?

I looked at Sonya who had stopped her play to examine me with her big, wise eyes. Then I went to her, picked her up and tickled her until she couldn't stop laughing, doing my best to reassure her that Mommy was ok, and so was she.

Not having heard anything from Mike in two days, I feared the worst and called the State Department to ask if there was news of an American citizen evacuation.

"Be assured that the American Government is doing what it can to monitor the situation," was the response.

The following day my brother-in-law called to say that he had seen Mike on CNN. He was getting on a bus looking happy, healthy and unharmed. A temporary ceasefire between the rebels and the Philippine military had been reached, allowing all civilians in the Makati area the chance to evacuate. A few hours later I received a collect call from Mike who was at the Manila airport saying that he was on his way home.

We were ecstatic to see each other again, anxious to get on with our new life. I had worked non-stop while he was away, boosting my settling-in efforts with nervous energy and the knowledge that he would be home soon. Almost all the pictures had been hung and things put away. The house looked beautiful. All we needed now was a Christmas tree and logs for the fireplace to enjoy a perfect holiday.

Mike and I renewed our love for one another, expressing gratitude for our relationship, our beautiful baby, and our life together. We were in this euphoric mood one celebratory evening when we decided to seal our love by having another child. Since I was still breastfeeding and hadn't menstruated for about three and a half years, the possibility of getting pregnant right away was remote.

But, once again I turned to God for His blessing.

On December 18, 1989, another miracle child was conceived. Another angel. It was a perfect Christmas.

CHAPTER 36

With a toddler, pregnant wife, daughter in college and new house, Mike felt we needed the security of a steady income. He sought a permanent job with a firm rather than continue his own business as an independent consultant, especially now that Fred was gone. Mike started interviewing in January, and by February he had accepted a job with an international accounting and management consulting firm. The job wasn't exactly what he was looking for, but Barter & Biddle was an excellent company and the assignment would provide an opportunity for him to get back into multinational work. Almost immediately he was assigned work on the Hub River project, requiring that we spend four years in Karachi, Pakistan.

It was February 1990, a Geng Wu Year, or year of the Yang Metal Horse. The year provided an endless supply of Metal, Fire and Earth and along with it, tensions in the Middle East, which mounted rapidly. Iraq increased its threats to invade Kuwait. The U.S. had already been invited by the Kuwaitis to intervene on their behalf, and the Saudis offered the U.S. their airfields to launch attacks against Iraq. The news reports were ominous, providing daily accounts of failed diplomatic efforts to resolve the crisis, offering little hope that the conflict could be dissipated before our imminent departure.

I was tired, scared and pregnant and didn't know if I could muster the energy to make another move so soon, this time to what sounded like the ends of the earth. From what I knew, Pakistan was a place where modern civilization had been forgotten and the value of human life was not to be assumed. Growing up I had always wanted to go as far as I could from Dyersville, but this wasn't what I had in mind.

My husband left for Karachi in March, then returned in

April for a few weeks before leaving permanently in early May for the four-year assignment. The timing of his departure meant that he would miss Sonya's second birthday. Once again I packed up our belongings and memories and reflected on the tectonic shift that was reshaping our lives. I debated what to do with our beautiful new home, which we had lived in for only a few short months.

The snow melted and the weather warmed sufficiently for Sonya to spend a few hours each day outside where she easily made new friends. She was a social, affable child who had something to tell everyone. She knew the names of all the foods she ate, the dolls she played with, the characters from her books and the landmarks we passed on the highway so that Mommy wouldn't get lost. Of course, I was the only one who could understand, but that didn't prevent her from disseminating her knowledge to all those who listened. Sonya was beautiful, but she also had an adorable smile, insatiable curiosity and charming, versatile demeanor, which made her irresistible. She played mother to the babies and baby to the older girls who carried her around the community or strolled her up and down the sidewalks.

Sonya had settled into her new home and had become attached to her surroundings. She was happy with life and approached every day with excitement. She was agreeable, pleasant and loving, and she rarely cried. Yes, she was almost two years old, but she was digesting . . . processing every activity, every person, every emotion and every change. In the beginning she didn't understand why there were so many people who came to look at her home and her room and why they were going into her closet. Then it became clear. She, too, sensed the unsettling change that was taking place in her life, and put up as much resistance as possible to prevent it from happening. She liked her home and became determined not to leave. When prospective buyers came to look at our house, she stood at the front door with her little outstretched arms, trying to block their entrance. I was still the center of her universe, but now she had a few demands of her own.

Jia Wood Day Masters have as much of their tree growth below ground as they have above ground. This makes them difficult to move. No wonder Sonya wasn't ready to "uproot" her home so easily. Jia Wood Trees need nurturing from all the elements in the same way that Yi Wood Vines do, the most important element being Qui Water, which comes from the clouds as opposed to Ren Water, which comes from the ocean.

Sonya turned two mid-May as I approached my fortieth birthday later that month. I wanted to celebrate this birthday with Mike in Pakistan, even though to do so meant moving quickly. I had gotten my real estate licenses in D.C., Maryland and Virginia, but had limited experience. Although I worked tirelessly to sell the house while preparing for our departure, it was impossible to accomplish. The market was depressed in suburban Maryland, unlike the rest of the area. In the end I decided to rent instead of sell, and to turn the specifics of the house rental over to another agent while I focused on the overwhelming details of an international move.

Our departure date was getting closer. Frantically I organized the immunizations, visas and packers. We sold our new Volvo to my friend and old roommate, Belinda, who allowed us continued use of it until our departure.

According to USAID's Community Liaison Officer in Karachi, there were neither Western clothing stores in Karachi nor any of the baby paraphernalia that we would need for a newborn and toddler. Although we had commissary privileges, which provided access to most grocery items found in a Western market, these items were limited. The Liaison Officer advised us to come prepared with basic requirements for an entire year. This meant purchasing a year's supply of clothes, underwear, medicines, ointments, toys, diapers, Tupperware, make-up, face creams, and whatever else fell outside of the guideline designated as "food stuffs."

I purchased several maternity outfits, sufficient until the baby was born in September. That was five months out. Beyond September I couldn't think. The outfits I chose were modest, Western garments that I deemed sensitive to a Muslim culture.

We rationalized the decision to have the baby in Karachi instead of in the United States. For one, airline regulations prohibited pregnant women from flying after the seventh month and they prohibited infants less than two months old from flying at all. In other words, if I delivered in the States, I would be convalescing stateside with a toddler and an infant for four months before I would be allowed to return to Pakistan. There wasn't anywhere to go for that length of time where we would not have been a burden. Sonya was already feeling insecure from the many recent transitions and I was concerned by the perceptible anger she directed towards her father. She was too young to express the pain she felt from his long absences, and acted out her feelings by rejecting him. If I delivered in the States, it would mean another long separation. I couldn't do that to either one of them.

Since Sonya had been born by cesarean, it was presumed that our second child would be delivered cesarean too. This important detail concerned me, but a Pakistani delivery was further rationalized by assuming that we would have a competent household staff to help out. By all accounts the Agha Kahn Hospital had an excellent reputation.

"Based on the birth rate," Mike noted, "doctors will have had considerable experience performing cesarean operations."

"Easy for him to say," I thought to myself.

It was difficult to be upbeat about this adventure no matter what spin was put on it. My younger sister, Leona, called with periodic updates on the violence and threat of war in the Gulf and said that we shouldn't be going there. However, she had no solution for where the babies and I should live had I decided not to go.

No one was cheering me on or excited for me. One after another they shook their heads like I was crazy. Interestingly, I never questioned the decision to accompany Mike to Pakistan. Karachi would never have been my first choice, but I assumed my role as his wife and partner and had confidence in his experience and wisdom that everything would work out. He was the breadwinner. Having been on my own for many years before I got married, I respected the effort necessary to provide financial stability. I trusted that Mike did the best he could to support us and I did not feel that I had the right to tell him how to make a living under the circumstances. Instead, I offered my full support as contribution, just like my mother, and did the best I could, too.

The only positive thing about this move that I could see was that as difficult as all this disruption and effort was, a move to Karachi meant that I could extricate myself—at least temporarily—from the debilitating, triangular relationship between Victoria, Mike and me. I looked forward to enjoying my husband as his wife, without the complicated dynamic that existed between the three of us.

CHAPTER 37

The night we arrived in Karachi thirty people were killed. Tensions heightened with every threat Iraq made to invade Kuwait, threats that were all met with international outrage and condemnation. Sonya and I arrived the end of May 1990 as we had planned, only a few months before the Persian Gulf War officially began. Angry, tense military men with machine guns stood on every corner.

I was a nervous wreck from the moment we arrived. Descending from the aircraft we were bombarded with the hideous sights and smells of an impoverished society. My cute little American maternity outfit, one of the most discrete styles I had been able to find in D.C., was out of place in this country, particularly under these circumstances. Although I was covered from neck to toe, I looked every bit of six months pregnant. I was the leading public spectacle as I stepped from the plane. Ignorant men gawked at me with their mouths hanging open, exposing red, rotted teeth, made so by chewing foul smelling betel nut, or *paan*. They may have meant no harm, but their vile expressions frightened both Sonya and me. My impression was that we looked deliciously vulgar to them and I shuddered at the thought of being fodder to their imaginations.

Sonya clung to me. Where had Mommy taken her? At this point in her life she had already moved several times and her cheerful disposition was being eroded by the stress. Because she didn't know her father very well, her security was with me.

Mike met us at the airport, beaming from ear to ear. I could tell that he was excited to have his family with him, anxious to introduce us to our new life. He had made arrangements for us at the Pearl Hotel, where the suites were large and where he thought we would be most comfortable. I was so happy to see him again, eager to bury myself into his shoulder, longing for the caresses I had missed over the months. Since he had last seen me, my stomach had ballooned in size. I yearned to know that he found me attractive. Sonya was timid in his presence, still adjusting to the flight, the environment and to the daddy she had not seen in a very long time.

Karachi is the largest city in Pakistan with a sprawling urban and suburban population of over ten million people. The Pearl Hotel was located in the center of town, about forty-five minutes from the airport. As we drove through one run-down neighborhood after another, I kept waiting for the nice part of the city to appear but everywhere I looked, things were dilapidated and falling apart. This decay was not the result of a recent war, just the fallout from decades, if not centuries, of harsh environmental conditions, poverty and neglect. I couldn't help but notice the layers of dust that stuck to the trees and the black, plastic garbage bags that got caught in their branches.

The day after we arrived, curfew was enforced throughout Karachi. Incomprehensible local and international political problems and religious misunderstandings exacerbated an already volatile situation, making Pakistan a virtual time bomb. According to local rumors, India did what it could to stir up trouble by shooting a few people and leaving the mess behind. As if those conditions by themselves were not enough, there was a chronic water shortage. Water had to be trucked from the northern part of the country and then made potable.

In retrospect and after having lived in many Third World countries, I've observed that the worst poverty comes to those without water. It is one thing to be poor and it is another to be poor without water. As long as there is water, basic needs can be met. There are fruit trees and wild berries, roots and shrubs. Without water, tempers easily flair and chronic hunger and thirst provoke desperation to a whole new level. The average yearly rainfall in Karachi is four inches, leaving the dried, cracked earth as stricken as the people. There are various brands of poverty that exist throughout the world, but poverty without water is the cruelest of all.

Curfew turned out to be a relief as it gave me an excuse not to leave the hotel. Tensions eased somewhat over the following days and weeks when eventually the curfew was lifted. I began to venture out and acquaint myself with the large ex-pat community, making new friends from Pakistan, the U.S., Europe, South America and Asia.

Expatriates in Third World countries bond easily and quickly, all relating to one another in their struggle to adapt to their surroundings. If you are an expat you are included automatically in invitations to lunches that are set up by embassy personnel and various women's organizations to help orient the newcomer. At one of these lunches I met an American woman named Carol who was married to a Pakistani man. Carol and Rumi had met years earlier in Texas, and had since returned to Pakistan where Rumi worked in the family business. Carol was also about six months pregnant and had another child who was Sonya's age. I was delighted that she invited me to have lunch with her at the private Sindh Club where they were members, and I looked forward to commiserating with her on children, life in Karachi and what to expect with the upcoming delivery.

On the day of the luncheon, I chose my outfit carefully, deciding on the blue pant suit that I thought would be most appropriate. My tank-like maternity top had three-quarter length sleeves, high neck line and the hemline of the tunic came below my buttocks. The pants themselves were loose fitting and calf length.

When Sonya and I finished getting ready, we went to the lobby to meet Carol, her daughter, Alia, their maid and her driver. After introducing the two children to one another and organizing them and the maid in the room with toys and books, Carol and I drove directly to the club for lunch.

We had been seated for perhaps half an hour when we became aware that the waiter had not come to our table. He walked past us several times casting disparaging glances, but did not stop. I was annoyed by this lack of attention and strange behavior since the restaurant was not crowded and I was getting hungry. Carol became equally impatient. She had married into a prominent family, accustomed to having servants scampering around her. The waiter's attitude was offensive, which she told him in Urdu. But he rebuked Carol's scolding and arrogantly held his ground, regardless of the obvious class difference. His complaint was that she dared to enter the club with me, a visibly pregnant woman, and he was the one who was offended.

I was covered from top to bottom and was wearing two pair of support stockings to keep my legs from bursting in the intense Karachi heat. Apparently, it wasn't enough to merely cover one's body in this country; you had to make the belly's protrusion disappear. Pregnant Pakistani women do not show themselves in public. They either stay at home or conceal themselves with veils and fabric so that their bulging bodies are hidden.

Carol had lived in Karachi for many years already and was familiar with their customs. She was wearing the traditional *shalwar kamees* with the huge, formless *pajama* bottom and extra lengths of fabric in front of her. A *dupata*, which is a sort of shawl or scarf, draped around her neck and hung down her back. Carol felt perfectly comfortable with my appearance and would have said something had she thought that I was inappropriately dressed.

She became angry, mortified that her guest was refused service. I wanted desperately to leave, but face-saving is an important part of Asian culture and Carol could not give in so easily, lest she be diminished in stature by a lower class. The only resolution was to have me evaluated by the manager.

The waiter led us to the next room where his boss was having lunch alone. His enormous body hovered over a heaping plate of food that contained every selection from the buffet. He lifted his dispassionate eyes from a stooped head while shoveling food into his mouth, watching us approach the table. His head remained motionless while his eyes moved up and down and back and forth. All the while he continued stuffing his face without breaking rhythm to his feeding. Then, without saying a word he used his fork to make circles in the air, indicating that I should turn to the side; then another twirl of the fork indicated he wanted to see me from behind. He surveyed my fullness from every angle, pushing food into his big, unmoving head while doing so. When he was satisfied that I wouldn't offend the other diners by my appearance, he again used his fork to motion our dismissal. There was no apology to Carol and me, nor reprimand to the waiter.

The last word on an otherwise humiliating incident came months later when our friend, Joe, told me about the sign he had read at the entrance of the Sindh Club tennis courts which read: "No women or dogs allowed beyond this point."

* * *

Sonya became ill with dysentery almost immediately after our arrival in Karachi and lost about five of her twenty pounds. We went from doctor to doctor looking for help, filling one useless prescription after another. She fought back the illness, attempting to run and play, but she was too sick. She used what little strength she had to sing and dance, dismissing her weak body until she no longer could. I admired her when she broke into a frail song, but a song nonetheless.

Finally Dr. Rafiq, who had a clinic at the Pearl Hotel, referred us to Dr. Bhally, a Pakistani pediatrician married to a British nurse. Dr. Bhally advised that Sonya be taken off all the medication she'd been prescribed and instead be given a preparation of yogurt and *kichurei*, a concoction made from rice, lentils, chicken and broth. She responded well to this simple remedy, and after weeks of being ill, she started to regain her strength and to feel better.

We continued to live at the Pearl Hotel until the end of
August when our home was expected to be ready for our arrival.
Meanwhile, on August 2nd Iraq made good on its threats to invade
Kuwait. The U.N. initiated sanctions against Iraq immediately and
the U.S., together with Saudi Arabia, led a coalition of forces against
the invader. Tensions across the Middle East escalated by the day. It
was difficult to know for sure how Americans would be affected.
Facts, I have come to realize, have little to do with perception. The
literacy rate in Pakistan is reported to be around thirty percent,
which I estimate to be high. Consequently, poor education and
poverty provide the perfect combination to manipulate the masses.
Although historical facts indicate that the U.S., part of a coalition
of thirty-four nations, had been invited by both Kuwait and Saudi
Arabia to avenge the Iraqi invasion, such details were distilled and
distorted as necessary by those who would exploit them to make the
U.S. the villain and target. As a result, Americans living or traveling
in the Middle East during this time became more vulnerable.

CHAPTER 38

USAID had lined up a group of houses for Mike to look at before
Sonya and I arrived. After much deliberation, Mike chose a house
that turned out to be huge, ostentatious and impractical. Mike was
careful to describe the properties to me in detail over the phone,
wanting to select something nice. In the end he accepted a property
that required extensive work, trusting the USAID folks to fix the
problems as they had told him they would do. It's difficult to say
if there were better choices, and there was no benefit in second-
guessing this decision, so I resisted the temptation to do so. Mike
wanted to do the right thing for his family and no doubt thought I
would like a big, showy house.

Still, it was a bit of a shock the first day I visited our new
home. Sonya and I went by ourselves while Mike was at work.
Shauket, our driver, took us to the area known as Defense IV, where

House in Pakistan

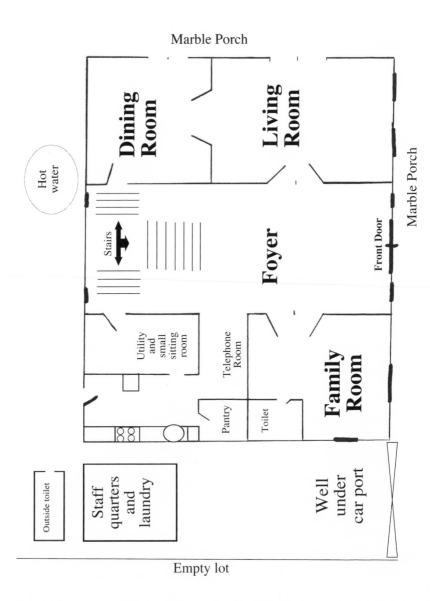

The garden before our mali *used his green thumb.*

Front of the Karachi house.

Foyer view from front door shows marble staircase; living room is on the right; family room and kitchen on left.

Side of the house; balconies are off of our bedrooms. Double doors open up from living room and dining room.

our house was located.

Shauket swerved more than once to avoid hitting pedestrians and bicycles barging into traffic. Entire families buzzed around together on a single moped, transporting as many as seven people between the handlebars and the bike's fender, all oblivious to any potential danger. Camels appeared out of nowhere and open manholes were flagged with no more than a stick or tree branch poking up out of them. As the car rocked its way through the city, Sonya clutched my hand in both of hers and snuggled more deeply into me, pressing her face against the round firmness of my growing belly.

Squatters lined many of the streets, making homes out of anything they could find. Men and children showered in plain view along the dusty street, which was somewhat shocking, and ran contrary to the pretense of modesty that I had experienced at the Sindh Club. However, I found their ingenious, makeshift shower contraptions more interesting than the public display of nudity. Somehow they plugged into the water main with a piece of hose or pipe and ran it up into a can into which they had poked holes, simulating a shower-head. The can was dangled from a scrap of rope or string tied to a stick.

"Wow, how clever," I thought to myself. "If these people had had proper educations, imagine what they would have accomplished."

Stopping at a light along the way, Sonya heard a rap on the window and sat up to see what it was. Beggars crowded intersections, waiting for the red lights that provided opportunities to beg for *baksheesh* or payment. A tiny woman had come to the car, pressing her face against the tinted windows. She tried to get a response to her tap by using the middle finger knuckle on the back of her hand to knock at the window, mouthing a pitiful request. She belonged to the waterless poor, displaying all the features of her hopeless plight. I estimated that she was somewhere between forty and seventy merciless years old. Her emaciated face was dried and shriveled, and her cracked, thin lips opened weakly to reveal the familiar rotted teeth. Her unkempt hair was partially hidden underneath her *dupata*, but there was nothing to hide the expression of her ravaged existence.

Sonya shrank back from the window terrified, confused by what she saw.

"Mommy," she asked curiously, "is that a monkey?"

CHAPTER 39

The development that included our house was in a residential area inhabited by ex-pats like ourselves and wealthy Pakistanis. As we got closer, the scenery and street mayhem did improve slightly. All the houses in Defense IV had walls around them. After what we had seen on our drive, I could understand why. People created their own oases to buffer themselves as much as possible from the grim reality that dwelled outside their gates, perhaps subconsciously fearful that the hopeless condition could be contagious.

The car stopped at a corner house with a vacant lot next to it. We had arrived. I noticed how unsightly that lot was, full of trash and pools of filthy, standing water. I would soon learn that people used it to dump their garbage since there was no collection service available in the city. Beggars were the first to pick through the trash, hoping to find something of use, maybe even something edible. They tore open the bags in their search, taking what they wanted and leaving a scattered mess for the dogs and cats to forage and scatter further.

The walls surrounding our house were about ten feet from the road, and inside the gate it was another fifteen feet to the front door. Nothing was growing in the yard, neither flowers nor grass. Where we were at sea level, a salty residue prevailed over the dry earth, sucking whatever moisture there was from the already parched ground. Still, I had imagined our house might have a garden and hoped that would be achievable despite the odds against it.

The house itself was white stucco, with a grand wraparound porch that encircled the front and one side. The side porch opened onto the yard. Towering, two story pillars majestically supported the roof, creating an impressive entrance. "I'll bet it's lovely inside," I encouraged myself, trying to be optimistic. I stepped onto the portico with Sonya in my arms, and carried her to the front door.

Ornately carved, heavy wooden double doors opened to a thirty-foot high foyer that ran from floor to roof the entire length of the building, separating it in two. From the front door I could make out the house's layout. The downstairs foyer was about twenty-four feet wide and stretched before us a good one hundred twenty feet. A huge staircase started about twenty-five feet in front of us, and led halfway to the second floor before splitting into two and continuing up a few more steps where it opened onto a large landing that separated one side of the upstairs from the other.

Dust was everywhere from the repair work that was underway, and USAID workers scurried, readying the house for our arrival. I just stood there for a few minutes, overwhelmed both by the size and condition of what I was seeing. When I tried to set Sonya down, she protested, her body a storm of kicks. With her determined legs glued to my hip and her frightened face buried in my chest, I ventured forward.

Off the downstairs hallway on the right were several rooms: a huge living room and a spacious dining room. I was struck by how dark everything was. The living room had a row of windows with heavy white, wooden shutters that were closed, blocking the light.

"How strange," I thought. "It would be so much more pleasant if they opened the shutters to allow some light to come in."

The living room and the dining room both had double doors that opened up onto the marble porch, reminiscent of a southern veranda. Three steps led down into the barren garden.

Separating the living room and dining room were glass folding doors that could be opened up to make one large room for parties. Though everything was dark and grimy, I could imagine the potential in that feature, especially for entertaining.

On the left were a den/office and a bathroom. A small, open sitting room separated the family area from the kitchen located at the back of the house. As I made my way toward the kitchen, one of the workers came out through the swinging door and greeted me tentatively in Urdu with the traditional salutation *"Absalam malekum, Memsab."*

In response, *"Malekum absalam,"* stumbled awkwardly out of my mouth. I was still trying to learn a few expressions.

With difficulty, he was able to convey that the USAID officer who was supposed to be meeting me had not yet arrived. I thanked him and continued on my tour with Sonya, still stuck to my hip.

I sized up the kitchen as being somewhat small, but functional once we got it clean. Off the kitchen was a pantry or storeroom where presumably our food would be stored. It had high windows covered by bars on the inside. Peering up at the light coming in, I realized there was no glass in these windows, just the bars.

There were many structural problems with this house. The window frames were one of them. They did not fit tightly, exposing large gaps between the frames and the masonry, which allowed an endless amount of dust to blow in. Fortunately, I suppose, I did not notice this particular detail on my first visit.

As I peered into the other first-floor rooms a second time, I made a mental note of the number of windows that needed curtains. There was a lot of work that needed to be done before this house could be turned into a home. Trying not to feel discouraged, I ventured upstairs.

The entire house was made of marble including the staircase. The design looked grand from one perspective, I suppose, but there seemed to be considerable wasted space and few possibilities for making good use of it. I imagined a sofa and chairs in the upstairs foyer that separated the four bedrooms, thinking this would be a nice place for an upstairs sitting room. The downstairs foyer area was trickier. Until I figured out what to do with it, I would let Sonya ride her tricycle there.

Wooden pickets on the staircase and landing rails were set at least a foot apart, wide enough for Sonya to walk through *and,* I fantasized with horror, drop twelve feet onto the marble floor below.

I shuddered at the thought and made a mental note to ask the work crew to address that hazard.

The bedrooms felt nearly as vacuous and unwelcoming as the rest of the house, but at least the children's bedroom was connected to the master bedroom, which was a relief to me. I could never accept having them sleep far from me.

This first visit was a look-see, intended to familiarize myself with space and window requirements. I needed to get a feel for the house so that I could plan how to decorate and make this place welcoming. For now I'd seen enough. It was time to digest what I had seen and figure out next steps.

As leader of his project, Mike was careful not to make unnecessary waves with USAID. He was new to the job, determined to create a positive impression on his team. The Hub River project was the largest Public-Private Partnership ever attempted in the world and the first to achieve completion in the developing world. It involved USAID, The World Bank, Israel, and several Arab countries, which brought to bear cultural, social and religious differences, all contributing to a complicated and stressful assignment.

Over the next few days, Mike and the USAID folks helped me piece together the house's story. Apparently, our Pakistani landlord's wife was dying of cancer and the family couldn't afford to live there. Her treatments consumed their financial resources, leaving nothing for home maintenance, improvements and repairs to the crumbling infrastructure. Their strategy was to rent a smaller place for themselves and lease out their large white home to an ex-pat family who they hoped would rehabilitate it for them. Lucky us.

CHAPTER 40

My first summer in Karachi was filled with repeated trips from the Pearl Hotel to Defense IV to check on the progress of the repair work, measure windows, and select curtain fabrics and upholstery materials.

Poor Sonya. Her health continued to worsen, presumably from the unfamiliar food and water. She continued to lose weight and suffered from alternating bouts with vomiting and diarrhea. With so much to do, our routines left little time for play or the attention I felt she needed from me.

Tensions all over the Middle East simmered to a slow boil after Iraq bombed Kuwait City, making life more dangerous for the ex-pats who lived in Islamic countries. It was impossible to predict from one day to the next if there would be a street uprising or how it would affect us.

On subsequent visits to our house, I zeroed in on the details room by room. It was difficult to get things done with Sonya underfoot or in my arms, but I knew that facing these tasks with both an infant and toddler would be impossible, so I pushed to have as much work completed as I could before I left for the hospital. One great fortune was meeting Shorty, a master tailor and part of the USAID team assigned to help us. Shorty was less than five feet tall, but what he lacked in height he made up for with his big personality. He was extremely talented and every inch a professional. He and I communicated well, in part because we were both aesthetically sensitive and enjoyed being creative. I genuinely appreciated his excellent work, and he appreciated my efforts to turn the dreary living room into a beautiful, welcoming space. I spent hours and hours shopping for fabrics, comparing colors and textures until I was satisfied they worked well together. Shorty did his magic with the fabrics, sewing intricate pleats on valences that hung above the shuttered windows.

We decided to keep a baby bed downstairs to avoid unnecessary climbs up the staircase, which was impossible to traverse quickly. I had had an amniocentesis while in the States, and knew the baby was a girl, information that proved useful while shopping for baby clothes and for creating a beautiful, feminine bassinette. I was delighted to find a rattan basket that sat inside a bamboo frame. The bassinette added a charming dimension to this otherwise cold room and was a small but promising solution to make life simpler.

Shorty used some of the fabrics from our living room curtains and upholstery and combined them with lace to make a cover that hung sweetly around the frame. He made a mattress by stuffing cotton into a hand-made sack that he covered with a pink and white flowered fabric. The whole look reminded me of what I imagined princess beds to look like from thousands of years ago. The bassinette was so precious that I planned to keep it in the corner of the den and use it for stuffed animals after the baby got older.

Shorty worked diligently so that almost everything was completed before my delivery. He was unique among the workers for his artistic sense, skills and work ethic. Unfortunately his professionalism did not extend to the other members of the team.

Furniture and area carpets were provided by the USAID project, along with a budget to upholster the furniture and make curtains. I happened to be at the house the day the largest carpet was delivered and was shocked to watch the workers roll it out on top of filthy, dusty floors. I couldn't believe my eyes. When I stopped them from what they were doing so that the floor could be cleaned, they looked at me like I was crazy. After all, what was the point of cleaning the floor if it was just going to be covered up with carpet? From their perspective, if you couldn't see the dirt, it didn't exist.

I had expected to work with a thinking, rational supervisor who managed this crew, and could never have imagined that it would be necessary to intervene. As a pregnant woman in this strange country, it was difficult to direct these barely educated men who didn't speak English. I sincerely did not want to offend anyone, but for the life of me couldn't understand or accept their way of doing things.

We had asked to have a phone installed in the downstairs sitting room off the main hallway. To accomplish this meant running phone wire from the connection box outside. Instead of tacking the wire as inconspicuously as possible to the baseboards or running it along the seam where the walls met the ceiling, the workers ran the wire right across the middle of the walls with total disregard to presentation. Because the connection box was a good distance from the sitting room, this meant that the wire ran through several of the downstairs rooms on the way to its destination, conspicuously displayed in the middle of our walls.

Then there was the plumbing. On one of my visits, I discovered to my dismay that most of the water pipes had rusted and were leaking. One could literally swing the pipes from side to side. There were so many leaks throughout the entire house, that streams trickling along the sides of the smaller pipes compromised the water pressure from the main pipe. To repair the holes, the crew wrapped cotton thread around the pipes. When the cotton eventually gave way and the water started pouring out again, more cotton thread would be applied.

Plumbing in Karachi in 1990 was, in my opinion, nonsensical. Under each sink, in the bathrooms and the kitchen, the pipe came from the drain and then went straight down toward a hole in the floor. This pipe was not continuous. It was cut short, leaving a gap of about six inches between the end of the pipe and a strategically placed hole in the floor where the wastewater headed for the sewer system. This precarious design attracted cockroaches and released foul odors, creating other maintenance issues that required constant attention.

Still worse, the Defense IV sewage system had a way of backing up every so often, creating filthy messes in our kitchen. The electrical system in the house was shot as well, causing four electrical fires in two years.

The USAID work crews were as good as any that existed in Karachi. They did their best to be obliging, but we spoke different languages in words, concepts and expectations. In order to have things done the way I wanted, onsite management was required which meant that I had to be present nearly every day.

Mike had problems of his own, making troubles at home secondary to what he was already dealing with. He feared that my demands and concerns would appear unreasonable, which would in turn cause problems for him at work. My job, however, was to create a home for ourselves before the baby arrived. At the very least our house needed to be made safe and habitable. There were only two months left to accomplish this daunting task.

CHAPTER 41

It was late August. As our moving day approached, my anxieties only increased. I absolutely dreaded the move to our house and would have preferred to stay in the hotel for the entire time we were expected to live in Karachi. The furniture had been delivered, the carpet was down and the curtains and upholstery were in progress, but the rest of our lives remained unsettled.

A much bigger concern than the ugly placement of the phone wires was that the phones themselves didn't work reliably. I needed to know that I could reach a doctor urgently if necessary. During our first week in the house, we experienced a ninety-nine percent drop rate in the middle of calls, and one-hundred percent of all our calls failed to go through on the first try. This accentuated my anxiety and the many challenges of life in Karachi.

Then there was the matter of the household staff. We hired all of the staff members at our personal expense, with the exception of the security guards, who were provided and paid for by the project. I hired three people from the pool of applicants maintained by the State Department's Community Liaison Office: a cook, an *ayah* or nanny, and a housekeeper. Our *mali* or gardener and *dobi,* the fellow who did the laundry, were hired from referrals. This responsibility was new to me. I had never hired household help or managed a staff, and nothing in my previous overseas experiences could have prepared me for the cultural and language differences that confronted me now. Pakistan is a complicated place for religious, cultural and political reasons, but I never imagined how our household would become a microcosm of these issues. As a Christian American woman, I pondered the potential problems that the Christian and Muslim Pakistani workers would have with me. Nothing was straightforward, and there was no way to anticipate what lay ahead.

With difficulty we adjusted to having three unfamiliar people with totally unfamiliar living habits in our home all day every day. There was Manuel, a highly recommended cook; an old lady, Nora, who was hired as our *ayah*; and Sikeena, a younger maid who was hired by Manuel to do the cleaning. She couldn't speak a word of English, but Manuel assured me that she was a good worker and I could depend on him to communicate with her for me. These three inside staff members happened to be Christian.

Muslim staff considered washing toilets and other aspects of household cleaning beneath them and refused to do those jobs, so it was not typical to hire them for inside chores. The outside staff, which consisted of the *mali*, driver and *dobi*, were all Muslim.

It was a week before my scheduled C-section, and all the domestic details were falling into place. Then, I received a phone call from Dr. Ibrahim, my surgeon, letting me know that he wouldn't be available to deliver the baby. He said that his brother, who lived in England, was sick, and that he needed to prepare himself for the flight to London that would be leaving in two weeks. Without apology, he said that his resident, whom I had never met, was available to do the surgery.

He then added flippantly, "It's routine. Anybody can do it."

"I've never met your assistant. I don't know who she is," I protested. "Maybe this is routine for you, but not for me. I've been seeing you for three months, and you've got to understand that I'm in Karachi . . ."

He could not have cared less that I was in Karachi or anywhere else for that matter. I imagined him rolling his eyes on the other end of the phone line while practicing basketball shots into a trash basket. Eventually he gave in to my pleas and agreed to perform the surgery as scheduled.

As the arrival of the baby drew closer, I became concerned about our belongings. Our shipment arrived at port the end of August, but we had multiple problems with the customs officials who angled to get *baksheesh*, a payment of some sort but in this case a bribe. According to stories circulating in the ex-pat community, it was customary for port officials to hold personal belongings hostage until these payments were extorted. Fortunately, USAID intervened. Our shipment was delivered to the house two days before I was scheduled to go to the hospital. My stress level reached seismic proportion after I unpacked the crates and discovered that the movers had left all our baby things in storage in the States. With two days to plan for the baby's delivery, I rushed to buy the necessary diapers and clothes.

We hadn't been able to decide on a middle name for the baby. Until then we could agree only on a first name, which was Sasha. So many unexpected issues had interfered with my plans to focus on quiet, pleasant things before the delivery, especially giving lots of attention to Sonya, who I was concerned about leaving for a week.

Dr. Ibrahim said that in Pakistan it was customary to spend from five to seven days in the hospital for a cesarean surgery. Five to seven days was a long time. Would Sonya be properly cared for by the house staff? It was a great relief when a friend with a little boy Sonya's age agreed to watch her during the daytime while Mike was at work. Nighttime remained an issue.

During those first days our household help had not inspired my confidence. Were they competent enough to manage without me? I knew at the time that I would have to deal with their poor attitudes directly at some point, but I didn't have the strength just yet.

Manuel presented problems from day one. Supposedly he was a masterful cook, but he resented working for me. He was lazy, arrogant, indignant and insulting. While embracing any attention Mike gave him, he scoffed at taking instructions from me. If I asked him to clean the fans in the kitchen, he wouldn't do it. When Mike came home in the evening, he had his scotch ready for him as he walked through the door. He'd serve my husband at the dining room table, but refused to serve me.

Manuel avoided speaking to me unless it was absolutely necessary. If he needed vegetables for something he was cooking,

he sent Nora to fetch me or notify me that he needed funds for
marketing. I had done most of the marketing myself, but in my
advanced pregnant state this became more and more difficult and
unsafe in the open markets. The vegetable shopping was one task
that I had to relinquish. Manuel sensed that I was naïve about life
in Pakistan and vulnerable for obvious reasons. Even though I had
hired him, he considered Mike to be the boss, and Mike's approval
of him was the only thing that mattered.

Manuel didn't like Sonya. She was having a difficult time
adjusting to our new life. Her sweet disposition was constantly
tested with one illness after another, and as a result she became
whiny and refused to leave my side. I was patient with her, which
annoyed Manuel. He took it upon himself to scold her when she
was fussy and correct her in my presence.

His reactions were out of line. I should have put Manuel in his
place right from the start, but I didn't. Instead, I wasted time trying
to figure out the "formula" for household management in Karachi, if
indeed there was one.

*The elements were against me, making it difficult to win that
battle or any other. I was surrounded by an onslaught of Fire, Earth
and Metal elements from the heavens, compounded by Fire, Earth and
Metal elements from the environment. Mike's chart had a preponderance
of Fire, Earth and Metal, too. If Fire wasn't scorching me, Earth was
absorbing my nurturing element, Water, or Metal found in the salty earth
was chopping at the roots of my Yi Wood.*

I tried reasoning and communicating our feelings to Manuel,
hoping to arrive at some mutual understanding and agreement as
to how the house would be run. This was possibly the worst thing
I could have done. Any attempt to show that you care about *their*
feelings was a further show of weakness and met with dissension. I
felt completely overwhelmed, not knowing what the "right" thing
was to do. I wanted a happy home but was unsure how to strike the
balance between children, husband, staff and my own needs. I hate
making excuses for myself, but honestly, it was difficult to know how
to manage in those circumstances. I tried to avoid making cultural

faux pas that would offend the help, assuming that as bad as they were it was better to have them than no help at all. I needed staff when I got home from the hospital, and Mike to back me up if I took any action to correct them. Given his determination to avoid conflict in the office and with the staff at home, I was at constant odds with myself as how to manage the complicated facets of our lives without his input. I needed him to understand the difficulties of household management in this country and how it affected our home.

CHAPTER 42

Shortly after we moved into the house, Manuel condescended to walk to the den where Sonya and I were playing.

"Madam, do you have glue?" he asked brusquely.

"Glue?" I repeated out loud, wondering why he needed glue, hoping he would offer to tell me.

"Yeah, glue," he snarled. "Do you know what glue is? Glue!"

I wanted to ask what he had broken, but was afraid to offend him by doing so. A bundle of mixed emotions prevented me from pursuing his request.

"Surely he would offer to tell me if he had broken something," I thought. *My "nice" get-along Yi Wood behavior surfaced once again, making me disgusted with myself for retreating and deciding against further questioning.* Manuel's aggressive behavior intimidated me. Regrettably I gave him a bottle of Elmer's Glue without demanding any explanation of why he wanted it.

I had forgotten about the incident until several days later when I was fiddling with the hemline of my maternity t-shirt and my fingers came across a smooth patch that was obviously not part of the soft cotton. It felt plastic-y, the way Elmer's Glue feels after it has dried, though I didn't make that association at the time. Curious, I examined the hemline more closely, noticing a long, black hair that was curled up and glued there. Although I thought it strange, I was not suspicious enough to imagine something sinister. Instead, I accepted Mike's explanation: "a manufacturer's defect."

Manuel's reactions to Sonya became more and more obnoxious and his miserable behavior towards me worsened. On one of our marketing excursions together, Manuel brazenly stole a biscuit off the baker's plate. The baker flashed him a nasty look, but said nothing because I was present. At checkout I paid for the stolen biscuit along with our other goods, which offended Manuel, causing him to snort disapprovingly. His cocky behavior had not gone unchecked after all. Manuel was becoming increasingly more arrogant to the point that he wasn't manageable.

Something was amiss between Sikeena and him, but I couldn't put my finger on it. Upon returning home from an errand one day, I could see from the front door entrance that Manuel, who was not allowed upstairs, had just emerged from our bedroom. I put down my packages and proceeded up the stairs to see what was going on. Manuel was now coming down the stairs. He passed me in his usual brusque fashion without saying a word. I continued up the stairs to find Sikeena crouched behind our bed, pretending to clean the floors. She was visibly shaken. I assumed her frightened expression had something to do with Manuel, but she was unable to communicate whatever troubled her. Later I found out from our driver that Manuel took a hefty monthly commission or "finder's fee" from Sikeena's salary—double the amount she had made while working for her Pakistani employers—a sum that he had negotiated for her. Now Manuel claimed ownership rights to her as well.

Manuel scared me. He was so arrogant that I didn't trust what he was capable of doing. Certainly he needed to be let go before I went to the hospital. I was not going to have him in the house with Sonya while I was away.

I spoke to Mike about firing him, but he didn't want to deal with it. Mike did not view Manuel's deficiencies and insolence the same way I did. Since he was a good cook, Mike wanted to keep him. However, I insisted on letting him go, and asked Mike to be there when I did. Preoccupied with his own challenges at work, he refused, telling me to, "take command of the house and do it on your own."

If we had been in the States, I would not have had a problem with this. I was thirty-six years old when I married and had always been independent, albeit naive. I managed every aspect of our complicated personal lives as a couple without difficulty, and was quite comfortable handling any and all practical matters. This was different. I could now speak from personal experience that Western women could not assume respect from male workers in Pakistan. Men normally deferred to men when it came to management, power and control. Respect was an ambiguous notion that warranted value only if it appeared next to fear. In fact, I would say that respect was confused with fear, and certainly Manuel did not fear me. His claims of being Christian did not make him less misogynistic, only more clever. He had no idea what it meant to be a Christian, a Muslim a Hindu or any other religious being. His male ego was his religion; the only thing he believed in.

Because I was pregnant and Sonya was so young, Manual smelled vulnerability, and schemed to exploit it. I was determined to get Manuel out of the house before I went to the hospital, so I took Mike's advice to fire him on my own. Fortunately, we had been assigned twenty-four hour security guards at the house. I enlisted their help instead.

The next day I instructed the security guard to keep Manuel at the gate when he arrived, and not let him near the house. The guard was to notify me immediately upon his arrival.

Manuel had waited ever so briefly before I came outside, but had already worked himself up into an agitated froth by the affront. As calmly as I could, I told him that he would not be working for us any longer because of theft and his bad attitude.

Even though the security guard was present, the firing turned nasty. Manuel became furious, huffing and puffing while shuffling his feet back and forth, and shouting strenuous denials of any misconduct. With only a few days before my delivery date, I was concerned about assaulting the baby with more stress. I handed Manuel his money in an attempt to limit further interaction, refusing him a letter of recommendation when he had the audacity to ask. His entire body clenched with loathing. Manuel stood in front of me with his shoulders raised, readying for an attack. Hatred brimmed his dark eyes as if to sear a curse into my heart. His heavy breathing slowed while giving me one last seething stare. Then, he turned abruptly on his heel to leave with his money clutched tightly in his fist.

He was gone. What a relief. Having Manuel out of the house would mean one less cause for worry while I was in the hospital. I felt better already.

I had come to realize that Nora was too old to be an *ayah* and besides, Sonya wanted nothing to do with her. It took me a while to put a finger on that dazed look Nora had in her eyes and the scent that lingered about her, but then I realized that old Nora was a classic *paan* head who got through her days on a low voltage buzz. I didn't blame Sonya for being uncomfortable with Nora's old, tired smile that had been permanently branded from the overuse of betel nut or *paan*. It made me feel uncomfortable too. There are several types of *paan*, but Nora preferred the addictive, tobacco variety that is held in a wad under the upper lip while a drug is slowly released from it. This substance mixes with saliva and provides the user with a mellow high. The continuous use of *paan* will eat through teeth and stain the mouth and lips a dark red color like it had with half of the people in Karachi. The smell of *paan* made me sick, but as long as Nora kept her mouth closed, I could live with it. Certainly she was easier to have around than Manuel.

I decided against having an *ayah* altogether, at least for the time being. Instead, I asked Nora to be our cook, which she accepted willingly. Nora felt far more comfortable in the kitchen than anywhere else in the house. She was relatively harmless in this capacity and certainly more pleasant, hygienic, reliable and manageable. To our delight, she was also a very good cook.

At last I could turn my focus back to delivery preparations, making sure that Sonya would be well taken care of and that the remaining staff had their instructions.

CHAPTER 43

I was frightened to have surgery in Karachi, despite the Agha Kahn Hospital's good reputation. Fortunately I had met a nurse, Ursula, at the American Club who volunteered to spend the first night after surgery with me at the hospital. Immediately I felt safer. I also asked the American minister's wife—who lived down the road from us—if she and her family would keep us in their prayers. I needed desperately to be with Him and sought prayers and blessings from others, still not confident that He would hear me.

Finally, the evening before surgery I called my mother to ask for her blessing. Normally it was impossible to get an international call through, but this time I had little trouble, thank God. I felt an intense longing to speak to my mother, wanting to hear her voice and to know that she would be thinking of me.

I felt that someone, some guide, was still with me, but not the Beings of Light I'd been so close to as a child. It was as though I was released to experience a life without Divine Light. Since embracing the supremacy of science years before, I had unwittingly relinquished that sacred connection. My mother was the one true link I had left. If my pleas for help were to be heard, it would be because God would never turn his back on her request, even if it were for me.

I still had childhood memories of Mom clutching yellow, worn-out sheets of prayers, crumbled from daily use. Surely after thirty years she had the prayers memorized, but she continued to page through sheet after sheet ritualistically, praying for our safety, our health and our care. I never doubted her connection with the saints and the various kinds of Blessed Virgins and Baby Jesus' she reported to, and now I asked her to pray to them for me and have them there with me during the delivery. I blurted out my fears along with my request. When I finished, there was silence from the other end of the line. I wasn't sure if the call had dropped or if there was just a delay due to the distance. Finally her voice came back to me.

"Oh, Mary, I'm worried about you. I don't know what to say, you are so far away. Of course I will keep you in my prayers, and I know that our Mother Mary and Lord Jesus will be with you too."

When I left for the hospital the next morning, I felt certain they were.

CHAPTER 44

Dr. Ibrahim arrived at my room before surgery eating an ice cream cone. He joked with Mike and cavalierly invited Sonya to the cafeteria to have a cone as well. Perhaps this was his way of reassuring me there was nothing to worry about.

The epidural hadn't yet found its way to Karachi. I was fully anesthetized, which meant that afterwards I recalled nothing of the actual birth. The surgery and convalescence period went well, although the anesthesia made recovery longer than I'd expected. Lingering fears of delivering in a Pakistani hospital dissipated. Dr. Ibrahim did not visit me during my stay. Presumably he made it to England on schedule. His assistant, who I met for the first time after the delivery, turned out to be every bit as competent as he had promised.

We were blessed with another beautiful, healthy daughter. *Another Yang Jia Wood, just like her sister, Sonya.*

After weeks of struggling to find a middle name that went well with Sasha, we finally found one. It was Alina, the same name Carol and Rumi had chosen for their baby girl. I had discussed Pakistani names with Carol, but none of them appealed to me more than the name they had chosen for their child.

"Sasha Alina." I listened to myself say the names together out loud, and thought they sounded musical. It was perfect: a combination of strength and femininity; powerful, yet gentle. Not only did it sound beautiful and resonate qualities that I thought were important in superior women, but it seemed appropriate to have her middle name be Pakistani.

Sasha Alina was a healthy child who resembled her sister at birth. She had a thinner, more compact body, but the same curly hair and clear blue eyes like her father. The similarities ended with looks, however.

She displayed a temper early on. Compared to Sonya's sweet disposition I couldn't help but notice how aggressive this little girl was. The hospital pediatrician called her a "hothead." Sasha was relentless with her demands, screaming madly until her needs were met. She seemed to be a tough child, for which I was grateful, figuring the resiliency would serve her well.

Ursula was a wonderful reassurance during my days in the hospital. She helped me walk to prevent blood clotting, made sure that my medications were given on time and that the baby was in good hands. If she hadn't been there, I would have been inclined to fret and languish. I don't believe that the hospital staff would have provided the assistance that she did.

Mike brought Sonya for daily visits, which gave me as much comfort as they gave her. She typically arrived wearing her shoes on the wrong feet and some red, garish dress she picked out by herself, which made me laugh. For some reason, Sonya had developed an obsession with the color red and thought she should own every red outfit she saw, oblivious to how unattractive they were.

Sonya was clearly frightened by the tubes that poked out of my arms and my immobility, but I couldn't tell how she was processing her sister's arrival. She mainly expressed sadness and concern for me by pointing to the tubes and asking, "Hurt, Mommy?"

I had wanted to wean Sonya prior to our move to Karachi, but with the numerous transitions and other struggles she faced it seemed cruel to do so. I read that the trauma that occurs from removing a child from the warmth of her mother's milk is not to be underestimated. Intuitively I knew this was true, especially under the challenging circumstances she faced in Karachi, not the least of which included her compromised health. The hot climate combined with the dysentery she had suffered made it imperative that I keep her well hydrated and protected from as much bacterial crud as possible. Nursing facilitated that.

I was concerned, too, that she would catch something from drinking the water, which was filthy. Sand and ugly microbial debris were visible in the water that emerged from the tap, unsafe to drink until it had been made potable first by filtration and then by boiling. Since I had little to no confidence in our staff being able to follow these instructions, I tried to shield Sonya as best I could from another bout with diarrhea by extending her breastfeeding longer than I had intended. Unfortunately, that led to her being weaned abruptly before I went to the hospital.

Despite fears to the contrary, I had plenty of breast milk for Sasha, even though I had nursed Sonya during the entire pregnancy. As a matter of fact, I had so much milk that the nurse asked me to pump for some of the other mothers on the maternity ward, which I did.

After five days in the hospital, I was eager to take our new baby home. Pakistan's weekend was Friday and Saturday, not Saturday and Sunday as in the West. Mike picked me up on a Thursday afternoon, but failed to ask the staff to work that weekend. They had left by the time we arrived.

Although I was feeling as well as could be expected, I wasn't prepared to be without help, at least not for the next two days. A dozen or more unexpected well-wishers from Mike's office and the neighborhood showed up over the weekend, all anxious to see our new baby. Unexpectedly, the sewer had backed up in the kitchen, which created a filthy mess. There was only so much I could do by myself to clean the floors before hobbling around the kitchen on slippery tiles while preparing cookies and tea. This was not how I expected to spend my first weekend home.

CHAPTER 45

Sonya had missed me tremendously while I was away. Now that I was home she felt safe to release her sadness and concern by whimpering into my shoulder while sitting on my lap. She saw my bandages and stitches, doubling up on her patience and good behavior. Sonya took my hand, offering two-year-old "help" when I moved so slowly.

I had tried to prepare Sonya for the delivery ahead of time, telling her that the baby would be hers as a way of heading off any potential jealousy. We had given her a life-like doll, who she named Veronica, before Sasha was born, and now she was excited to have her very own live baby. Sonya had practiced diapering and nursing Veronica. With all her experience, she figured that she was prepared to care for this live baby too.

It wasn't until I took a screaming and bewildered Sasha from the arms of Sonya as she attempted to nurse her that Sonya realized she had been duped. This baby wasn't hers after all, and now she clung to me more than ever.

One afternoon shortly after I got home from the hospital, we were sitting in the family room where Sonya was holding Sasha, examining every inch of her. She checked her ears, neck and hands, and investigated her clothes.

All of a sudden she exclaimed, "Mommy look at this!" Slowly and with great care, Sonya pulled out a two foot-long black hair that had been tucked into the baby's sleeve.

"Ugh, how did that get there?" I said, taking the hair from her. "We'll have to change our laundry techniques. I don't think the clothes are being washed properly."

I was baffled. Neither Nora nor Sikeena were allowed to handle the children. They prepared the food, cleaned the house, and the *dobi* came once a week to do the laundry. The hair remained a mystery until another hair appeared a day or so later, only this time it was curled up in Sasha's disposable diaper. At this point I ruled out coincidence or lack of hygiene. There was no way that a long, black hair could have gotten inside a disposable diaper.

Both the maids had long, black hair, as did every maid in the country. It wouldn't be unusual to find stray hairs, but highly unusual to find hairs in such strange places.

* * *

The entire day was weird. Both Sikeena and Nora went about their business as usual, but I noticed something strange about their behavior. Were they being more attentive than usual? Or did their watchful glances make them seem more intrusive?

Sasha had been sleeping upstairs since morning, and Sonya and I were working on puzzles. Nora and Sikeena walked into the room together. Since Sikeena did not speak English, Nora addressed me on her behalf. Sikeena watched, gauging the effectiveness of Nora's performance.

Nora's theatrical skills were quite impressive as she switched into woeful pleading, begging for a salary advance for Sikeena who, she said, needed money to pay for school uniforms for her children.

"Madam, her children *neeeed* to go to school and *neeeed* to have the uniforms," Nora implored, adding dramatic affect by writhing her body and twisting her face while extending her arms pitifully.

"School started about a month ago," I pointed out skeptically. "Why haven't they gone?"

At that, Nora intensified the urgency in her dazed eyes, opening them as wide as saucers. She stooped over, pretending to pick up a whip. With a grand gesture, she threw her arms over her shoulder as if to flog her back.

"That's what they do to children if they come to school without uniforms," she exclaimed. "They are beaten!!"
She continued her imaginary flogging until I asked her to stop.

The entire scenario was too bizarre for me to process. I just wanted them out of the room so I could be with Sonya who looked as dismayed as I.

Normally, I would have checked with Mike if one of the staff asked for an advance, but today I just handed over the money. Sikeena, now looking quite pleased, gladly took the money, and then asked to leave early.

"Fine," I said. "Go get uniforms for your children."

After they left the room, Sonya and I went upstairs to check on Sasha who had been sleeping for an unusually long time. She appeared to be fine so we returned to the family room to resume our play. An hour passed, and then another. Why isn't Sasha waking up? I was beginning to worry, but reminded myself that newborns sometimes do go into periods of deep, extended sleep. Sasha was twelve days old.

Every forty-five minutes or so we checked on her. After about six hours, we were excited to hear her hungry wails. We hurried up the stairs as quickly as we could. I picked up a screaming Sasha from the bed and rushed to change her so the screaming would stop. Sonya noticed how nasty her diaper rash had become. "Ouch," she said, pointing to the baby's red bottom.

Our supply of cotton diapers hadn't arrived in the shipment, leaving me no choice but to use the plastic variety until I could find something better. Although I didn't like using disposable diapers, I had not been able to find a nice cotton alternative in Karachi. The disposables—a very poor quality—chafed the baby's tender skin. Instead of putting another diaper on her, I decided to give her bottom a chance to breathe. Holding Sasha with the nappy unfastened, we all headed back downstairs to the family room where I nursed her.

CHAPTER 46

I put Sasha lengthwise on my lap with the diaper underneath her, watching every movement she made. As I tried to caress the little feet kicking around my face, she yelped.

"Sasha must not be in very good spirits today," I said to Sonya who giggled approvingly, delighted that I could find something wrong with her new sister.

As the afternoon slipped into evening, the baby's temperament continued to worsen. I assumed it was the diaper rash, but couldn't understand why that would affect her toes. Soon Mike arrived home from the office and found all three of us on the sofa, Sonya and I trying to humor our unhappy child.

"Sasha must not be feeling well. She has a terrible diaper rash," I said casually. I feigned mild concern even though I was worried about infection. Mike was not the type to respond to alarmists.

I continued playing with her little kicking feet, but my good-natured attention was rejected as she screamed in pain.

"There must be something wrong with her toe," I said to Mike. I grabbed her foot and held it close to my face so I could examine her toes more closely. One toe was a shade darker than the others. It was the middle toe on her right foot. The toes of a twelve-day-old child are minute, so I had to look closely. I knew I had discovered the problem when I touched only that toe, and again Sasha howled.

Sonya tried to hold the baby still so I could have a more thorough inspection. Yes, something was definitely there.

"Mike, I see something around her toe," I shouted, forgetting his disdain for people who over emote. I couldn't tell for sure, but it looked like a translucent white hair wrapped around her toe that caused the pain and swelling.

Ignoring Mike's tired expression from a hard day at work, I called Dr. Bhally. When I described the problem, he commanded, "Take her to the emergency room immediately. I will have a surgeon waiting for you. It must come off urgently!"

The Agha Kahn was a fair distance from where we lived. Mike wasn't keen on leaving home for a wild goose chase, especially since the driver had already left for the day and he would be the one to take us. Since the doctor said it was urgent, he mustered the energy to drive us.

Two doctors, a resident and an intern, had been briefed by

Dr. Bhally and awaited our arrival. They asked to see Sasha's toe. The resident remained reserved during the exam, but the intern was more inquisitive.

"How would a hair get on her toe? Who takes care of her? When did you notice the hair? Did anything strange happen today?"

I repeated the last question, "Did anything strange happen today?" I thought briefly before answering, "Yes, the entire day has been a bit strange." I understood what he was suggesting: Someone had done this deliberately to Sasha. I had suspected so myself, but why?

It took over an hour to remove the translucent thin fiber that was cutting into the baby's skin. By this time her circulation had been impeded, causing the site to be particularly sensitive. Anesthesia was not used to remove the fiber, resulting in painful screams and kicks from Sasha until the surgeons finally dislodged whatever it was.

After the translucent thread had been removed and the drama subsided, the doctors allowed me to examine it under a microscope. At first I did not observe anything unusual. As I looked more closely, it did indeed look like a hair, and it seemed as though the hair might have been knotted and that there was the tiniest bit of "something else" that was holding the ends together before it was snipped. When I asked the resident's opinion about this, he told me to contact Dr. Bhally the following day.

Mike wasn't particularly engaged with the evening's events. He was tired, obviously looking forward to returning home and forgetting about the incident. I wanted to dismiss it too, but for me it wasn't that simple. An uneasy feeling plagued me.

The next morning I called Dr. Bhally as the resident had instructed. He said he needed to speak to me in person at his office. I did not want to expose a newborn to the germs in a doctor's clinic or to the stress of another trip across a dusty city, but given the strangeness that was going on at home, I decided to take both the girls with me, afraid to let them out of my sight.

We had a short wait before being asked to step inside the

doctor's private office. "Sit down!" Dr. Bhally ordered, "I have something to explain to you."

Dr. Bhally must have considered his words carefully while anticipating our arrival. He found it difficult to look at me while he spoke. He proceeded slowly and carefully, "In our country there are practices with which you may not be familiar. In this particular case, someone has put a hair around your infant's toe as a type of black magic ritual. These things are usually done to revenge another. It doesn't really matter who is responsible for performing this ritual. The point is that someone who works for you intends grave harm against you and your family, and you have no choice but to return home, and fire everyone in your house."

Dr. Bhally didn't know that I had had previous experience with black magic and had already considered this explanation. What I found most horrifying was that anyone would target an innocent child. Unable to speak, I sat there numbly as Dr. Bhally continued.

"I don't necessarily believe in such things, but just in case there is something to it, I would encourage you to give alms to the poor during this week."

"I don't necessarily believe in such things," I repeated to myself. What does that even mean? Obviously you know it exists, you've seen it hundreds of times. So, if you know it exists, then what does it mean that you "don't necessarily believe in such things?" Do you mean that you don't understand it? You don't know how it works? And if you don't know how it works then you don't believe in it and it can't exist? I wanted to scream at him.

No one ever *believes* these things until it happens to them, and even then people are afraid to talk about it. That's the problem. No one wants to admit that black magic exists, or that they or someone they know has been affected by it, fearful that society will view them askance forever more. I looked at Dr. Bhally, hoping that he would give me some words of encouragement, or that he would say something to indicate his acknowledgement and compassion, but there was nothing more he would say. The meeting was finished.

"What? It's over? That's it? I need you to help me get through this. Someone tried to kill my baby and you want me to give alms? Don't you understand?" There was no point in getting upset with him. I prepared us to leave.

"Alms won't be enough," I thought tacitly.

I thanked Dr. Bhally, lifted a sleeping Sasha onto my shoulder, took Sonya's hand, and headed out of his office.

How would I explain this to Mike? He should have come with me to Dr. Bhally's office. My concern shifted from the well-being of my children to gaining the support of my husband. Somehow he would have to understand.

The girls and I returned home in silence. After putting the children down for naps I was grateful for a small amount of peace and quiet to reflect on Dr. Bhally's advice before Mike arrived.

CHAPTER 47

"No!" he fumed. "Statistically this can't happen, and we are not going to fire anyone. Furthermore, I won't be married to a woman who goes around talking about black magic and I refuse to discuss it."

"Statistically?" Who is talking about statistics? I am talking about reality. It is the *reality* that a hair was surgically removed from our infant's toe because someone in our home put it there. Was the statistical reference meant to throw me off? Was I supposed to feel less intelligent—maybe crazy—because I was speaking about *reality* while you pull statistic superiority out of thin air? Was I supposed to forget this happened to our daughter because it is uncomfortable to discuss it? Was I supposed to pretend this didn't happen?

I don't remember the level of detail I gave to Mike concerning my experience with Simone and the two psychics. He may have assumed that I had a parlor-game fascination with the occult, but I don't know if he knew the extent of my first-hand, personal experience with black magic. When it came to taboo subjects he seemed unreasonable, which I didn't understand. His intellectual curiosity was unlimited having read books on all kinds of topics, including the occult. He could discuss Black Magic from an academic perspective and come off sounding brilliant. Now when it affected our lives . . . our baby's life . . . he refused to discuss it. I did not understand why Mike couldn't—wouldn't—discuss this with me. If Mike didn't want the incident with the hair spread beyond the privacy of our family, the best thing would be for him to explore all angles with me. I needed his support, but clearly I wasn't going to get it. Somehow I'd have to figure this out on my own.

Although Nora gave the performance of a lifetime the day of the incident, I did not suspect her of doing something malicious to Sasha. She was far too timid, and I didn't believe she had been upstairs near the bedrooms that day. She was too busy cooking in the kitchen. Moreover, she could hardly see. Nora would have been physically incapable of putting that hair on Sasha's toe. It's possible that Nora colluded with Sikeena, I supposed, especially if she could benefit in some way, but she would never have taken the lead on this sort of thing. The only possibility was Sikeena, directed by Manuel.

The first hair had appeared glued to my t-shirt—with white glue, just like the one I provided Manuel—while he was still working for us, so this more recent caper had his fingerprints all over it as far as I was concerned. Most probably he was still taking Sikeena's salary. He must have put her up to asking for the advance, too, as another way of extorting what he could.

Instead of firing both maids as Dr. Bhally had suggested, I listened to my intuition and decided to fire only Sikeena. Sasha was less than two weeks old. I was trying to recover from surgery, got no rest during the day and slept little at night. The house had endless structural problems, which required heavy daily cleaning and constant attention. Plus, shopping in the intense heat was more than I would be capable of doing until I healed. In 1990 there were no grocery stores in Karachi. We bought our produce at the squalid, fly-infested outdoor vegetable markets like everyone else. After analyzing the daily demands of our household I came to the conclusion that I needed at least one maid. Not knowing how to fire

Sikeena without incurring further wrath, I sought advice from the USAID Security Division, run by a Pakistani. I hoped he would be more open-minded than my husband and would agree to help me.

CHAPTER 48

The head of Security was alarmed by the story I relayed to him. He was familiar with these kinds of things, saying that black magic was usually done to locals, not foreigners. After some thought the security officer came up with a plan. He suggested that the maids fill out employment application forms for a security check, knowing that Sikeena would never pass. She didn't have a surname, a husband, a proper address, nor a father who would vouch for her. Since she was a person without an identity, she would fail the check and subsequently be dismissed by USAID security without consequence to me.

The plan worked brilliantly. Little did I know, however, that after her discharge, Sikeena returned to her previous employer—the Pakistani family who lived next door! Sonya spotted her from our upstairs window while she was outside, sweeping along the wall that separated the two houses.

I tried to get information on black magic, needing to understand how and why it worked, but there was no public library where I could research this subject, nor apparent authority with whom I could consult.

Desperate for answers and at the suggestion of the head of USAID Security, I agreed to visit a mullah, an Islamic religious teacher, with him. This particular mullah was probably in his mid-thirties and unable to speak English so most of my questions went unanswered. The mullah offered a limited explanation, which echoed Dr. Bhally's.

Through the translation of the security officer the mullah explained that, "This type of malicious act is usually intended for revenge purposes and also to gain power over another," he said.

"The revenge was most probably directed against you, with the intent to 'drain the life out of the child' which would destroy all of your lives."

Thank God we found that hair in time.

CHAPTER 49

Sasha fully recovered from her toe problem, but Sonya's health problems worsened. She had never regained full strength since we'd arrived in Karachi. After recovering from the initial bout of dysentery, she'd succumbed to food poisoning several times, and picked up every flu bug that was around. After the flu she developed a constant, dry cough and slight wheeze. A never-ending cycle of illnesses disturbed her, making visits to Dr. Bhally's clinic become part of our daily routine. His expression changed when he saw us coming as if he knew that any medications and remedies he prescribed would not be effective. He tried his best, but there was a limit to what he could do.

Meanwhile, Sonya was becoming a child I didn't know. She, too, played with imaginary friends, but didn't seem to enjoy them as much as I had when I was a child. She asked us to set places for them at the table. At bedtime, I latched our bedroom doors before tucking the children into their beds. Invariably one of her "friends" would be left outside, which triggered fits of tears until I unlocked the door to let them in.

For reasons that eluded me, Sonya was not at peace with her imaginary friends. She clutched at me, devouring my attention. Some extra clinginess was understandable given Sasha's arrival—many children have a hard time sharing their mothers with new siblings— but Sonya's tormented demands seemed to be deeper. I wanted desperately to have my happy child return. Somewhere between imaginary friends, medications, and the new baby, I was losing her.

It was December 1990. The American Women's Club in Karachi hosted an annual Christmas bazaar where handicrafts, baked goods and items from local vendors were sold. A portion of the proceeds was given to the various charities that the Club ladies sponsored. Sonya, Sasha and I had just arrived with my friend, Rosella, and had stopped to speak to some of the other ladies. Sonya, who had been holding my hand, suddenly released it and dashed in front of me shouting, "I need that. Give me one of those!"

I chased after her until she stopped at a kiosk sponsored by an orphanage run by Catholic Nuns. Sonya grabbed a statue of the Virgin Mary that had been made by an orphan child, looked at the nun, and pleaded, "I need this."

The nun, taken aback by a two-year-old child requesting a religious statue, picked up another statue of the Baby Jesus and gave them both to her. Sonya was instantly content; her shouting stopped.

Sonya was only two and a half. I don't remember having any religious discussions with her, and there wasn't anyone else who would have. I don't know how she knew about the Virgin Mary, or what the image represented to her. She insisted on sleeping with her statues for the next two years until we moved. Regrettably, I tossed them at that time because the pieces of cracked plaster had been glued together so many times after falling from her bed onto the floor that they no longer resembled the statues that had been given to her.

CHAPTER 50

The Gulf War was brewing and strong anti-American sentiment erupted into hostile demonstrations. It was now January 1991. Sasha was four months old.

Tensions in Karachi mounted. Civic stress was even greater than what we experienced on the first day we arrived in Karachi the previous May, and the number of angry looking, machinegun-toting military men on the street corners had multiplied. Their scowls threatened warnings that they would shoot to kill if need be. One day I foolishly went to the market with our driver where a soldier told him that it was too dangerous for us to be there and asked us to leave.

Evacuation became a key topic of conversation at the American Club. We all anticipated an abrupt departure. I applied for Sasha's passport immediately after getting home from the hospital, and was becoming concerned by how long it took to receive her documents. It was taking months, and the delays tested my patience. The U.S. Embassy consul's office insisted on putting us through all the bureaucratic red tape it could to verify that our baby was, indeed, an American citizen. I could not understand the issue. Sasha was the daughter of two passport-carrying Americans whose births had been verified. Her father was an Air Force Academy graduate working for a U.S. government agency.

Fortunately I had brought our marriage certificate with us, and Sasha's birth certificate from the Agha Kahn Hospital was easily verifiable. Not to mention that the American community was small. We all knew one another. Our American friends, Mike's colleagues and even the Visa Consular had all seen me bursting with pregnant discomfort during the three months before I delivered. Some of these people even visited me in the hospital. Therefore, it seemed disingenuous and farfetched for the consular to insist on a copy of Mike's divorce papers from fifteen years earlier in order to validate our marriage certificate and, by extension, prove Sasha's right to citizenship.

The consular, married to a Mexican woman, knew that Mike was first generation American of Mexican descent, and assumed some "insider's knowledge" when it came to consular matters that dealt with Mexicans. With a wink and a nod, he thought it understandable to suggest that Mike may have gotten what he referred to as "a quickie Mexican divorce," that would somehow disqualify Sasha's right to citizenship.

To satisfy the consular's preposterous claims, Mike contacted his first wife, who provided a copy of their divorce decree. In the meantime, political tension mounted. Every day became a test of restraint and patience, and waiting for Sasha's passport only heightened my anxiety as I anticipated a possible emergency departure.

Mike arrived from the office one evening saying that there would be a security briefing the next day. All Embassy related personnel were asked to attend, including USAID contractors. Mike and I attended the briefing together. We were told that the U.S. would be attacking Iraq sometime during the following week to ten days. If we wanted to leave the country at government expense we would be allowed to do so. The amount of luggage we could carry was limited, however, and it was not certain when or if we would be able to return.

It didn't take two seconds for me to decide to leave with the children. Initially Mike thought he should stay for another week and catch up with us in D.C., but as the situation became tenser, he decided to go with us. Sasha's passport was finally issued. I packed the few warm clothes we had for Washington's winter weather and our photos, fearing that we would lose everything if we couldn't return. We were ready to go.

CHAPTER 51

I had never been so relieved to be in the States. Mike went directly to Washington, D.C. to work. Sonya and I took Sasha to meet her grandmothers, aunts, uncles and cousins in California and Iowa before meeting up with Mike in D.C. two weeks later. He had found us a lovely, small, corporate townhouse apartment in the heart of Georgetown.

This was a peaceful time, in sharp contrast to where we had been. I bought a double stroller to take both girls on walks through the neighborhood, reminiscent of the days I strolled Sonya around the National Cathedral. What a pleasure to finally feel safe in public, free of walls and gates and the necessity for security guards and drivers. It was a luxury to inhale fresh air, shop in stores, eat fresh fruits and vegetables and drink water from the tap.

Victoria, who was developing into a beautiful young woman, lived close by. She enjoyed meeting Sasha and seeing how Sonya had grown. It was nice to see her interact with the younger girls and to claim a relationship with siblings that she had always wanted.

It seemed like an eternity had passed. The charm and safety of this lovely little apartment helped me to feel hopeful about our futures once again. We stayed in D.C. for several months until the Gulf War ended, tensions had a chance to diffuse, and it became safe to return to Karachi and the big, rambling albatross that was our Karachi home.

We had laid off our house staff when we evacuated prior to the Gulf War, not knowing at the time if or when we might return to Pakistan. They all wanted their jobs back, which meant one less detail for me to manage. Nora returned to her post as the cook and Laxmi, who had replaced Sikeena after she was fired, returned to cover the cleaning duties. Laxmi didn't last long, however. She was caught filling Sonya's empty medicine bottles with booze from our liquor cabinet for her alcoholic husband.

Sadly, I was so desperate to find staff with a modicum of competence, that I would have kept Laxmi regardless of her stealing, if she had been trainable. Laxmi was a pleasant person, but was so deficient in cleaning and understanding cultural nuances that there was no hope to develop her. One day I walked into our bathroom to discover her at the sink brushing her teeth with my toothbrush. Needless to say, not long after settling back into our life in Karachi, I was faced with another round of interviews and hiring to find someone to take her place.

I was quickly reminded of what a chore it was to keep anything clean, attributable in part to the standards, experience and knowledge of the available help. Everything took effort. Eventually I became more realistic as to what I could expect and learned to feel more compassion for the help than irritation. In fairness to our cleaning staff—most of whom did their best—our house was also a problem. The windows did not fit tightly in their frames and there were huge spaces under the doors. The latter were so gaping that the customary American hardware store remedies would not have helped, even if they had been available.

During the summer, these gaps in the windows and doors provided easy entry for the Karachi mosquitoes, which were enormous. They loved tender baby flesh and feasted on Sonya and Sasha during the night after finding their way through the mosquito netting that was put over their beds. The combination of heat and mosquitoes made sleeping especially difficult in the hottest months, but there were big surprises to contend with in other seasons as well.

One crisp, cool morning, I gasped as I headed down the marble stairs with Sasha in my arms, alarmed by what I saw on the floor near the front door. Huge, dark circles were plunked and flattened on the marble tiles. Both inside the house and along the wrap-around veranda outside laid huge, black discs. They turned out to be dead bugs—piles of dead bugs—that had come in en masse seeking the warmth of the house within its concrete outer walls, which stored the sun's heat gathered during the day. They glommed together in cow-pie-like configurations and died in clusters. This ritual continued until their season of death had ended.

CHAPTER 52

The salted, parched yard that lay in front of our porch was another major challenge, but Mike harbored a fantasy of being a gentleman farmer and took on the gardening as his special project, for which I was grateful. The garden was one of those male jobs that commanded the authority to deal with the landlord and *mali*. Somehow Mike convinced the landlord to bring in topsoil to amend the problems that plagued our unfertile lot. Together, he and the *mali* planted colorful bougainvillea along the walls until slowly but surely the yard was transformed into a lovely extension of our indoor space.

As USAID contractors, we had privileges at the commissary, a store that supplied provisions to U.S. Government personnel. Contractors who worked for private businesses, such as those working for the oil companies, were not so fortunate. They brought their specialty items—such as chocolate chips, cheese, salami and jams—with them in their luggage when returning from business trips to the States.

Access to the commissary was a very special perk, one that we didn't take for granted. Flour, sugar, cake mixes and cereal had to be stored in a freezer to kill any bugs already present, and to prevent others from invading and multiplying. It took me a while to figure all this out. Until I did, pounds and pounds of food was lost to bugs. At first, I stored these dry goods in Styrofoam ice chests to protect them from the dust and roaches that were on the outside trying to get in. If that method succeeded in keeping bugs out, it did nothing to kill the bugs that were already *inside* the dry food packages and the eggs that were waiting to hatch. The freezer provided a secure place to store all of our meat, but wasn't nearly large enough to contain the flour, cake mixes and other dry foods as well.

Fresh produce was the only food item that was replenished regularly. Good quality fruits and vegetables were difficult, if not impossible, to come by. I hoped to find frozen vegetables at the commissary, but none were available there either. If we were to have vegetables at all, we purchased whatever was available in the local markets and made do.

All fresh produce was soaked in bleach and then cooked. If the bleach didn't destroy any existing nutritional value, the overcooking killed what was left, making attempts to stay in front of the health curve a never-ending battle.

CHAPTER 53

Sasha, now just over six months old, adjusted back to life in Karachi rather easily. She did not suffer from digestive problems or the bronchial and ear infections that typically affect young children. She remained hotheaded, however, and extremely independent. Even at six months she was able to defend herself against Sonya's harassment, climbing onto her older sister's back to reclaim her toys, and pulling Sonya's hair while attempting to bite her with toothless gums. Sasha never shied away from a good tussle, even though her sister was at least three times her size.

I continued to nurse Sasha, afraid to use the Karachi water needed to make formula. Instructions to the staff were to filter and boil all drinking and cooking water, but the results were unreliable.

Unlike Sasha, Sonya continued to be sick. A steady stream of illnesses plagued her. She had food poisoning several times, even though Mike, Sasha and I never did, and barely recovered from one thing before coming down with another. Food poisoning one day, a respiratory infection or some other ailment the next. Visits to Dr. Bhally resumed as part of our routine.

Shortly after our return, Sonya developed a horrible cough. Despite the chronic illnesses, she still had the spirit to play, which I encouraged her to do as a way of distracting her from her misery. The coughing got worse, however, and cough syrup and Tylenol were not having any effect on her symptoms. I was concerned, but not enough yet to risk perpetuating the alarmist reputation I had with my husband. I tried to keep my fears in check. Sonya tended to be dramatic by nature, which caused me to wonder if she might be exaggerating her condition.

By morning Sonya was sicker than I had ever seen her. She felt clammy to the touch and was listless with fever. I summoned the driver who picked up Sonya so I could carry Sasha. We rushed to Dr. Bhally's clinic where we took a seat in the reception area along with the ten or so patients who had arrived before us. Sonya seemed to be sleeping on the sofa, but I was now gravely concerned about her heavy, labored breathing, not knowing what to make of it. Fortunately, Dr. Bhally stepped out from his office to check on the workload, saw Sonya and shouted, "How long has she been like that?"

Frightened, I replied, "I don't know. She's been sick since yesterday."

"Get her to the emergency room immediately. Can't you see what's happening to her?"

"My God," I thought pitifully. "What *is* happening?"

Without asking any questions, I accepted help from one of the office assistants who carried Sonya so that I could manage Sasha. Together we bolted down the stairs to our waiting driver who raced us to the hospital.

Sonya survived what turned out to be an asthmatic attack. Fortunately we were given prompt attention at the hospital where she regained consciousness. A dozen "what if" scenarios passed through my mind as I realized Sonya had quickly drifted into that lethargic state that precedes death.

It was one thing to meet life's challenges by myself as a grown adult, but watching my children suffer was more pain than I could bear. My biggest concern had been to shield my children, a task that was proving to be beyond my control.

This was the first of many asthmatic episodes we experienced with Sonya. Years later we discovered that she was allergic to dust, an unavoidable fact of daily life in an arid, underdeveloped country. Sonya had been prescribed Ventolin, Zaiditin, Bricanyl, Prednisone and antibiotics. During the two years and three months we lived in Karachi she endured numerous IV drips and emergency runs to the hospital.

This previously vibrant child was slipping away and becoming someone I didn't recognize. The drugs were affecting her. Emotionally she became more desperate for my attention as I was the only person who showed her any patience. Her father judged her asthmatic condition to be the result of "over-mothering," an emotional problem that I had created. His remedy? Not to spend so much time with her.

Our friends also seemed to feel that she was spoiled. Perhaps, but how could any mother not be sympathetic under these circumstances? Sonya was barely three years old and had already experienced significant traumas. Was she spoiled ... or as scared as I?

CHAPTER 54

Mike tried to distance himself from what he referred to as "our problems" (meaning the girls' and mine) and buried himself in intellectual pursuits both at the office and at home. I recognized that his job was demanding, so I tried to be patient with him. Even if he hadn't been faced with so many professional demands, I still think he would have found it difficult to cope with the extraordinary circumstances that had become part of our lives.

While Mike was in Islamabad on business, I decided to take Sonya to see Dr. Rafiq, the kind doctor we befriended at the Pearl Hotel who helped us through our initial illnesses. Dr. Rafiq had instructed the hotel kitchen on how to make the tasty kichurie that cured Sonya's early bouts of dysentery, and he referred me to Dr. Ibrahim for the cesarean section. Now I hoped he would help Sonya again whose behavior had become more erratic.

When we arrived at the hotel clinic, Sonya was having one of her fits, crying and screaming and flailing about. Our driver stopped the car at the front door and came around to help us out from the back seat. He lifted Sonya down from the seat while I held Sasha. As he did so, Sonya threw herself onto the pavement, pounding and screaming. Dr. Rafiq came outside to check on the commotion, visibly shocked when he saw her. "What has happened to this child?" he asked in disbelief.

Inside his office I described the various episodes of our lives since we had left the hotel months earlier. We discussed Manuel, the delivery, the hair incident with Sasha's toe, the development of Sonya's asthmatic attacks, the Gulf War evacuation, and now this. I hoped for some advice that would put an end to our misfortune. Dr. Rafiq waited before he responded, first looking at Sonya, who was now quietly enjoying a lollipop he had given her, and then at Sasha who was lying contentedly in my arms.

"Mrs. Avila," he said softly, "Sonya isn't the same child I knew before. I've seen cases like this. As a matter of fact it happened to my own son. Sometimes people do things to other people to either cause pain or have power over them. The people who do these things think they can steal another's energy."

I wasn't particularly surprised at what he said next.

"It looks to me like Sonya is possessed."

Dr. Rafiq told me about his son, why a curse had been put on him and how he overcame it. Apparently it was a situation similar to Sonya. He, too, was a beautiful child, and the source of considerable jealousy among the household staff. Dr. Rafiq was no expert, but he suggested that the hair that had afflicted Sasha had affected Sonya or that she had been cursed separately.

Dr. Rafiq believed that the curse could be removed successfully. We needed only to find the correct way to do it. He had taken his son to a mullah for healing and suggested that I do the same. Then he told me to go home and wait for him to contact me after he had made arrangements.

I left the doctor's office with my children, not knowing what we were getting into, but hoped this would be as simple as providing a bottle of my favorite perfume had been years before. What caused the onslaught of physical ailments that plagued my darling Sonya?

How could I protect her from what I couldn't see, understand or identify . . . and couldn't prove existed?

How am I going to explain this to Mike? Truth is, he didn't want to see this issue any other way than as a statistical aberration. Suddenly, I became angry with him. "That's a good way to keep your distance," I thought to myself resentfully. "Throw some math at it. Sound intelligent. Be above it all." Intellectual information was so much neater.

If I ignored the hairs, the illnesses and Sonya's behavior, would the craziness stop? Believe me, I too wanted to ignore it all, but this was my child we were talking about. I didn't have the luxury of denying the truth. Sonya needed me. Sadly, I'd have to face this problem alone. Mike would never understand. It would just become another one of "my problems."

CHAPTER 55

Dr. Rafiq contacted me several days later, asking me to bring Sonya to his office. Excited at the possibility that this ordeal would soon be behind us, I took only a few minutes to get ready, leaving Sasha with Nargis, our latest ayah and housekeeper. Nargis was a Bangladeshi woman who was charming, young, vital and pretty and had a beautiful smile, which was an anomaly. Her presence was a relief for me *and* Sasha who loved her. She came with good references and provided the physical strength and competence I needed to help with the children.

When Sonya and I arrived at the clinic, there were several men with white robes, turbans and long beards waiting in the reception area. Dr. Rafiq introduced us to the mullahs, who he addressed as holy men.

Sonya sat quietly on my lap as the men looked at her intently and then conferred among themselves before speaking to Dr. Rafiq in Urdu. He translated their diagnosis.

"Yes, this child is possessed," they had all agreed, "but it's too strong. We cannot help her."

I groaned audible disappointment. She is being good today, I thought. How could they determine just looking at her for a few minutes that they couldn't help her? How could they possibly give up so quickly? They're supposed to be holy men.

"Noooooo . . . please don't refuse us," I thought desperately.

Dr. Rafiq watched my optimism deteriorate into frustration. He groped for words of encouragement that would make me feel better, if only temporarily.

"Don't worry," he said. "There's always hope. These mullahs are inexperienced and I shouldn't have asked them here in the first place. There is another holy man outside of Karachi with a reputation for dealing with these matters. I'll make arrangements to take you there."

A few days later Dr. Rafiq and his driver picked up Sonya and me for a visit with the holy man located about two hours out of the city. The squalid, arid landscape provided little distraction from my thoughts. Dr. Rafiq found it difficult to humor the two of us. I tried to be pleasant for his sake, nodding my head to acknowledge his various points of interest along the way. I wanted some quiet time to try to connect with God while Sonya drifted in and out of sleep.

It was late when we arrived. Throngs of people had already lined up to see the holy man. It would be hours before our turn and no one was about to let us jump to the front of the line. Exhausted and disappointed, we made our way back to the city after scheduling an appointment.

The following week we made our way once again through the noisy, densely packed highways and dusty suburbs before arriving at the mullah's mosque. Similar throngs waited in line, but this time we were ushered to the front, where we were met by an elderly gentleman with a long, white beard, dressed in a classic white *shalwar chamiz*. He was much older than the mullahs we had met with previously, and hopefully wiser. Without asking me any questions, he examined the lines in my hand before saying in English that other curses had been put on me before, but later removed. He described the person responsible for this crime against Sonya, our former cook Manuel, and expressed his sympathy for her condition. His accurate observations inspired confidence, prompting me to readily accept a special *taviz*, an Islamic script from the Koran. He wrote the script on papyrus paper in saffron ink and then held it over a flame to make the dried writing turn brown. The mullah instructed me to read the *taviz* at certain times during the day for a prescribed number of days. Finally, I was to put the saffron script in clean water to wash away the negativity. I accepted his "cures" and obediently followed his instructions.

After days and then weeks of waiting for results, despite my committed practice of his instructions, I had to accept another disappointment. Sonya's illnesses worsened and so did her behavior.

I wanted to tell Mike of our activities. It concerned me that no one knew of our whereabouts when we were on these sojourns with Dr. Rafiq. Tensions from the Gulf War lingered and expatriates were not allowed beyond the city limits.

CHAPTER 56

We were now in our second year of living in Karachi with no relief in sight for Sonya's unrelenting illnesses. Emotionally, I was worn thin from sleepless nights and restless days. Stress was taking its toll. My once tall, lithe frame dwindled to scrawny proportions. During the two years we lived in our house I had not slept one complete night without being awakened. I was up an average of five to six times a night to breastfeed Sasha or comfort Sonya during nightmares. Even when the girls slept, I was often yanked from sleep by the voices.

Sometimes these voices would call "Germaine," taking on Mike's intonation. At other times they would call out "Mary," sounding like my mother. There were also times when they blew in my ear or imitated the cries of the children. I sprang from bed to tend to the girls only to find they were sleeping soundly. The voices were annoying, as if they wanted to wear me down. I felt certain that Sonya heard them, too.

The craziness and constant lack of sleep were debilitating. I ached to speak to Mike, to hash out what was happening to our lives and to end the loneliness between us, but I had been dismissed so many times that I didn't dare subject myself to further rejection and risk whatever credibility I may still have had with him. Mike steadfastly refused to talk to me about "our problems," disclaiming any possible threat of involvement, but I held out hope that somehow some way he would come to understand that his rejection would not end the nightmare.

As the family of a USAID contractor, the children and I were living in Pakistan under the umbrella of Mike's passport. I had not realistically considered leaving Mike, but I was at a loss to understand how the girls and I could survive if we stayed.

I didn't expect Mike to accompany us on the trips to the

mullahs, but I did want to tell him what I was doing without fear of condemnation. I weighed my prospects for survival in the States without Mike and concluded that there was nowhere I could go with two small children in tow. There was no one I could impose upon back home, no career to fall back on at this point, and there was no way to support myself and the children. It was difficult to determine how badly my health had been compromised and whether or not I could physically handle a job and the care of two small children. I had become pathetically weak during the two years that we lived in Karachi, finding it difficult at times to lift my arm to comb my hair. I felt as if a straw had been put to my veins and the life was being sucked out of me. Leaving Karachi with my children would have been a physical impossibility.

My Yi Wood element struggled to survive against the odds. The small amount of Water in my chart was needed to nurture my children, my home and my environment. Yi Wood vines can use all the elements, including Jia Wood, a massive tree. Jia Wood is the Day Master for both Sonya and Sasha. In the same way that a vine can climb a tree trunk to reach the top for sunshine, my Yi Wood vine climbed the Jia Wood tree to see the Light. My love for them kept me going, just like my mother's love kept her going. Love is a healing vibration.

Despite everything, I loved Mike. I believed we belonged together against all odds. I was committed to our family and our marriage, a unity that was sacred to me. For whatever reason, I loved a man who fathered our two miracle children and moved us to this strange part of the world. I accepted the facts as they were and that I was where I was supposed to be. Somehow I was determined to survive the forces against us, and begged God to heal Sonya and to let me live long enough to raise our children. I decided to follow my heart and listen to the subtle urges that had always guided my decisions. I gathered the strength to manage within the dysfunction that developed between us, believing our problems would be resolved one day soon.

CHAPTER 57

The girls fell asleep early one evening, a rare event. Exhausted, I collapsed into bed with Mike, who was reading. Recognizing that I needed sleep, he closed his book and got up to go to the bathroom next to our bedroom. Before reaching the bathroom door he turned around and said to me, "Did you say something?"

"No," I answered lightly.

"But did you hear that? I thought I heard someone call my name."

"Yes" I said, "but it wasn't me."

"That's strange, are you hearing voices lately?" he asked. Hallelujah!!!

"Yes, I'm hearing voices and have been for months," I wanted to shout with happiness, but tried to control my excitement for fear of blowing an opportunity to have a conversation. I was anxious to tell him about Dr. Rafiq, the visits to the mullahs, and the failed attempts to remove the curse. I wanted him to understand what we were going through so that he would show some compassion for Sonya and patience with me. I wanted him to be part of our lives, our struggles. This was not all going to happen in one evening, but the fact that he could hear the voices, too, was a beginning.

CHAPTER 58

Pakistani culture was complex. I couldn't understand the distinctions between the Shiite and Sunni Muslims nor the disdain that the Muslims and Christians held for one another. How did the role of the mullah compare to that of a Christian priest? Most importantly, how could Sonya, a child, be affected by Black Magic? The minister's wife down the street gave me pamphlets to read about the devil and possession, which I found interesting, but they didn't logically explain why or how it could happen. How could an innocent child, incapable of making religious or any other choices, be made prey to the devil? It didn't make any sense.

The minister's wife introduced me to Luke Parker, a Christian Pakistani and reputed authority on both the Bible and the Koran. I invited Luke to our home for discussions on religious differences in Pakistan, hoping that the conversation would appeal to Mike's intellectual nature and we could enjoy the discussions together.

Luke started visiting around the time Sonya developed a hideous staph infection, one in a sequence of many we contended with at the time. The first of these staph infections appeared as a large boil that festered on her leg. After it had been treated and thought to have disappeared, it moved to the bridge of her nose, right between her eyes. The boil was huge, adding a quarter inch of thickness from eyebrow to eyebrow and flattening out her bridge, which made Sonya look deformed. The boil was lanced, antibiotics were given, and again we believed Sonya had recovered. Not so. The boil reappeared on her cheek, and then on the very tip of her nose in the shape of a giant soap bubble. Now people shrank from this once endearing child, hoping that whatever she had wasn't contagious.

The last and most hideous of the boils was in full bloom the night Luke Parker came for our Koran discussions. It appeared as a large egg on both her upper and lower eyelids. It looked grotesque and was extremely painful. Sonya interrupted our exchange with one of her tantrums, diverting our conversation to her unsightly, painful condition. Luke, concerned by what he saw, asked how long she had suffered and how it had all begun. Given the chance, Mike would have told the story beginning with the first boil on Sonya's leg. I spoke first, however, and started with Manuel, the fired cook.

As I told Luke about Manuel, the hairs and the mullahs, Mike sat quietly. He frowned when he learned that I had not consulted him before taking the children out of the city, which was not only dangerous but a security violation. Luke listened intently to every word I said, and then asked simply, "Why haven't you taken her to see a priest?"

I was somewhat taken aback by this obvious question. Why hadn't I sought out a priest? My response was inadequate, even to myself. Perhaps I assumed that since we were in a Muslim country I should seek a Muslim solution? I had no good answer for him. All I could say was, "I don't know any."

"Tomorrow I will take you to see Father Jerry, an old Jesuit priest. He will know what to do."

CHAPTER 59

Sonya needed to see a doctor. The sty was enormous and had begun festering. I was worried that it would affect her eyesight. Since Luke was going to pick us up in the morning, I thought that I could take Sonya to the clinic when we returned from the church.

It was another long drive through dusty streets before we arrived at the Catholic Church. Sonya was in full form that day, swinging her arms and kicking her legs. The priest was waiting for us. Noticing that I had Sasha in my arms and that Luke was having difficulties managing a turbulent Sonya, he walked down the long center aisle that connected the foyer to the altar to meet us.

At the sight of Sonya's hideous infection and hysterical flailing, Father Jerry d'Sousa said he had no doubt that Sonya was possessed. He held his hand above her head as if to offer a blessing. Her fits and shouting subsided long enough to ask me a few questions before we entered the sanctuary.

"Are you hearing voices?"

I was so excited by this question that I temporarily forgot where I was and shouted enthusiastically, "Yes, yes! I hear voices all the time!"

As if my credibility wasn't sufficient, I added, "Mike hears voices, too."

I don't know how much Luke had told Father d'Sousa before we arrived, but the good priest recognized my desperation and could see that I was counting on him for help. Not wanting to hold out false hopes, he said that he had done exorcisms before but could offer no guarantees. He suggested that he come to our house that weekend to see what he could do.

Father d'Sousa gave all of us his blessing before we left the church with renewed hope to put these troubles behind us.

CHAPTER 60

After we got home, I took Sonya to the doctor. By this time, Dr. Bhally was very familiar with Sonya's staph infections, perplexed as any of us as to why they persisted. This infection was nastier than the rest because it was enormous and located on both the upper and lower eyelids. He didn't think a course of oral antibiotics would be strong enough to address the infection, recommending instead that Sonya spend a few days at a nearby clinic on an intravenous drip.

This was not something I wanted to hear. Sonya despised hospitals and I strongly suspected that she had contracted this infection in the hospital in the first place. I didn't know how I would physically cope, knowing I would take Sasha with me. Nargis was a good ayah, but Sasha was still nursing and I would not consider leaving her overnight with anyone. Having Sonya stay alone in a Pakistani hospital or clinic was out of the question, too.

I returned home to get Sasha, packed bags for the three of us and headed to the clinic which was located in Clifton, a suburb near our home. It was fast approaching the end of the day when Dr. Bhally was finishing up with his patients. He met us at the clinic before going home for the evening. He had ordered us a private suite, instructing the attending resident, a woman, to give us special attention, which seemed to annoy her. Dr. Bhally then departed, leaving us in the care of this young doctor who led us through quiet, empty corridors before arriving at our special room.

In the late afternoon setting sunlight, layers of dust particles glistened on the furniture. The bathroom mirror was so filthy that our reflected images appeared as impressionistic expressions. When I commented on the room's condition to Dr. Bhally's resident, she was again irritated, but sent up two tiny "cleaning ladies" to tidy things up. From personal experience I had no reason to expect the cleaning ladies to be different from who arrived. Their red *paan* smiles and rotted teeth announced their identities. They came with*out* a bucket, a broom or a dust cloth, and were uncertain what I wanted them to do. Since they couldn't understand a word of English, I did my best to gesture cleaning movements and showed them the mirror as an example of what was generally wrong with the entire room. They seemed to have gotten the message. In an attempt to impress, one of them looked at me confidently while pulling a long length of toilet paper from the holder. Then she dampened it under the faucet. With deliberate gestures, the tiny little cleaning lady maintained eye contact and her most reassuring smile while making large circular motions on the lower half of the mirror—she was too short to reach the upper half—like she had watched me do when I was trying to communicate that the room needed cleaning. She finished her job and stepped back to look at her masterpiece with pride. A muddied mess had been created on the lower half of the mirror. Our impressionistic images quickly became a childlike finger painting. After "cleaning" the bathroom, the little ladies took more toilet paper and dusted off the lamp tables.

It was no use. Years of grime had settled on the curtains, the tabletops and the floor. It would never be clean. At least not that night. I had a choice. We could either stay or return home, but there was no value expending precious energy on cleaning, a futile activity. I opted to stay because I was already there, hoping for the best.

Mike came to the clinic for a visit on his way home from the office.

I told him about my meeting with Father d'Sousa, our scheduled exorcism, and that I had invited him to the house for lunch that coming weekend. Confident that Mike would like the priest, I described Father Jerry as a kindly, interesting old fellow who had come to Karachi from Goa many years earlier.

Mike, like me, was raised a Catholic. I never got the impression that his immediate family was particularly religious. Certainly he was not. Mike had abandoned Catholicism and rejected religion in general early in life. After studying the Crusades in a college history course, he refused to accept that Christ would encourage rampant death and destruction in His name and reasoned that all religions were about control. There was no point arguing that Christ, who died in 33 A.D., had nothing to do with the Crusades that began in 1095. The Crusades were political in nature and Christ's name had been abused. Religion can be about control. It can also be about guidance. We do have intelligence, Free Will, and a conscience to help us with that distinction. Control comes in when *every* word is expressed as an absolute, *both* by those who would have you believe in religion and by those who argue against it. I couldn't understand why it was necessary for Mike to throw the baby out with the bath water on this subject, or why he adamantly deferred to a position he crystallized as a youth. I judged this to be his safe harbor from emotional and religious involvement, and from discussions with me that he didn't want to have. I wanted to know how he felt about the weekend's scheduled exorcism at our house, but he looked down on what he considered drivel and refused to talk about it.

Sasha, Sonya and I spent the first night at the clinic in tight quarters. Sonya awakened periodically with nightmares, only to find the drip tube taped to her vein and her bulging eye throbbing with pain. I looked down at her, struggling for relief. She had been a lovely child, blessed with the effervescent spark of life that made her eyes twinkle, feet dance, voice sing, and heart love. And now she lay there with tubes in her arm and ugly boils on her face.

As I stroked Sonya's forehead and cheek to comfort her, I struggled through tears to visualize the child I once knew. The loose curls, big blue eyes, rosy cheeks, and chubby legs that gave her an angelic, yet mischievous look were gone. Instead of curls, matted hair smashed against her head and an enormous festering eye caused her to look more like one of Karachi's neglected, unloved street urchins than my darling cherub.

Her screams and cries awakened an unhappy Sasha, who nuzzled my breast looking for milk. After two days and nights without sleep, I was physically, emotionally and mentally drained. The dysentery and chronic asthma attacks had nearly taken Sonya's young life, but it was this hideous staph infection that was breaking my heart. The cruel sight of a once adorable Sonya was crushing, and the mounting demands on my energy exceeded my capabilities. Having soothed her back to sleep, I broke down and wept bitterly, begging for mercy.

"Please God, forgive me," I pleaded. "Show me the way to save our lives."

CHAPTER 61

Almost immediately after getting Sonya home from her two days at the clinic, I could sense some improvement. The most recent boils were clearly healing. I suspected that we weren't completely out of the woods in terms of her health, but at least this one, potentially disfiguring symptom had been arrested. For the time being I could turn my attention back to managing the house and preparing for our upcoming visit from the priest.

Father d'Sousa, or Father Jerry as he preferred to be called, arrived on Saturday morning for the healing. Fortunately, this exorcism was not dramatic or frightening like in the movies. First the priest blessed Sonya, Sasha, Mike and me. Then he went through the house room by room, going through every closet and cupboard, sprinkling holy water and saying prayers as he went. He stopped periodically to examine one thing or another, said a few prayers while making the Sign of the Cross, and then went on. Without drama he focused his attention on the job at hand, not engaging in questions or descriptive commentary.

Mike remained downstairs, anxious for the priest to finish so that he could have lunch.

The exorcism completed, we went downstairs to be with Mike who was already seated at the dining table. Father Jerry sensed Mike's misgivings, appreciating that he might require some explanation. Patiently he tried to explain the differences between ghosts and spirits in a way that we could understand, before being dismissed by Mike. He explained that, "the spirits living in your house are not ghosts. Ghosts are manifestations of the deceased, whose souls or spirits refuse to leave the earth. They refuse to pass on."

Father Jerry looked at Mike for acknowledgement before proceeding. Mike didn't budge.

"Spirits, on the other hand, never had bodies. Angels and demons are examples of spirits that can actually be created by focused energy such as thoughts, prayers, rituals and black magic." He explained that what we had in our house were spirits of a lowly or negative variety, presumed to be demonic. According to Father Jerry, negative spirits had been created or conjured up by rituals done in our home, specifically in our bedrooms, causing our sleepless nights and misfortune. We were experiencing spirit hauntings as opposed to ghost hauntings."

"However," he explained, "in the same way that evil or dark spirits can be created, so can light spirits. By invoking the name of Jesus Christ through ritual," as in his exorcism that day, "Darkness is cast out by bringing in the Light. Light always prevails over darkness in the same way that an opened door allows light into a dark room. The reverse is not true."

Father Jerry said that we could expect unusual spirit activity for about three days, but after that he hoped that our lives would return to normal and that Sonya would recover.

Mike seemed satisfied with the explanation, respecting the old man's point of view. He quickly changed the topic of conversation to Indian history, asking Father about his Goan ancestry, terrain Mike could relate to more easily.

Within a week or two after Father Jerry's visit, I felt like a new person and Sonya's nightmares lessened. Her staph infection healed completely and never returned. Best of all, Mike was being transferred to Manila in the Philippines, and we were scheduled to leave within the next few months.

Every chance I had I expressed gratitude for the mercy that

had been shown my family and me, and I offered continual thanks for the good things in our lives. I began reading the Bible at night, sitting on the bathroom floor for hours after Mike went to bed. I repeated prayers over and over, begging for protection for my children, reminding myself of my mother and the way she repeated the prayers of her pages when I was growing up.

"Please, God, keep my children safe," I implored.

I renewed my faith and love in Christ and felt "born again," not knowing or caring what that meant relative to the Born Again Christian Movement. I felt like I had been dipped into a vat of springtime and emerged with sunlight streaming through my pores. I felt rejuvenated. To me, born again meant that I was back in God's good graces.

Part Two

SCIENCE

CHAPTER 62

We flew directly from Karachi to Manila in July 1992. The first thing that struck me as we touched down at the Manila airport was the contrast between the two cities. It was as if somebody had flipped on a light switch. I felt like I was emerging from some crusty, filmy darkness into the light. What this might mean to our life ahead lifted my spirits. We had survived the desert environment and had been delivered into the lushness of the tropics. Trees were everywhere, and so much water. *The Wood element of Sonya, Sasha and I absorbed our surroundings like a dry sponge in a bucket of water.*

Mike's company, Barter & Biddle, booked us at a resort hotel near Mike's office. The hotel was located on the oceanfront with palm trees all around and lovely breezes coming off the water. Life began to reshape itself. In the evenings we ate in the dining room with live music, usually a mariachi-type band playing upbeat, familiar international tunes. Music in the Philippines is pervasive, an ingrained part of life. There could be three combos playing at the same time in different parts of the hotel, ranging in size from full-scale orchestras reminiscent of the big band era to individual soloists performing in smaller, more intimate settings. Over centuries, the Filipinos have evolved from a blended cultural mix to become a distinct hybrid that enjoys music of all kinds. If they aren't able to play, sing or dance to their music, Filipinos are just as satisfied to listen and watch.

The band in the dining room where we ate took pleasure in singing our requests, one right after another. They entertained us tirelessly with beautiful renditions of *Besame Mucho, Love Me Tender,* and *My Way.* My heart drifted back to our wedding day when they played the first strands of *Begin the Beguine,* the song that accompanied our first dance as husband and wife:

> *When they begin the beguine*
> *It brings back the sound of music so tender,*
> *It brings back a night of tropical splendor,*

It brings back a memory ever green.

I'm with you once more under the stars,
And down by the shore an orchestras playing
And even the palms seem to be swaying
when they begin the beguine.

To live it again is past all endeavor,
Except when that tune clutches my heart,
And there we are, swearing to love forever,
And promising never, never to part.

Their interpretation of the sentiment was lovely, and the words seemed to be written for that moment. Mike and I sang along to the tunes, allowing them to carry us back to simpler days. We loved music and dancing together. Music was our salve, the magical ointment that cured all.

I'd like to think that Sonya inherited her intuitive rhythm and passion from me, for no other reason than she had great moves and a natural ability to perform. She danced happily by herself at the table for our pleasure as well as her own, until the band members graciously welcomed this charming little four-year-old girl on stage to rock the rhythms with them. She joined them without looking back and danced and shimmied to her heart's content like the world was expecting her. It was a joy to witness Sonya's happiness once again. Our little girl with the rosy cheeks and big eyes had returned.

CHAPTER 63

The contrast to our former life in Pakistan was striking. In part, I saw the cultural differences as a direct reflection of the influence that religion has on a society; Pakistan, a predominantly Muslim country, compared to the Philippines, a predominantly Christian country. Besides education, the most immediate characteristic that caught my attention was the music, beginning with the melodic chime of church bells, a welcomed contrast to the woeful call to prayer that began at dawn every day in Karachi.

Karachi did not have venues where adults could enjoy dancing and music, and certainly there was no such place to take our children. There were no public spaces like parks to enjoy an activity that communed with the local people or where we could enjoy bright, cheerful customs that celebrated life in an uplifting way. Yes, it was possible to find singers and dancers on stage, mostly men, but not occasions where the public could spontaneously interact in celebration of a life's event, or share with the larger group of humanity.

For Westerners like us who were trying to establish a family life, Christian society was less threatening and more inviting. Life in Pakistan required being covered up and hidden. Life felt morose.

The Philippines and Pakistan are both considered Third World countries, loosely defined as those countries that receive Western aid. Lumping them together under this label is misleading. The reality I experienced was that Pakistan was medieval compared to the Philippines, attributable to literacy and religion. By comparison, The Philippines has a high literacy rate, about ninety-five percent, compared to the recorded literacy rate in Pakistan which is around thirty percent. Eventually we were blessed to find a very good staff including an ayah with a bachelor's degree in mathematics and a cook with a teacher's degree. It was a relief to have people in our home who brought all the attributes of education with them to the job. This isn't to say that Manila did not have its own issues, including a high rate of poverty. I'm simply saying that education wasn't one of them. And once again I was struck by the fact that poverty in the presence of water—plenty of water—never seems as dire as poverty in an arid environment.

Immediately after our arrival I began researching available housing. Budgetary constraints limited our options and monthly losses on our rental property in the States further affected our disposable income. I wanted to live in a protected area, but properties within the gated communities or compounds where most U.S. government employees resided were out of our price range. Eventually, I narrowed our choices to a few candidates and took Mike to visit the finalists with me.

Housing in foreign countries, I have learned from plenty of experience— particularly in Third World countries—is the single most critical factor to consider when settling a family. One's home must be in a good location and feel safe, protected, and clean with everything working properly. Something else about housing in Third World countries: it should be pretty. I attributed many of our problems in Karachi to our home and was cautious not to repeat our mistakes. I wasn't being difficult, just matter of fact. Any housing we chose had to be pleasant, or have the potential to become so without expending two years of precious emotional, physical and financial resources to bring it up to an acceptable standard.

From experience I knew, too, that it is emotionally debilitating to cope with visual poverty both inside and outside the home, *and* deal with all the other settling-in issues. I added "pretty" to my list of requirements asserting that—as homemaker—I was the one who determined what that meant.

Although I had found the house we settled on, Mike chose it. I favored a house in Das Marinas Village, but we were not able to negotiate the USAID budgeted price with the landlord. The house on Lapu Lapu Avenue in Magallanes Village was the next best one on the list.

Right from the beginning the house did not feel right to me. Mike liked the size—six bedrooms—and the big swimming pool. I resisted, but we were running out of time to find something better. Mike's work contract offered a limited number of days at the hotel to allow us time to get organized, but they were soon to expire. We decided to take the house on Lapu Lapu Avenue and make the most of it.

I was eager to get our home set up so that we could enjoy life as soon as possible, longing to create a normal existence for our family, whatever that meant. Manila appeared to be an hospitable and welcoming environment that I was anxious to explore.

I should have listened to my initial reservations about this big house. Its location on Lapu Lapu Avenue outside the village compound is what troubled me most. Lapu Lapu Avenue was off-limits to State Department and USAID personnel as a place to rent because it was considered a security risk. As contractors, we did not fall under the State Department's concern so if we wanted to live there, they would not object. Mike was confident we'd be fine and proceeded to negotiate the terms of the lease.

The house felt unprotected and the security risk felt real. There was a steady stream of traffic along busy EDSA Avenue, which ran parallel to Lapu Lapu Avenue and the front of our house. A tall, iron picket fence separated us from the street, but did not offer the security I wanted, especially after hearing accounts of robberies from several neighbors. We were used to having solid walls around our yard and not feeling so exposed.

Safety was one issue, but I felt there was something else that I just couldn't put my finger on. The house was newly remodeled, light-filled, huge and lovely, and the landlord seemed to be a great guy, so what could be the problem?

The first clear hint that we should rethink our decision came when Mike submitted a bid of one thousand dollars per month less than the asking price and the landlord accepted without countering. It didn't seem natural that he wouldn't at least try to negotiate, even though the house had been sitting empty on the market for over a year while being renovated. Still, the price was right, and I could not come up with a convincing argument not to rent it.

USAID did not provide furniture on this assignment. Instead we were given one budget to buy furniture, a second to make curtains, and a third to purchase air conditioners and appliances that are not typically included in a rental property.

There were no furniture stores in Manila where one could purchase a ready-made sofa and have it delivered to the house. There were only showrooms. Everything was custom built. Many women complained about this system, but I rather enjoyed working with the artisans and designing our own furniture and curtains. Granted, this required a lot of work, but the activity nurtured a creative outlet in me that was rehabilitating. My biggest challenge was creating something lovely within the budget that had been allotted.

Even before our lease was signed in late August, I set to work to organize the fabrics, sofas, bedroom sets and dining room furniture. My goal was to make sure that everything was in place before the girls and I departed for my brother's wedding in Montana in mid-September. We moved into our house on September 1, 1992, before our shipment arrived from Pakistan.

CHAPTER 64

The phone rang while I was preparing for bed the first night in our new home. Mike answered, listened briefly and said, "I'm sorry, but Laura doesn't stay here. She is at the hotel." He assumed the caller was asking for Laura Fishbein, the Barter & Biddle advance person. Then I heard Mike say, "Thank you very much, but I'm a married man. No thanks, I'm not interested."

I came out of the bathroom, still brushing my teeth, to listen more carefully, but Mike had already hung up the phone. He sat there with a funny smirk on his face before saying, "That was the strangest phone call I have ever had!" The piece of conversation I had missed was a solicitation from the caller saying to my husband, "Well, you sound interesting, perhaps I should be speaking to you instead."

Mike and I laughed at the call. We didn't know that Filipina women were so forward. Nor did we realize that we were getting a glimpse of the house's sordid past.

Daniel, an American, and his Thai wife, Nam, lived next door to us with their high school daughter and his elderly mother. Daniel worked on a third party contract like Mike, so they had a lot in common. Daniel and Nam had lived in Manila for about fifteen years, during which time they had learned a lot about the city, its people, the ex-pats in the community and other interesting trivia. After so many years, they considered Manila their home and intended to stay. Daniel and Nam were excited to have American neighbors move near them and invited us to lunch the very next day.

Nam came out to greet us when we arrived at their gate. She smiled warmly, chirping her enthusiasm in the charming way that comes naturally to Thai women. "Oh, so you are living in the *yakuza's* house," she said, followed by giggle, giggle, giggle.

"*Yakuza?* What's a *yakuza?*" I said, offering a spontaneous giggle in reply, like she had told us a joke that I didn't get but should have.

"You don't know what a *yakuza* is?" (Tee hee hee.) "A *yakuza* is a Japanese Mafioso. An underworld character," she laughed.

Nam filled in more details. Apparently, the former occupant of our new home was a Japanese gangster who had run a brothel from the premises. We told Nam and Daniel about the phone call we had received the night before from someone looking for "Laura." Presumably Laura was one of the girls who had previously lived there and had worked for the *yakuza*. According to Nam, fourteen "maids" had lived in the house; all were being trained for overseas work in Korea and Japan.

This was turning into a very interesting afternoon. It was now clear why the landlord was anxious to close the deal, why extensive renovation was necessary, and why we had received a strange phone call our first night on Lapu Lapu Avenue. I was still processing this extraordinary bit of information when Nam blurted out the next thriller.

Punctuated by more giggling, she said, "Yes, and there was a double murder committed in your house, too!"

I was speechless. Her giggling became less charming. "Is that really funny?" I thought.

Without prompting, Nam described the murder scene enthusiastically.

"Yes, the *yakuza* was a very bad man. He had some work done in his house, but didn't pay."

According to Nam, the worker who was being stiffed came every day to collect his money, but the *yakuza* kept giving him the run around. The maids were ready with excuses, usually that he was out of town or at the office. The worker became more and more angry, not willing to accept the usual stories. He had not been paid *and* the lies and excuses were insulting. The day that the murders were committed, the worker came prepared. He saw the *yakuza*'s car parked in the driveway, disbelieving that the *yakuza* was out of the country. The usual excuses had all worn thin, and he had already worked himself into a rage. He forced himself past the maid who opened the gate, and ran into the house and down the hallway to the end of the corridor where he stabbed a maid in the back room, now our children's playroom. The houseboy tried to stop him but he was also slain.

More giggles. "You moved into the *yakuza*'s house."
"Stop that darned giggling," I thought, becoming irritated.

Now what? We had already paid two year's rent in advance. This customary real estate practice made sense under the circumstances. With everything else on my mind, I couldn't adequately digest the moment. Another sick or bad house? What would that mean for this next chapter of our lives?

I decided not to dwell on that question further, but instead turned my focus on preparations for the upcoming trip to Montana with our girls. I was looking forward to seeing my family and to some semblance of sanity after the two long years in Karachi. There was nothing more I could do about the house at this point anyway, except to make the best of it.

CHAPTER 65

By the time we returned to Manila after the wedding, our furniture had been completed and the house was falling into place nicely. My seventy-eight year old mother-in-law, Josephine, would arrive soon. The timing was perfect.

Mike and I planned a small dinner party for his mother and his boss, who had arrived from Washington, D.C. the day after Josephine's arrival. Josephine started preparing herself early in the afternoon so she could relax before the other guests arrived. While stepping from the tub, she somehow scraped her foot along the metal rail that guided the sliding doors and removed the tissue-paper-thin skin from the top of her foot, exposing her bones and tendons.

Blood was everywhere. Somehow she'd also cut herself behind her ear, perhaps by hitting her head on the faucet when she fell. Blood dripped down her neck and onto her chest and back where it mixed with water, making the gash look much worse than it actually was. Fortunately our cook, Flora, grabbed a clean t-shirt to wrap Josephine's foot and stop the worst of the bleeding.

Sasha, who had just turned two, became hysterical. Not understanding the chaos she feared the worst: "The kidnappers had arrived!" During our stay in Karachi I had lived in constant fear that our children would be kidnapped, an all too common occurrence. Unwittingly I passed this fear onto both Sonya and Sasha who had no idea what kidnappers were, but who dreaded them all the same.

Frantically I scooped Sasha up and did what I could to calm her fears while I ran outside to hail a taxi from the stand across the street. The cabbies ignored my signal. They were upset with me for filing several complaints with the Village Association for parking too close to our house and loitering outside our gate. Since then they refused to drive me or charged exorbitant fares when they did. The cabbies continued to ignore my pleas until they saw Josephine being led out to the gate by the maids. The sight of an old woman with a bandaged foot and blood-smeared face must have evoked their sympathy. In no time flat one of the cabbies pulled up to the gate so we could get in more easily and drove us to Makati Hospital in record time.

The emergency room was jammed with people suffering from all sorts of problems. The grieving family of a child who had just died from viral meningitis was there and a tired, worn out child-mother with a premature infant sat quietly until a doctor would see her. She was too young and poor to accept her new responsibility. With despair in her eyes, she offered her sleeping newborn to me, hoping that I could be the one person who would possibly save her. Despite the deep compassion I felt for them both, I could not accept being a mother to either one. At this point I was so weak that I could barely take care of my own children and myself.

Josephine waited stoically for several hours until the doctor was available to clean and wrap her foot before sending her home. It was a nasty wound. I thought the doctor would stitch it, but he advised against stitching saying that it would be best to wrap it, keep it clean and hope the skin would graft back on its own. Josephine had worked in a doctor's office for many years before her retirement and was comfortable with the care that had been prescribed.

A series of incidents, harbingers of many more strange days to come, caused me further pause regarding our housing decision. During the first month in our house on Lapu Lapu, we witnessed a drug bust on EDSA Avenue, which ran parallel to our street. Three bank robberies and a kidnapping followed in the years ahead. One of the bank robberies happened at nine o'clock in the morning. We couldn't miss the excitement; the stakeout point was at our front gate.

A more amusing Lapu Lapu memory was the day a fellow drove up to our gate in a taxi with his bags in hand, looking for "the General," and expecting to spend the night. He was shocked to find that the General—and his houseful of lovely maids—no longer lived there.

CHAPTER 66

After my mother-in-law's accident, she stayed with us for most of the next six months. She was bedridden for the first three months and made plans to tour Asia for another three months after that. Josephine's extended visit compounded other problems. It wasn't just her foot injury that needed tending. She required a considerable amount of continuous medical care as well as entertainment, responsibilities that fell to me. Josephine could be a domineering woman. As self-anointed matriarch of her Hispanic family, she displayed pretentious and condescending airs, expecting treatment consistent with presumed aristocratic lineage.

She engaged in gossip with the maids, enticing them with extra money here and there, and implicated herself into our personal lives where she had no business. She postured as would a royal who did not participate in public emotional displays, and spurned my feelings if they conflicted with her own.

I was annoyed when Josephine told me to stand up straight and hold my stomach in. She dared to use her seventy-eight-year-old self as an example of how I should look. Josephine preened in front of the mirror while standing sideways with her stomach sucked in, oblivious to the excess thirty-five pounds she carried around her hips and midriff. If I could have joked with Mike about the preposterous comparison I wouldn't have been offended. Certainly there was no excess fat on me, nor did I have poor posture. I was tired, however, and looked it. Standing united against me, Josephine and Mike dismissed my ill-health as an attention-getting device.

Chronic health problems continued to drag me down. Sleep deprivation, inadequate nutrition, and years of living an extraordinarily stressful life were taking their toll. My weight dipped to a puny 105 pounds. Something I couldn't understand was that no matter how much I ate, food didn't seem to nourish me or stick to my bones.

I had been to the doctor for a series of tests, which revealed a large cyst on my kidney, cystic amoebae and anemia. These discoveries helped to explain my distended stomach, for which I was prescribed a treatment of three powerful sulfa drugs, but not the general malaise, weakness and chronic aches and pains.

One weekend we visited a friends' home near Laguna, about an hour's drive from Magallanes Village. The area is known for its hot springs, where natural and man-made pools capture, drain and replenish themselves with clean spring water. The water was so fresh that you could drink it. We lazed away the afternoon in the pool under the hot sun, and kept cool with San Miguel beer at ice-cold temperatures while snacking on pork rinds and *adobo*.

When we got home that night I started to feel ill, and continued to feel poorly throughout the next day. I was dizzy, another symptom to add to my list of medical complaints that no one wanted to hear about.

The two years we spent in Karachi had taken a toll on my health. I was desperate to feel well again, but recovery was difficult with the never-ending challenges we faced in the Philippines. Twelve-hour electrical brownouts—scheduled outages as opposed to unscheduled, *blackout* outages—were a regular occurrence. Without air conditioning, the 100+ degree temperatures were unbearable, a seemingly plausible explanation for both my dizzy spells and weakness.

CHAPTER 67

After Mike and the children were sleeping and the maids had finished their work, I would escape to the privacy of our bathroom, where I sat on the cool tiles of the floor to pray and read the Bible or some other spiritual material. I wanted to connect with God, investigate my spirituality and educate myself on black magic. I have always believed in the adage that, "there is nothing to fear but fear itself." I feared black magic and truly believed that if I could unravel the shroud of mystery that threatened me, I could make that fear disappear.

Every night I prayed, too, for good health and the strength to raise my children. I thought I was dying. I pleaded with God over and over again to spare me until the children were grown. I wasn't afraid to die myself, as I truly believed in an afterlife that would be so much easier, but the thought of leaving my young children behind to face the perils of life without a mother was more pain than I could endure. Something beyond amoebae, anemia and cysts was making me so ill.

Before finishing, I threw in another request. I asked God to intervene on my behalf; to make it impossible for me to fly to Hong Kong with Josephine, who was back to her old self. Now that she had recuperated in bed for three months, she was ready to travel. I resisted the arm-twisting invitation to go with her. The incessant, pontificating lectures and opinions that were her style of conversation drained me of precious energy I needed for myself. I would do anything to avoid being exclusively in her cross hairs. Plus, I didn't feel comfortable leaving the children.

I slipped into bed, careful not to awaken Mike. I was more tired than usual and fell asleep almost immediately. At some point I woke up freezing, but too weak and in too much pain to pull up the blankets. My left arm felt as if a horse had kicked it and the persistent, overall weakness overpowered me. I rolled into my husband for warmth. As I did so, I remember whirling off, traveling into the blackness, not knowing the destination. Then I arrived at this place . . . an awful place.

The depressing, lifeless scenery reminded me of my first glimpse of a Karachi landscape when we drove from the airport to the hotel: dirt encrusted trees dangled black, plastic garbage bags from their leafless branches. The desert sand that appeared everywhere in Karachi created a beige, muted impression that caused me to squint when I went outside. Here, too, I squinted to adjust my eyes to the dimness. Where was I?

Thick gooey mud was all around me. Then, just as I thought there was no life, I saw people off in the distance. How strange, they're not wearing any clothes, I thought. I could see only their backs, not their faces, but I sensed hopelessness in their bent heads and heavy steps. They were all walking in the same direction with no apparent destination. In their slow procession to nowhere, they reminded me of Jewish prisoners being marched off to the gas chambers. They, too, seemed to have accepted their fate and had given up on life.

Unexpectedly, one of the men in the back row turned his head to the side. It was my husband.

"Mike?" I thought. "What are you doing here? What is this place?"

At that moment I became aware of my "guides," the ones who were giving the tour. Although one was on each side of me, I was never able to see their faces.

Steering my attention away from Mike and without saying a word, they directed me to look at the densest part of the spongy quagmire. As one of the guides pointed to the mud pool that lay in front of me, the second stooped to pull off a net that was laden with inches of gooey earth and soaked, decaying leaves. As he threw back the net, a cat sprang from the detritus with the power of a gushing geyser. It was as though the cat had been waiting to be released. It was so quick that I only glimpsed it as I heard its frenetic squeal when it raced past me. I marveled that the cat emerged from the slimy mire perfectly clean. How had it survived? How had the cat remained fresh and alive, untouched by the soulless environment? Somehow the cat was determined to live. It didn't belong there.

The guide on my left interrupted my thoughts as he motioned me to look inside the hole. Without stepping forward, I stooped over to peer inside. How strange. There lay a once beautiful woman, bloated from having been there for so long. "At least ten years," I thought to myself. Why hadn't the body decayed? Then, I noticed that the woman was wearing a one-piece denim jumpsuit that zipped up the front. It looked like the same one I had worn in Switzerland when I lived there but had abandoned years earlier. The woman's hairstyle was similar to my own, too.

I shuddered as the reality became clear to me.

Then, I squeezed my eyes shut and put my hands over my ears in an attempt to stop my thoughts, sensing the guides could read them.

"Nooooooooooooo! No moooooore!" I screamed to myself while pushing back any acknowledgement that would make it real. The fight within me was useless. There was no choice but to acknowledge the horrible truth.

I was in Hell. The woman was me.

CHAPTER 68

The splashing noise from Mike's shower awakened me. I was disoriented, not knowing where I was. I looked around to see the familiar walls of our bedroom and realized that I was at home in Manila, and my husband was preparing for work. I tried to piece together what had happened the night before—where I had been. "What happened to me, and why did I have this excruciating pain in my left arm and along my left side?" I shivered from cold, despite the warm temperature of the room.

Mike finished his shower and came to sit next to me on the bed. I told him how I had awakened with cold and pain on my left side, needing his body for warmth. Briefly, I told him about the dream, eliminating the part about him. I waited for his comment. Familiar with my husband's emotional orientation, I wasn't surprised when he said almost casually, "Germaine, it sounds like you had a heart attack. I think you should see a doctor."

Yes, he must be right. I had had a heart attack and a pre-death experience. I wasn't nearly as troubled by the heart attack as I was by seeing Hell instead of Heaven. Instead of Light, there was darkness. Instead of beautiful music, choirs of angels, and an overwhelming feeling of love, I experienced dreadful quiet, naked, desperate people and overwhelming hopelessness.

Why? I was filled with the love of God and felt closer to Him than ever before, trusting the deep, personal relationship we had developed once again. As I reflected on the previous evening, my most painful thought was that my devotion to God was a mockery, and I questioned His existence as well as my sanity.

I was comforted by the realization that I had not died. I survived to care for my children as I requested, and I had a good excuse not to go to Hong Kong with Josephine.

Slowly I got out of bed and walked to the bathroom, startled by my reflection in the mirror. My eyes were bright red and there were tiny red spots all over my body. I combed my hair, the excruciating pain in my left arm made it difficult to raise. Carefully, I put on my bathrobe and joined Mike downstairs for breakfast.

As I sat at the breakfast table, Flora came in to serve coffee. She took one look at me and gasped while taking a step back.

"Are you ill, Madam?" she asked alarmed.

"Could be better Flora," I answered, assuming I really did look as bad as I felt. Just then Josephine joined us. After a polite exchange of morning greetings, Mike gave her a matter-of-fact description of my symptoms and said that I was going to the doctor. Josephine offered to go with me. I was hoping Mike would offer, but he did not. He went to work, and Josephine and I prepared for the doctor's office.

CHAPTER 69

A colleague of Mike's recommended an internist who had an office at the Makati Medical Center. Supposedly the doctor had an impressive academic pedigree that included Harvard Medical School. We found our way to his office, where we waited for well over an hour. Finally, Josephine asked the receptionist if I could be next since I was very ill. Shortly thereafter, I was ushered in to see the doctor.

Without examining me, the doctor asked if I had regular menstrual periods.

"No," I said, confused by his question.

"How old are you? Are you going through menopause?" he asked.

It became clear where he was taking this so-called examination. He assumed that I was suffering from some emotional female problem, the kind the little woman gets when she either doesn't receive enough attention, usually sexual, or simply can't cope with the stresses of being a spoiled expatriate wife. He ignored my red eyes, broken blood vessels, elevated blood pressure and the excruciating pain on my left side. He claimed that my unusually high blood pressure was caused by frustration from the long wait, and apologized for the inconvenience. The doctor reasoned quite simply that since I did not drink excessively or smoke and my body type was not that of a heart attack victim, I couldn't possibly have heart problems. I should, however, "gain a little weight," and maybe "do some volunteer work to take your mind off yourself."

In desperation and naiveté, I blurted out something about my strange dream without going into the details, hoping he would show some interest or concern that would provoke a more thorough exam. That was a mistake. Now he was more convinced than ever of his diagnosis: female problems of the emotional type.

The exam was over.

I went home feeling beaten up emotionally, mentally and physically, but remained more concerned about the dream from the night before than the fact that Mike and Josephine agreed with the doctor's diagnosis. What was this dream really about? I had always had vivid dreams, but woke up knowing they were dreams. This time it was different. I actually had been somewhere else. This was . . . real?

CHAPTER 70

Recognizing my pain and hopeless resignation, the maids wanted to do something for me. Since the medical profession had written me off, they suggested that I see what they called a "quack doctor." Quack doctors don't have degrees of any kind, but rather rely on psychic auras, intuitive information, and centuries-old ancestral wisdom to arrive at "diagnoses." According to our maids, quack doctors are the be-all and end-all for diagnosing problems of every variety. They also offer remedies. They are a one-stop shop for anything that ails you.

Vivianna was a new maid who I did not know very well yet. She suggested that she go to the quack doctor in my stead since

I was too weak, and persuaded me to give her a photo of myself so the quack doctor could read my face. I could have considered this amusing prior to our Pakistani experience, but since then my newfound respect for paranormal beliefs and activities didn't allow me to take anything for granted. I was touched by our maids' concern, which caused me to override my better judgment. A medical doctor had just dismissed me, and my husband and mother-in-law thought my health problems were caused by some sort of female hysteria. By comparison, here were these sweet women who offered compassion and assistance in the only way they knew how. In my weakened state I gravitated toward their kindness and acquiesced to their suggestion.

Vivianna was hardly out the gate when I regretted my decision. During my research on black magic, I read that the practice of using psychics and the like can disable one's own intuitive abilities by relinquishing power to another. I assumed quack doctors were of the same ilk. During my nighttime prayers I promised God that I would work towards developing my connection with Him. I was concerned that this visit to the quack doctor would violate my promise. Suddenly, I felt ashamed for my weakness and asked God to forgive me. Since the incident in the laboratory I knew what it meant to be without God, and I never wanted to live without Him in my life again.

Hours passed before Vivianna returned home. She claimed to have waited in a very long line. The quack doctor explained to her that two days earlier when I was at the Laguna baths with my family, I had gone to the toilet and offended a fairy.

Good heavens this was hilarious. I perked up by this delightful story and couldn't stop laughing. I begged Vivianna to continue, now anxious to get the report, eager to hear every word of what she had to say.

Filipinos believe in a variety of little people, akin to elves, who live in damp, tropical areas. It would not be unusual for these fairies to inhabit toilet spaces in a place such as the baths in Laguna. Vivianna explained that Filipinos are accustomed to excusing themselves to the little people whenever they use the facilities. She said that she did so routinely, even in our house! Apparently I had forgotten my manners while tinkling and had inadvertently offended one of them. Insulted, the fairy blew in my face to teach me a lesson, resulting in the heart problem.

The story was so enchanting that I no longer was upset with myself for sending her to the quack doctor. From the medical doctor's perspective, I had "female problems," and from the quack doctor's perspective, I had offended a fairy. I had always felt that God had a personality, but now I was getting a sense of His humor as well. I was willing to concede that the quack doctor may have known something that I didn't. With a sigh of relief I became optimistic that there could be another explanation for what had happened. Somewhere between medical science and quack doctors there had to be an answer. Maybe there were several explanations that led to the same conclusion, but from different perspectives.

CHAPTER 71

Marianne, a new friend, shared my developing interest in metaphysical sciences. We had many conversations about energy, the occult, interesting books and points of view that challenged and stretched my way of thinking. We were both in search of answers to the why, how and wherefore of man's existence, and enjoyed exchanging thoughts and perspectives. Marianne offered comfort and a sympathetic ear, though she had no explanation for the dream. She suggested that I call her friend Francis, a lawyer who was very well versed in metaphysics. I phoned him immediately.

Though I never met Francis, I remain forever grateful for his gentleness, patience, understanding and wisdom. Marianne was correct. He had a vast understanding of many things and gave me an explanation of the dream that resonated indisputable truth to the core of my being.

Francis shared my belief that I'd had a pre-death experience.

Over the phone he took me through the dream step by step. Yes, I went to Hell in the dream, but it was my personal hell, not necessarily the hell of another soul. "Hell is the absence of Divine Light or Life," Frances explained. I felt this absence while living in Karachi, a city made beige from the dust storms and lack of rain. To me, Karachi symbolized a place without light or hope, which invited darkness.

The hopeless looking people from the dream were just that, people without hope. If we do not have hope, we do not have life, which is death. To be alive physically but just going through the motions of an existence without joy or hope is a form of hell.

My husband was in my dream because without realizing it I had assumed a role for his spirituality, which impacted my own. Anxious to receive his compassion, support, understanding, and respect, I made continuous attempts to explain my thoughts and efforts to him, which were consistently rebuked. As a result, I was left feeling angry, even bitter. The constant rejection put me in a dark place emotionally, which translated into the spiritual equivalent of Hell. The dream indicated that Mike needed to go his own way spiritually, and that it was not up to me to assume responsibility for his choices or direction.

"One's spiritual growth is a personal journey," Francis admonished. "Now it is time to heal, and to direct your attention and energy to loving yourself."

The jumpsuit I wore in Switzerland symbolized my experience with Simone and her voodoo dolls and the first time I encountered my worst fear: Evil in the form of a devil.

In one way or another, arrogance challenges the God within. The day I denounced the existence of God in the laboratory in favor of intellectual self-importance I created a Light vacuum. In so doing, I invited the Light to leave, which created the void where Darkness entered.

The cat was my Soul, and the cat was alive. The dream represented a death of my physical body and the resurgence of spirit. The message I received from the dream was that I needed to put the past behind me. Indeed, my body had died, but my soul was alive and vibrant. A new beginning awaited me. Yes, I had been through hell, but now it was time to get on with my life.

CHAPTER 72

Unwilling to accept the internist's diagnosis, I scheduled a second examination with a female cardiologist a few days later. She gave me a heart monitor to wear and performed the exams that one would expect after complaining of a heart problem. Tiny red dots from the broken blood vessels still peppered my body, and my blood pressure remained high, when it was normally low. Her diagnosis was "disulfirum affect," a liver reaction to the three sulfa drugs that had been prescribed for the cystic amoebae.

"Yes," she confirmed, "I believe that you had a pre-death experience. You are lucky to be alive!"

As I understand it, my liver was unable to process the sulfa drugs. This resulted in a sort of "liver implosion" that created the same symptoms as a heart attack. The strong sulfa drugs should not have been prescribed. Considering my low weight, chronically low blood pressure and chronic anemia, the heavy dosages and combinations of medications themselves could have been dangerous for anyone, particularly someone in my condition. Drinking San Miguel Beer in a warm pool under the hot sun did not help matters either.

Reflecting on the circumstances that led to the dream, I recognized that however painful the past years were, I needed those experiences to understand something about life that I could not have learned any other way. I attracted those experiences to myself to *experience* Good vs. Evil in order to *know* the power that Good has over Evil.

I only wish that Sonya and Sasha had been spared the pain they endured during this time. *My Yi Wood vine climbed the trunk of their Jia Wood tree trunk to get to the Light, the wisdom. Cosmicly speaking, they saved me.*

My entire life had been sprinkled with countless, magnificent, miraculous blessings. There had been the school Christmas play, the scholarship to attend the University of Chicago, the conceptions of my daughters. The list of inexplicable blessings that came as a direct result from prayer was a long one, and had still not been persuasive. What would it take before I understood how great the power of God is? The dark experiences, as horrible as they were, were the ones I invited to myself to provide the most convincing and conclusive proof that Light prevails over Darkness, and that Good prevails over Evil. I now realized that it was I who attracted the unfortunate circumstances that trailed me, and it was I who would have to change them.

My current health crisis may have been threatening, but it had been accompanied by an other-dimensional message. It was my wake-up call. The dream clarified what I needed to know in order to move forward. My future lay in front of me. It was time for me to take command of my life and make changes in myself. I needed to focus my energy on healing physically and spiritually.

Just like the exquisitely vibrant cat, my Soul had survived. I was once again filled with hope.

How does one rebuild a life after being given a second chance to live? Where should I begin?

CHAPTER 73

Josephine left the Philippines in April 1993. Shortly after her departure, Mike and I began making arrangements for an extended trip to the U.S. where Mike would have hip replacement surgery. For several years he had been suffering from excruciating pain that he attributed to an old football injury. We could have done the surgery anywhere, but decided on Dubuque, Iowa, where there was a hospital known for its excellent orthopedic care. Dubuque is located about thirty miles from Dyersville, where my mother lived. I asked my mother if we could stay with her during Mike's surgery and convalescence. She agreed.

I was excited to be going back to the States. I needed to see my family again and have Sonya and Sasha get to know their large extended family of cousins and aunts and uncles. The eleven siblings made it a point to get together each year for at least a few days of picnicking and fishing. This year would be no exception. The difference is that this would be the first year that my children and husband would be participating. I may have rejected Dyersville and this way of life when I was younger, but now that I had seen the other side of the world, Iowa *was* Heaven.

About twenty years after I graduated from high school, big excitement came to sleepy little Dyersville when it was chosen for the filming location for the beloved baseball film, *Field of Dreams*. In fact, the "if you build it, they will come" farm adjoins the sweet corn field where I hid out as a child. The irony of it all.

CHAPTER 74

Mom and Dad had sold the farm to my brother and his wife about fifteen years earlier when Dad retired so they could purchase their dream home in a new housing development in Dyersville. Dad lived there for only a few years before his untimely death from a heart attack. Now Mom lived in the house alone. She lovingly tended to her plants and flower garden, and enjoyed the freedom she had acquired once we were all grown. I looked forward to having my mother to myself for a while without competition from ten siblings and I hoped, too, that the girls could bond with her during this time. Unfortunately however, the old tensions between us resurfaced.

Mom was now seventy-one years old and nursing her own health problems. It was hard on her to have us stay in her small, tidy home. We arrived with huge overseas bags, paraphernalia and our personal problems and requirements that complicated her serene life.

She generously offered Mike and me her bed, and the girls stayed in the bedroom next to ours. Mom slept in the third bedroom. She was recovering not only from a recent bronchial affliction, but from a lifetime of struggle. All she sought was the solace gleaned from the pretty, comfortable home she was finally able to enjoy and the children and grandchildren who adored her.

I imagined that whatever it was that I was going through, it couldn't compare to the hardships she had already endured. She had done her job. There was only so much she had left to give.

I think she saw me as a rich woman who had an accomplished husband and everything I could possibly want or need. Yet, here I was, camped out with my convalescing husband and two young children in her home. Although she never said so explicitly, I sensed that she felt we were staying with her to save money at her expense.

Without realizing it, Mike reinforced this view by presenting a rosy picture of our lives to my family, giving them the impression that we lived an exotic, five-star life abroad. From his perspective that was probably true. Not wanting to contradict him, I didn't reveal the details of our struggles. The Internet did not exist then and international phone calls were ridiculously expensive. Consequently, it was almost impossible to stay in touch with my family and friends in between our infrequent trips to the U.S. Besides, I don't know what I would have shared if they had been ready to listen. All they knew was that I lived abroad, had maids and a driver, and a husband with a good job. In their eyes I was doing well.

If we could have let go of the past and had learned not to take things so personally, perhaps Mom and I could have enjoyed a more wholehearted visit. Sadly, this was not the case. There were too many meals she felt obliged to prepare, too many visitors she felt expected to entertain and too much frenetic activity with kids, doctors and husbands that unnerved her. Overall, there was too much tension to tell Mom what was in my heart and on my mind, which was that I needed her. I needed to be close to her for her comfort, to feel her love. More than anything I wanted her to know how much I admired and respected her, and how her example and words of love helped me through the most difficult time of my life. I wanted her to know that because of her selflessness and generosity she had prepared me for whatever life had in store for me. I wanted her to know, too, that whatever I knew about being a good mother, she taught me. Mom's lifelong acts of kindness filled the reservoir I drew upon when I needed courage to protect my children and move on with life. She left the spiritual imprint I recalled and emulated. Despite the differences between us, she was the embodiment of what I cherished and the legacy I wanted to pass on to my children. I wanted Mom to know that if there was anything good about me, it was because of her.

We were the proverbial ships passing in the night, she and I, caught up in time and space where we didn't understand one another.

CHAPTER 75

While Mike was recovering from his hip replacement surgery, I developed an infection in my right breast. Antibiotics were prescribed without success. The node had swollen to the size of a lemon by the time the doctor suggested that I have it removed. This particular infection was unusual. Normally an infected area feels warm, but this one was cold, a phenomenon that I pointed out to the surgeon when we met prior to the operation. He had no explanation for that anomaly, nor could he understand the post-op pathology report that revealed "benign, multi-nucleated, undifferentiated giant cells of unknown origin." Although I was relieved that the test results showed nothing more sinister, I would have liked an explanation for my general malaise and this unseemly infection, which was responsible for the loss of a big chunk of breast tissue.

We left Iowa in September and detoured through Washington, D.C.to visit with old friends and Victoria before returning to the Philippines. Mike was recovering beautifully from his hip replacement. The infection in my breast returned the week we were scheduled to fly back to the Philippines, but I decided to wait until we were back in Manila to have a second operation.

Surgery was scheduled for a few days after we arrived. This time the result of the pathology report was conclusive. The benign, multinucleated, undifferentiated, giant cells of unknown origin were Langhans cells, indicative of tuberculosis. I had mammary TB, quite common in the Philippines but not in Dubuque, Iowa. This explained the "cold" node, the resistance to antibiotics and why the Iowa surgeon had been unable to assess the problem definitively.

Of course I wasn't happy about the diagnosis, but relieved to have one. Finally there was an explanation for my weight loss, anemia, and overall weakened condition that had plagued me for so long. This made so much sense. Now I could undergo treatment, rebuild my body and get on with life.

My doctor suggested that I hold off on the drug treatment since I was in my forties and there were no symptoms or evidence that the TB existed anywhere else but in my breast. The advice was welcomed. I was afraid that the drugs used to cure the TB would assault my liver further after the disulfirum/heart/liver episode.

CHAPTER 76

Our landlord, Dr. Sandres, was health advisor to Philippine President Fidel Ramos and operated a free acupuncture and traditional medicine clinic. I called him regarding some house-related problem but ended up mentioning that I was diagnosed as having mammary tuberculosis, and told him about the malaise that afflicted me.

Without seeing me, he was able to describe my symptoms better than I could. "Are you dizzy? Do you have 'floaters' in your eyes? Are you feeling weak?" he asked.

Dr. Sandres invited me to meet with his partner, Dr. Jennifer, sometime later that week. She used acupuncture, an ancient Chinese therapeutic technique, to direct chi or energy to diseased parts of the body by puncturing certain "points" with fine needles. The concentration of energy at the affected site can provide results without medication. This was what I was hoping for. By examining my pulse and tongue, she determined which organs were weak and targeted them specifically. Dr. Jennifer offered to treat the TB with a special series of acupuncture treatments over several months.

After a few sessions of acupuncture augmented with herbal remedies, I began to feel much stronger. I found it amusing that my watch, which had a mechanical system powered by wrist movement as opposed to quartz crystals, had a tendency to run slow. But, now it was running fast, reflecting the sudden improvement in how I felt.

CHAPTER 77

During the first year we lived in Manila, mysterious night torments made bedtime drudgery. I analyzed these dreams with concentrated zeal as was my nature, awakening each morning to a new set of symbolic images that needed deciphering. After sifting through these thoughts and experiences, I evaluated them once again, seeking plausible explanations for whatever it was in my subconscious that was disrupting my sleep.

Our lives were inexplicable by any sane standard including my own. I supposed that my tortuous slumbers reflected an inability to reconcile the craziness. How did we manage to select a yakuza's house and a house in Pakistan with spirits? There had to be an explanation for this just like there had to be an explanation for the episodes of black magic I had experienced during my life. How and why were these things happening to me? What in the world could that be about, and why me? Why my babies?

Why could Mike and I not find peace together without one problem after another? I loved him. Although he was not emotionally demonstrative or forthcoming, I knew he loved me too. I accepted that there was a dysfunctional kink to our lives that needed to be resolved, but surely it wasn't worse than the kinks of the smiling, happy couples that I envied. We were decent people who treated others with respect. We accepted our responsibilities to family and society and managed our lives accordingly. We were well educated and hard working. Still, our friends were not experiencing the travails that we were, and I couldn't help but wonder what we were doing that was so wrong.

Once again I turned to God. This time I asked Him to clean our lives mentally, spiritually, and physically. I prayed for pure thoughts for myself so the horrible nightmares would stop.

It was right around this time that I developed an obsession for pearls. Although the prices varied widely depending on quality, I could buy them for as little as two dollars a strand. Since I had never particularly liked pearls that much before, I was curious why they had become so important to me. The Philippines is full of pearls, either from local farms or imported from Hong Kong. My first tentative purchase was of a single strand of the small, elongated variety known as rice pearls. Before long, I expanded my search for pearls with unusual colors and distinctive shapes, and bought five to ten strands of these beautiful gems at a time. Eventually I'd buy an entire hank, a bulk of strung pearls without clasps that were similar in shape, size, color, luster and quality. Sometimes these hanks had five strands on them. Sometimes they had twenty, fifty or even a hundred.

I just couldn't get enough. They looked delicious. Feasting with my eyes I became a pearl glutton, unable to push myself away from the table for fear someone would take one of these delectable morsels from me. My appetite for pearls became insatiable until I found myself with bags full. I stashed them away like a greedy child, bringing them out when I was alone just to have a look at the piles of scrumptious, gleaming treasure. At night I draped them over my shoulders to feel their smooth texture and coolness against my skin.

I realize this may sound self-indulgent. Perhaps it was, but in truth it was easy to justify any indulgence. Pearls cost relatively little, and I had to have them. No, I was compelled to have them and could not have stopped buying them if I had wanted. I felt myself healing. Literally, there was a biologic reaction that was occurring within me, one that I could feel. It was like busy, nimble little fingers were knitting shredded fibers back together again. I assumed the pearls were a big part of that; they nourished me. Bedtime suddenly became a pleasure when dreams of this spellbinding treasure pampered and spoiled my psyche, ending the months of nightmares.

I went to every corner, nook and cranny of Manila looking for pearls, cherishing the time spent in hot stalls speaking to the fishermen and small shop owners who shared my appreciation for these mesmerizing gems. They, too, were captivated by the pristine loveliness that pearls possess. While feeling the thousands of pearls strung on hanks that went through my fingers, I compared their texture, color and luster, admiring the various shapes that made some more interesting than others.

I decided to take a gemology course hoping to learn something more about this newfound obsession. However, the professor's knowledge was strictly academic and limited to what she could see through the lens of a microscope. The fishermen understood the enchanting character of pearls that they could experience just by holding them in their hands with their eyes closed. They would bite the pearl, feel its coolness and use their fingertips to examine for pits and bumps. The gemology professor explained refractive indices, nacre depth, and the importance of specific gravity for culturing purposes. Taken together, the two perspectives gave me a new dimension of understanding and appreciation for the pearl's captivating qualities. Pearls are the only precious gemstones that come from a living creature and not directly from the earth. They come from Water! That alone makes them unique and special. Was it any wonder that I should be attracted to them?

I couldn't help but notice that the theory of light—so relevant to the study of gems—kept recurring in thoughts and daily activities. Light had left my body when I had forsaken God in the laboratory. Light was absent in my hell during the pre-death experience. I began to see "Light" as a general theme to my life. Pearls seemed to be replenishing my life with Water and Light at the same time.

The dreams about pearls continued, taking on an entirely

different dimension. I now dreamt of lustrous, milky, yogurt-looking vats of pearls displayed in Fantasia fashion. The pearls were strewn for my pleasure or made into voluptuous creations. In my sleep I designed lavish necklaces set with large mabe (ma-bay) pearls and other gemstones. I bulked twenty strands together before attaching them with beautiful golden clasps. These designs were not only for long, thin necks with pretty décolletage. Some roped elegantly down the backs of women wearing stunning, revealing evening attire.

My nighttime creations didn't end with the dream from the night before, but dominated my thoughts when I woke up in the morning when they became my daydreams as well. The only way to settle the restless activity within me was to create a channel for buying and selling pearls, the only solution to having them in my life both day and night.

CHAPTER 78

The metaphysical, the paranormal and the phenomenal were now officially part of my life's experience and belief system, and I was open to learning about other so-called taboo subjects, such as crystal energy. Actually, I couldn't understand why these were considered taboo at all. It was so normal; so scientific.

The metaphysical perspective that accounts for Heaven and Earth had to hold the key to infinite answers. Were other people not equally curious? Or did the curious just keep their interest silent? Manila is a place where one can explore many interests, including metaphysics. I assumed this was because of the country's yin, feminine nature, which lent itself to new ideas and spiritual awareness.

Eventually I was able to find a group of women who shared my interest in the supernatural, relieved to know they were also searching. We read books, shared our experiences, took day trips to healing spas outside the city and explored and discovered the unusual together. To uphold our image as mainstream women to the outside world, we remained discreet as a group. We trusted one another with our confidences as we sought answers to the unknown. We practiced Pranic healing on one another and experimented with African chants and drumbeats, meditation, and Indian dancing, and we read books by Edgar Cayce. We analyzed the book *The Celestine Prophecy* as a group, and read about angels and extraterrestrials.

By the time I was introduced to Maribelle, I was completely open to learning about another facet of healing. Maribelle was fascinated with uncut gemstones and their unique characteristics, and how different gems had healing qualities. She had written a book on the subject. She also set these beautiful uncut stones in gold to create exciting pieces of jewelry.

When I explained my obsession with pearls to her, she told me about the special and unique qualities of specific gemstones and the effect they have on us as individuals.

"Pearls," she said, "represent purity. For whatever reason, your soul, through your body, is purifying."

She showed me a beautiful book on crystals, *Love Is in the Earth*, written by a woman known simply as Melody, who writes "The pearl symbolizes purity and can stimulate that condition in one's body and mind; hence, providing a clear vehicle for the advancing states of wisdom, as well as a clean channel for receipt of spiritual guidance."[1]

I read books on the metaphysical meaning of crystals and about their piezoelectric energy field. Crystals are formed over thousands of years before they are mined, during which time they absorb energy from Earth's pressure. Lasers are powered by quartz crystals, which are used in woofers, stereo equipment, computers, checkout counters, clocks and watches. Quartz crystals also have a memory. Learning these facts appeased the more scientifically oriented part of my mind and helped shore up my confidence in the applications I was learning from Maribelle and from my books. If crystals could play a profound role in technology, then why couldn't their energy fields be effective in healing our bodies? It wasn't much

---

Melody, *Love Is in the Earth: A Kaleidoscope of Crystals*

of a leap for me to trust in such therapeutic powers.

When I had asked God for a cleansing, it never occurred to me that it could or would be done with gemstones during my sleep, or that I could carry this dream state into real life.

With Mike's encouragement I did create the necklaces of my dreams for myself, donning as many strands and rings as possible. I hired *plateros*, goldsmiths, to create the clasps for me, and before I knew it I was known in Manila as "the Pearl Lady," besieged with requests to create designs for others.

Mike, the children and I visited a pearl farm on Palawan, an island just a short plane ride from Manila, and we vacationed in the Philippine cities of Zamboanga and Davao, places known for their pearl farms. This preoccupation with something so beautiful swiftly displaced the negativity that surrounded me for so long.

As the nightmares disappeared and my thoughts shifted, so did my perspective on life. Mentally and spiritually I was being cleansed, which helped me to improve physically. The acupuncture treatments along with my discovery of pearls were the first of many steps taken in a long healing process. Finally, I was on an upward rung of the spiral.

CHAPTER 79

As a child I was at the broadest, most expansive part of the spiral, pictured in my mind as a type of coil that resembled a funnel or a cone. Fresh air, wholesome food, caring parents and Christian values nurtured me. I was soundly supported by elemental richness to become fearless and confident. Unfortunately, arrogance and ego displaced self-confidence, projecting a path that abandoned the spiritual richness I had known since birth. My search for the elusive caravan without spiritual guidance led me to the narrowest part of the funnel until I ultimately hit rock-bottom.

Past experiences had whittled me down, but once I made the decision to get back on my feet and take responsibility for the choices I had made, only then could I begin the healing process. In the same way that it takes years—in my case forty three—to reach the bottom of the spiral, it can also take years of hard work to undo the belief systems and habits that bring one to that point. Another journey is embarked upon while you climb back up the rungs until you ultimately return to the top of the spiral and God's grace.

Spiritual Spiral

As you can see in the above figure, the Spiral is wide at the top and eventually becomes narrow until it arrives at its smallest point, which is rock-bottom. In the same way that reaching a low point is a process that spans many years, so is it a process to climb back up to the top of the spiral.

CHAPTER 80

Sometime in September, a woman from our metaphysical studies group mentioned seeing a flyer announcing a lecture on Feng Shui. Margaret Milton, an internationally renowned speaker, would be in Manila shortly after Mike, the girls and I returned from a trip to

Moscow. I had never heard of Feng Shui before, but couldn't ignore the compulsion that prompted me to attend.

"Feng Shui is the ancient Chinese science of harmonizing energy," the flyer said. I marked it on my calendar, anxious for that date to arrive, sensing that Feng Shui was important to me.

I had been attending seminars that Dr. Jennifer, my acupuncturist, was giving on the macrobiotic diet, discovering an aspect of nutrition that I had never considered before. The diet itself is basically low fat, high fiber and predominantly vegetarian, but in some cases foods are selected for their "hot" or "cold" qualities to bring balance to one's physiology. For example, foods that grow under the ground like carrots and potatoes are considered "hot," while those that grow above ground are described as "cold."

Dr. Jennifer's lectures included an introduction to the core Taoist concept of Yin (negative) and Yang (positive) energies, which she applied to nutrition, reinforcing the concept that we are literally what we eat. Hot climates such as the Philippines are Yang, but the people who live there tend to be Yin because they eat more Yin (cold) foods to keep cool. Likewise, people from colder climates are Yang because they tend to eat more Yang (hot) foods to stay warm. These preferences also reflect food availability, a reflection of nature's brilliance in providing what is needed in each case. And, along with Yin and Yang determinations, personality characteristics follow.

To help me rebalance my Yin/Yang energy to regain my health, I needed to address my eating habits. It wasn't that I didn't eat well nutritionally. It was that from a Chinese perspective I wasn't eating *appropriately* to heal my many physical ailments, symptomatic of an energy imbalance.

Dr. Jennifer lectured on Chinese medicine and beliefs and about the flow of energy or chi that exists in all facets of life. She practiced Feng Shui, too, another facet of the same Chinese system. While she didn't go into any great detail about it, I was fascinated that I would hear about this Chinese practice from two different sources at almost exactly the same time.

CHAPTER 81

We traveled to Moscow in October 1994, completely unprepared for the freezing temperatures we encountered there. The city's centralized heating system is turned on after the outside temperature remains below 8 degrees Celsius (46.4 degrees Fahrenheit) for more than five days in a row, which is usually mid-October. We happened to be there right before the temperatures dropped. It was so cold we could see our breath while inside. The frigid temperatures made it difficult to take showers or for the children to play. You would think we would have been miserable in such conditions, but for some odd reason we weren't. In fact, we absolutely loved it. For one thing, we were so used to being hot all the time, it was a lark to be struggling with the cold for a change. The frigid temperatures provided the perfect excuse to cuddle under the blankets in the big bed, forcing us to play together as a family in a way that we did not in Manila.

We took tours of the city and visited the open markets, examined old brass samovars and selected antique religious icons. We introduced the girls to the beautiful art and oil paintings for which Russia is famous. Sasha found a two-inch by four-inch oil painting of a log cabin that had smoke curling from the chimney. The house had one window upstairs and another downstairs. Red flowers rested in the meadow in front. I was touched by the simple serenity of the painting, the antithesis of our life, and asked Sasha to tell me what it was that appealed to her about the house. She had turned three only a month earlier, so I wasn't expecting something particularly profound, but was curious if she could articulate her thoughts just the same. Sasha thought for a second and looked at me with her blue eyes and curly lashes like I was supposed to intuitively understand without asking. "The painting makes me feel good, Mommy. May I have it?"

Sasha was fascinated by the possibility of taking the "underground," a train with glass windows from which she expected to see ant and mole tunnels. The famous Moscow metro system, known for its elaborate crystal chandeliers and mosaic-tiled floors that decorate the metro stops, was small comfort for her disappointment. She was equally disappointed when we were unable to locate a tusk from a woolly mammoth.

Russian people are highly educated and well versed in music and the arts as well as politics, history, science and economics. Therefore it was quite startling to realize that Russia was considered a Third World country, even though it had emerged on the other side of an industrial revolution. Under Communist dictatorships, beautiful public spaces were erected while residents suffered abject poverty at home. Russian people look western. This resemblance created a sense of familiarity and confusion at the same time. I didn't expect those from Third World countries to look like me, nor did I expect this level of sophistication from a Third World country. I erroneously associated countries lacking in natural resources with poverty, low literacy rates and Third World status. However, all three countries: Pakistan, the Philippines and Russia are rich in natural resources. Therefore, I amended my observation by adding politics and government corruption as the main contributing factors to Third World economies. Politics, government corruption and Third World status all go hand in hand.

CHAPTER 82

We enjoyed an exhilarating two-week stay in Moscow before returning to Manila with some lovely paintings and fond memories. Upon arriving home, I went upstairs to unpack our bags from the trip. I walked through the interior security gate and down the hall, cognizant of the stifling, enervating heat, a sharp contrast to the freezing temperatures in Moscow. Then, for some reason there was an ever-so-slight chill. Every few yards I felt the little chill again, and noticed goose bumps causing the hair on my arms to stand up. I looked around, like I had done many times before, for a clue to the strange chill. The windows were closed, and the scheduled brownout pre-empted any possibility that the air conditioner could have caused it. I was the only one upstairs. There wasn't a breeze from someone who had passed me in the hallway. That chill always had me stumped. Where did it come from?

Nam and Daniel, our on-going fountain of uplifting information, seemed to know everything that went on in the neighborhood. Our house's history with the yakuza, the murders, the bank robberies—all historical data registered safely in the annals of their institutional memory. Now there was another piece of trivia. The village where we lived, Magallanes Village, was built on a graveyard. I would have to ask them if they knew where that chill came from too!

We lived in an attractive house that was nicely decorated. Regardless of how nice it looked, I had always felt uncomfortable. The maids were constantly fighting with one another, making it difficult to manage them, and Sonya and Sasha became prone to crying and whining. For some reason we were never able to settle in like we had wanted.

Mike did not have any problems with the house and was oblivious to any problems the girls and I may have been having. He loved the big rooms, large windows and glass doors, and was in a world of his own when swimming laps in the pool where he taught the girls how to swim. Sonya became a particularly good swimmer who eventually proved she was as graceful in the water as she was on the dance floor. Sometimes on the weekends Mike and Sonya played Dolphin together. Mike threw coins into the deepest part of the pool where the daddy and baby dolphin dove for them. Sonya held onto his trunks while he took her the ten feet below to grab the coins before coming up for air, a practice that helped strengthen her lungs after her episodes with asthma.

Our evenings were spent in the family room, where we shared thoughts about the day before moving to the dining room for dinner. Having our meals prepared was indeed a luxury. I loved that I could have those moments of peace both before and after dinner with the family instead of worrying about meal preparation and cleanup.

After dinner we listened to music, mostly Latin. Sonya entertained us with her skirt flipping Salsa moves on her "stage," the hallway that separated our dining room from the sliding glass doors that led to the pool. Sometimes Sonya danced alone, sometimes Mike and I danced together, and sometimes Mike took turns dancing with the girls. Sasha stood on top of her dad's feet and clung to his legs while he taught her the box step.

CHAPTER 83

Nothing changed while we were in Moscow. I don't know why it should have, but I was disappointed to return home to the same maid issues from before we left. Vivianna, the maid who visited the quack doctor for me when I was so ill, continued to cause trouble with the others. She was a terrible gossip who liberally spread ridiculous stories around the neighborhood about her previous employers and me. Mike's business associate and wife confirmed my suspicions about her after they stayed in our house during Mike's hip replacement surgery. Upon our return from the States they reported the malicious fabrications—all lies that Vivianna was known for.

Vivianna was a nasty woman I kept far too long, mistakenly thinking that Sasha was close to her. In my defense, I wanted to finally provide the girls with some stability and continuity in our home life and hesitated doing anything to upset that balance, including getting rid of Vivianna if Sasha liked her. Managing household staff is a tricky business. Vivianna was competent at her job and did not present a physical threat that I was aware of, arguments that justified keeping her if Sasha was happy.

However, she wielded influence and power in the community with her wicked tongue. I risked retribution of one kind or another by firing her. When she wanted to make life miserable for me, she had her friends and cronies among the night drivers, security guards, maids, and other hired help in the Manila metropolitan area call our house during all hours of the night. An unsatisfactory solution was to remove the phone from the hook. The danger in estranging her was twofold: first, that she would badmouth me to other potential maids, making it difficult to find someone to work for us based on reputation; and second, that nobody would agree to work for us because they knew if they crossed her, she would target them. Vivianna needed to be let go in a safe and appropriate way that I felt certain would reveal itself.

Vivianna knew the rules. Rule number one was that the children were not permitted to play in front of the house. The metal picket fence allowed far too much exposure to passing strangers and heavy traffic along Lapu Lapu Avenue, a risk that we could not afford to take.

Despite my absolute instructions, Vivianna defied them. I happened to circle back around the block one day after leaving for an appointment. To my horror and disbelief, Sasha and Vivianna were in the front yard. Sasha was climbing the fence wearing only a panty while Vivianna sat on the front steps portraying the image of a beaten down, forlorn victim. This was her way of announcing to the world that I was a horrible mother and abusive employer, any attempt to create a negative impression of our home and me.

I got out of the car shouting, "What do you think you are doing?"

Vivianna scrambled to get up. She pulled Sasha down from the fence and hurried to open the gate so I could enter. She sputtered some incomprehensible excuse, holding herself out as powerless against the demands of a three-year-old child.

This incident occurred on the heels of another that already had me upset. Flora, our cook, was away on leave, but had prepared soup made from left over turkey, intended for that day's lunch. With Flora away, Vivianna was expected to serve the mid-day meal.

Shortly before noon Vivianna brought me the pot of soup and asked, "Madam, is this the soup you would like for lunch?" It registered as a strange gesture since she had never asked this type of question before, and there was only one soup in the refrigerator.

"Yes, Vivianna, that would be fine," I answered curiously.

A little while later she called me to the table and set a bowl of the hot soup in front of me. The steamy broth wafted deliciously to my nostrils. I stuck in my spoon, anticipating the tasty combination of vegetables, herbs and turkey. Instead, out came *not* a piece of turkey, but a two-inch long cockroach, a length that didn't include the antennae.

Over the years I had become quite knowledgeable about cockroaches, creatures that fascinated me. Cockroaches are enormous in Asia and in abundant supply. I spent hours watching them on the floor of our bathroom while reading at night and came to identify some of their habits and weaknesses. I knew that if I flipped them on their back, they couldn't turn upright unless they wiggled to the cupboard or wall where they got some leverage to turn themselves over. I learned that roaches fly, strategize—after being flipped on their backs for a few hours—and even attack. I knew that cockroaches molt—and was scared to death the day I found an enormous, sluggish, white roach crawl out of the sink drain. I knew, too, that cockroaches have an identifiable odor that I could detect quite easily if one crawled across a brownie mix box in the pantry.

I sniffed the bowl in front of me and examined the cockroach on my spoon very carefully. It was fully formed with its antennae still intact. After looking at it from all angles and making sure all its parts were attached to his body, I weighed the impact of its presence in the soup which otherwise looked delicious. The roach looked fresh and there was no lingering cockroach odor that I noticed, every indication that its death was quick and could not have harmed the food. Was I really going to throw away a pot of this delicious soup because of a cockroach?

"Nope," I thought to myself, "I've lived in Karachi where all kinds of gunk floated in the water. A cockroach is nothing to me."

Feeling like a seasoned warrior, I very carefully laid the cockroach on the plate underneath my bowl and then put my spoon back in the liquid for another mouthful, anticipating Flora's delicious preparation. I watched as my spoon dipped under the vegetables until it contained a little something of everything. A piece of carrot, a piece of celery, a bit of onion . . .

Then, I lifted the spoon a second time from the broth.

Eeeeewwwwwwww!!! There it was. Another gigantic, fully formed, freshly dead cockroach.

There was no doubt in my mind that the cockroaches had been recently added to the soup. The condition of their bodies was exactly the same—perfectly intact and unaffected by the heat, stirring, or having been buried under chunks of turkey and vegetables. Their presence was not a coincidence. One cockroach? Maybe. But two? There was no way that could have happened by accident.

I called Vivianna to the dining room.

"Vivianna, what are these cockroaches doing in my soup?"

Feigning bewilderment while wringing her hands and stepping back and forth in rehearsed movements she whimpered disingenuously, "Oh, oh . . . I don't know Ma'am."

"Boy, oh boy," I thought to myself, "she is really a crafty one."

"I didn't put them there, Ma'am. You'll have to ask Flora how they got there."

Vivianna's conniving made me sick.

"Liar!" I shouted at her. "*You* put them there. You put those cockroaches in the soup so that I would fire Flora. You are the one responsible for the discord among the staff."

Vivianna's scheming mind had done her in. I imagined how she calculated the "right" number of roaches that would be believable, considering the likelihood that one could be present but not two, or that two could be present instead of one. Or maybe she thought that I would eat one without noticing it, so she added the second roach for good measure.

After a year of struggling with her negative, divisive energy and bad attitude, I'd had it. The latest incident with Sasha was a spiteful security violation that I could not accept. Retribution or not, Vivianna was gone.

I filed a formal complaint against her at the American Woman's Club, minimizing her chances of causing grief to someone else.

It goes without saying that it's nice to have someone prepare meals for you and do your household chores, but these services can come at a price, depending on who is working for you. The system for living in Asia is different than what we know in the U.S. It's not possible to manage an efficient household in Asia without help. If I could have, I would have.

CHAPTER 84

I did not go out in the evening primarily because Mike preferred staying home. Parties and dinners were for couples. It wasn't fun to go alone. *A vine or blade of grass Yi Wood enjoys the companionship of others and tends to be social. One blade of grass is unhappy alone, but a garden of grass is a party. Bing Fire, the Sun, on the other hand, has no problem shining on his own. The Sun beams beneficence, and relishes in the adoration of others for being so. Bing Fire doesn't need the companionship of others like Yi Wood. Bing Fire simply is.* Mike made it a point to be in bed by eight o'clock p.m., the same time that I put the girls to bed. We did not attend parties or invite guests during the week, and socialized infrequently on the weekend as well. There were times when I yearned to do couple things. I wanted to enjoy the fun side of Manila with my husband, and expatriate life in general, but Mike didn't enjoy socializing, always using work as an excuse. Far too much energy was expended before he agreed to accompany me, which took away the fun we could have had. Eventually it became an expectation that I give in to his sighs and refusals, which I generally did.

The Feng Shui lecture was different. I desperately wanted to attend whether Mike did or not. I asked him to go with me, more as a courtesy than anything else, knowing that he would have one reason or another for saying no. The compulsion to attend the lecture gripped me despite the sighs and excuses that normally prevented me from attending. A lecture is something I could do on my own. I had to go. Whatever Ms. Milton was teaching, I needed to learn it, even though I had no idea what Feng Shui was.

Margaret Milton presented different floor plans of houses as she described the impact of doorways and directions on the occupants' lives. She presented an example of a floor plan where the entry opened to a bathroom near the front door. The toilet was the first thing you saw when the door opened. There was also a bathroom on the second floor immediately above the front entrance. She explained how these detrimental features and others might affect the residents of such a home. *The foyer of a building is the mouth of the building, and is called Bright Hall. The foyer area should be open, clean and light-filled to allow Yang energy to accumulate. The toilets represented Yin energy in a Yang location, an energy violation. The existence of the toilets, Yin elements, and the flushing of them, represented the flushing away of wealth.*

Although that particular plan bore no resemblance to that of our Manila house, from her presentation I was already starting to understand the impact of a house's layout, positioning, and design on the inhabitants. At some point during her discussion, everything clicked. Intuitively I felt that Feng Shui would help to make sense out of what was happening to me and to my family. I could not ignore the urgency to know more about this science. In the same way that pearls and acupuncture had initiated a physical healing for me, I sensed that Feng Shui would help solve the problems with our house, which I believed affected our lives.

After the lecture was over, I approached Margaret at the front of the room and waited in line to show her a crudely sketched floor plan of our home that I had quickly drawn during her lecture. I was excited to have discovered something that was within my control, something I could do myself that I believed would make a difference. This was an ancient science, proven effective over centuries by practical people. This science was accessible to me; one that I could study, learn and apply.

Ms. Milton gasped when she looked at my sketch, exclaiming that it was worse than her worst example and asked to have a copy of my sketch for herself. We had a U-shaped house, known to cause

House in the Philippines

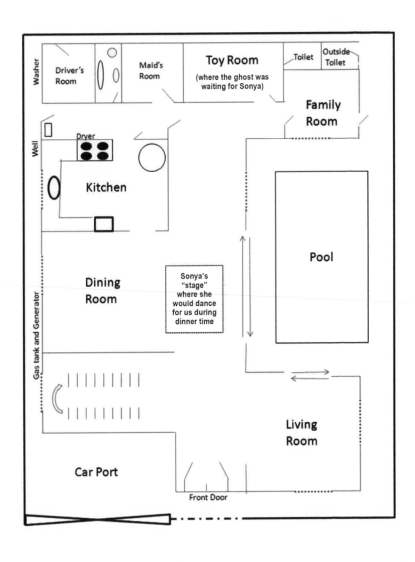

special problems. Along one side of the U there were four interior doors in a straight line that opened up to one another. The first of the four doors was the outside entry into the maid's kitchen. Directly across from it was the door leading to the hallway. From the hallway one could walk in a straight line to the family room door, and directly on the other side of that door was another door that led to the outside.

"Two doors in a straight line represent loss in the form of health, finances and relationships," Margaret said. We had four doors that lined up in this way. A death-knell.

We had lived in our Manila home for less than a year. I had already experienced a "heart attack" episode and tuberculosis. Mike had a hip replacement and Josephine suffered a horrible accident in the bathtub. Two dogs met terrible deaths, and an untold number of pet birds had died. And then there was the house's jaded history that had preceded us.

A huge swimming pool occupied the heart of the property, or the center of the U-shape. According to the Feng Shui Bagua—an eight-sided diagram used in Feng Shui to map out a home's energy—the center of a space is an Earth element. A Water element located in an Earth element space creates a conflict.

Ms. Milton pointed out that the placement of our bedroom furniture was problematic because our master bathroom door was in a direct line with our bed. Energy travels in a straight line. She said this positioning caused us to be sick and recommended that I change the position of the bed as soon as possible.

Margaret explained these phenomena without my grasping the new concepts. Her explanations resonated with my own feelings, which I had come to pay more attention to. In my gut, I knew she was right. The next morning I rearranged our bedroom according to her advice, feeling better immediately.

"This is a difficult house to correct because the Yin energy—negative energy—is so strong that you would literally have to reconstruct parts of the house to change it," Margaret explained. "You are very lucky to be doing as well as you are."

I hadn't told her about the *yakuza* or the graveyard. What I understand now after years of studying Feng Shui, is that the house's structural design, location and position on the lot attracted other negative yin energies. It's also true that the yin energy of the location might have attracted an architect who would design this type of home, and a certain Dr. Sandres who would build it. It's also true that our natal charts—our destiny—allowed for the possibility that we would be drawn to this arrangement.

In Feng Shui, everything is connected to—and potentially affecting—everything else. Therefore, it's important to look at the whole and all the various influences at play, including the personal natal astrology of the family members. The natal chart, which is based on your birth date, must be brought into harmony with the property if balanced Feng Shui is to be achieved. This balance refers to a person's position between Heaven and Earth and the dynamic influences that both Heaven and Earth have on an individual. Consequently, a home may be nurturing and supportive for one person, but not for another. The polarity of a home literally associates itself with the polarity of one's DNA.

After rearranging our bedroom and feeling a positive effect immediately, I wanted our entire house professionally analyzed. I asked our landlord to help me find a consultant. His laboratory had been optimized using Feng Shui principles, so he offered to give me the name of the fellow who had done it.

CHAPTER 85

Dr. Sandres introduced me to a Feng Shui practitioner referred to as Windy. Unfortunately, Mr. Windy was not immediately available for a Feng Shui session so he sent his partner. It was interesting to watch the Feng Shui practitioner make his analysis and then place two-inch square mirrors in different arrangements on the walls. Personally, I would have enjoyed more explanation of how and why these mirrors could shift energy, but he was not the chatty type.

When he finished, he asked us to leave the house for a long lunch. We returned about two hours later, giving the energy a chance to settle after his adjustments. He determined that the energy of our house was too yin. According to his calculations, his corrections could only bring the level up to about twenty-five percent. Coincidentally, he had also Feng Shuied the house next door and the mirrors he had placed to deflect their negative energy were affecting our house. As if we needed that.

When we returned from lunch, there was a noticeable difference in the feel of our home, definitely a positive change. I felt stronger immediately—like I got some wind in my sail—a feeling that continued to grow over the ensuing days. The downside was that Mike and I began to bicker openly. Whatever it was, we fought about it. The extra strength I acquired from the new energy helped me to take on disagreements with Mike that before I would have let slide. Yes, I detected that the Feng Shui adjustments caused the house's energy to shift, and it was much better, but I also felt that the Feng Shui practitioner's work required some tweaking.

I explained to Windy that his partner's Feng Shui adjustments had made a noticeable improvement, but that something more needed to be done. Windy's schedule opened up. This time he offered to do the adjustments himself. Windy rearranged some of the mirrors and asked us to switch the guest bedroom—which had the best energy in the house—to the family room. The best energy needed to be shared by the entire family. As it was, the guest bedroom was empty most of the time and benefitted no one.

We also moved furniture that created energy blockages. Unfortunately, he said there was a limit to what could be done without filling in the swimming pool to create a flower garden and relocating one of the outside doors to disrupt the four doors lined up in succession. He elaborated on the weaknesses of the U-shape design of our house that Margaret Milton had mentioned, helping me to understand how the various features and orientation were likely affecting us.

Windy was much more open about his work than his

partner had been and didn't seem to mind my endless questions. He explained that one of the mirror arrangements was called "the Lotus," intended to attract opportunities into a home when positioned correctly. There was also a "Sun" arrangement that was used to add the Fire element to an area where Fire was needed. He further described how energy placement had a cumulative affect and would build over time. I asked him to teach me Feng Shui, but he was very reluctant to do so. He said that men normally practice Feng Shui. Not intending to be discriminatory, he wanted to honor the integrity of the system.

"Women are considered Yin," he said. "Their predominant characteristics are soft and receptive and are more vulnerable to others' energies which can affect their own." The practice of metaphysical sciences is also a Yin activity. A yin woman practicing a Yin craft creates an imbalance. He knew of my recent health struggles, and that if I studied Feng Shui I wouldn't be able to resist practicing it, which could potentially make me more ill. He didn't want to be responsible for doing me a disservice.

For many years I had been searching for logical, scientific explanations for my bizarre life. There was no way that I was going to let this opportunity get away. I was desperate to probe every detail he shared with me, pushing to know the principles that lay behind the corrections he had made, so I could carry the knowledge with me to wherever we moved.

I pleaded with him to teach me more. Few books were available on Feng Shui in the early nineties. None were textbooks. At that time the ancient Chinese texts had not been translated to English nor made available to laymen. Instruction was done on a master/apprentice basis without study materials. After some cajoling, Windy finally agreed to teach me some Feng Shui basics. For the next few months he came to the house when he could spare the time, using the floor plans of our Manila house and our house in Pakistan as case studies. I took notes and gleaned as much information as possible during the short time that we had together. I was not in a position to become a formal student but was determined to learn what I could from Windy while I had the chance. He refused to accept money for his instruction so I gave him pearls for his wife instead.

What Windy could not predict was that as a result of the Feng Shui corrections, the other occupants of our home would become unhappy and make their appearances

CHAPTER 86

We knew about the *yakuza* and the double murders and that our house was built on a graveyard, but up until this point, Mike and I had not seen actual appearances from ghosts. What we had experienced were the unaccounted for sounds, smells, and creepy goose bumps that occurred when walking into a draft in stifling, hundred degree heat when neither door nor window was open, nor air conditioning on. Sonya and Sasha spoke of the scary people in their bedroom, but I was never sure how much was real and how much was imagination.

Because of the Yin nature of the house, the women who lived there were affected more than the men. As a result, Mike's interest in Feng Shui was nominal since he didn't notice the problems and couldn't understand what it meant to have "the energy adjusted" or "why" we needed to have our energy corrected.

"Nothing is wrong with *my* energy," he was quick to point out.

After Windy did the Feng Shui adjustments, it was Mike who had the sleepless nights and who felt uncomfortable. The maids, children and I were feeling much better. I wanted to feel sorry for him and maybe I did a wee bit. To tell you the truth, I was so relieved to feel better myself that his discomfort didn't register all that much with me. Mike wasn't a Feng Shui believer yet. Until he was prepared to discuss a compromise, I was prepared to let him live with the discomfort.

Meanwhile, I studied privately with Windy who taught me a little more each time about this fascinating science. I continued to make executive decisions on the various changes to be made in our house based on Windy's advice. Mike went along with these decisions, but was still not convinced.

CHAPTER 87

It was always in the middle of the night, usually three o'clock a.m., when the noises started. Our bedroom and office rooms were located on the long hallway. The upstairs security door that had been installed before we moved in was closed and locked every night as added protection. This door was positioned at one end of the hallway while our daughters' bedroom, guest bedroom and upstairs family room were on the other end. My husband's office was next to our bedroom. Once the security door was locked, nobody could get inside the second floor area. Opposite our bedroom along the hallway was a wall of sliding glass doors with a balcony that opened onto the pool below. These doors were not accessible to anyone from the ground.

One night out of nowhere an incredible noise jolted me awake. The noise barreled down the length of the hallway. Just as "it" arrived at the end of the long corridor, the noise reversed and barreled down to the other end of the hallway. The racket was so loud that it sounded as though someone were shoving all the furniture back and forth, though there was no clashing or banging. It was like a train looped continuously without stopping, or a dozen bowling balls rolling down an alley that reversed at the door before rolling back.

When I heard the noise the first night, I did not open the door to see what was out there. I was too scared. Whatever it was, I knew it wasn't human and that I couldn't do anything about it. I just lay awake all night long without making a move. The next night— again at three o'clock a.m.—the same thing happened, and again the next night and the next.

Mike heard the noises too. The first night he lay awake

without saying anything to me. The second night he nudged me, "Germaine, do you hear that?"

Already awake, I answered, "Of course I hear it,"

"Did you hear it last night, too?" he asked.

"Yes, I did," was my tired response. We lay awake the entire night as we did many more countless, sleepless nights until the noises mysteriously stopped some weeks later.

From the beginning an ayah slept with the girls. This practice was as much for my benefit as it was for theirs. If the girls awakened in the middle of the night, I wanted them to feel comforted by the ayah's presence before coming to our room. Sleep deprivation remained a problem, making it difficult to recover from the tuberculosis and other stresses, let alone this latest situation. We instructed the ayah to stay in the room with the girls when these noises occurred and did not want her to open the door. Since we didn't understand what we were dealing with, we preferred that "it" remain in the corridor as opposed to coming into the bedroom. Whatever "it" was, we were not prepared to confront it.

During the period when we were having our three a.m. noise episodes, we had invited several expatriate and Filipino couples for a dinner party. Among the latter were Jun and his wife, Mercy, Mike's office manager. Mercy and Jun had recently married, and very sweetly found a way to include all four of us in their wedding. Sonya and Sasha were flower girls, and Mike and I were "assistants-in-waiting" for the bride and groom.

The day after our party, Mercy and Jun returned to our house to speak to us, proceeding cautiously. "We don't know how to tell you this, but when we were at your dinner party, we saw ghosts."

They were timid about sharing their sighting with us, believing that Americans are less receptive to the paranormal. However, Mercy and Jun had become as close to us as family. We appreciated that they felt comfortable sharing something that could have been viewed unfavorably. We understood how they felt. Mike and I hesitated to speak about the ghosts outside our home for the same reason, uncertain that anyone in the expatriate community would believe us.

Fortunately, Jun and Mercy now knew our little secret. Mike had a business meeting in Hong Kong, and I wanted to go with him, feeling in need of a respite. Unless there was someone to stay with the children, I wouldn't consider going. Up until then, I had never left the children out of my care, even for a night. The ghosts made it particularly difficult to do so. Jun and Mercy were the only couple I would consider entrusting with that responsibility. Sonya and Sasha adored them, and they were far more knowledgeable and better equipped to handle the strangeness in our home than we were.

What a relief to be able to discuss the ghosts and the noises in the middle of the night with our dear friends who had an understanding of these phenomena, and were still kind enough to stay with the girls while we were away.

Our maids were intimately familiar with the paranormal activities in our house, too. They experienced numerous nighttime visitations from the ghosts who appeared to them in their bedroom, just before they went to sleep. We talked freely with one another about these strange occupants like we were discussing unwanted houseguests. By this time, Mike and I were more annoyed than frightened with the ghosts. The maids responded in the same way.

The Philippines is a mix of Filipino, Chinese, Malaysian, Spanish and American cultures that have integrated their varied beliefs, religions and values over centuries. Spirits, afterlife, ghosts, fairies, metaphysics and other dimensions were all on the table for discussion without condemnation.

CHAPTER 88

We called home the first night we were in Hong Kong, anxious to hear that everything was okay. Jun and Mercy had not been spared from the racket that inhabited our hallway. They, too, heard the clamor of "it" as the noise raced furiously down the long passage, and they, too, were afraid to open the door.

Since we were away, both the cook and the ayah slept in Sonya and Sasha's room with them, and on the second night, Jun and Mercy stayed there too. All six of them huddled together as the ghosts appeared. These entities were dark with distorted faces and ragged clothes whose intent was indeed to frighten. Desperate to escape the ghosts, Jun, Mercy, the maids and our children moved to the guest bedroom on the third night, but no escape was possible from the hauntings that followed them. Needless to say, our friends were relieved when we returned home.

Until Mike and I had a solution for the hauntings, there was nothing else to do but move the girls into our bedroom with us. Fortunately our room was large enough to accommodate both of their beds as well as ours. It was easier for me to lie awake at night knowing that Sonya and Sasha were close by. The children continued to sleep in our bedroom until we left the Philippines.

Sonya and Sasha became less and less afraid of the ghosts as time went on. I explained to them that ghosts could not hurt them; they could only frighten. Once they accepted that they wouldn't be harmed, they realized that there was no need to be afraid either.

Bizarre events that had previously taken place during the middle of the night were now occurring at all hours. The ghosts were becoming more assertive. The most poignant episode was the day Sonya had an encounter with the "floating lady." Dora, the ayah, first recounted the tale to me after finding a mess of broken glass in the playroom. The explanation was so fascinating that I had to hear it from Sonya herself.

Sonya, who was about six years old at the time, described the details of her visit with wide-eyed innocence and animation.

"Well," she said, "I was coming out of the kitchen, and I was going around the corner, you know, right there by the dining room, Mommy? And there was this lady, and she was wearing a white dress, but she was floating. And she had like an animal under her arm, and I saw her Mommy! I was scared. I jumped back behind the kitchen wall, but I knew that she was looking for me. I could tell!

But when I poked my head around the corner to see if she was still there, she had gone away. So, I walked down to the toy room. And when I got down to the toy room, there she was. She was waiting for me Mommy! I knew she was waiting for me. And when she saw me, she flew up and hit that mirror off the wall, and flew right through the ceiling and she didn't crack the ceiling or anything!"

"Wow," I thought, "this is incredible! Truly incredible!!"

There were many questions about the incident, but most importantly: "She flew up and hit that mirror off the wall."

Sonya was referring to the Feng Shui mirrors that the Feng Shui practitioner had placed in the toy room. The mirrors were nearly to the ceiling. It would have been impossible for Sonya or Dora to reach nine feet up, and even if they could, they would not have been able to dislodge them. The evidence was obvious. A mirror was missing from its placement, and broken glass lay scattered on the floor. Since the floating lady had disrupted the mirror arrangement, I was concerned that the destroyed Feng Shui cure would bode unfavorably. I got a ladder, climbed to the disrupted arrangement of mirrors and tried to pry the remaining mirrors loose without success. They remained tightly fastened to the wall.

The floating lady must be communicating with us through Sonya, and it had something to do with the Feng Shui. I couldn't see the ghosts, but Sonya had described numerous encounters with them. I felt them, heard them and smelled them, but could not see them.

I recalled the incident at the Christmas bazaar in Pakistan when Sonya grabbed for the statue of the Virgin Mary, and the morning she awakened in Sasha's bed. When I asked her why she was sleeping with Sasha, she answered quite matter of fact while wiping the sleep from her eyes that, "Jesus put me here."

I fully believed Sonya saw the floating lady she described. There was no other explanation for the fallen mirror and there was no reason not to believe her. After all, Mike and I were hearing furniture move during the night!!!

According to Windy, the floating lady in white was complaining about the new Feng Shui balance in the house. The adjustment caused the Yin-Yang ratio to tilt. The ghosts became uncomfortable in much the same way that we had been before the adjustments were made. Houses don't usually have this kind of paranormal activity, at least not of this magnitude. Our house was unusual because of the graveyard and murders.

Our Yang to Yin Feng Shui ratio remained less than twenty-five percent Yang after the corrections, far lower than a balanced home should be. This was the best we were going to achieve without redesigning the property. According to Windy and other spiritual advisors I consulted, this home belonged to the ghosts. We were the intruders. I'm not sure why this was so, but we had no other choice but to leave.

CHAPTER 89

We moved into our house on Lapu Lapu Avenue in September1992 and moved out in December 1995. When we became aware of ghosts I tried to manage the problem as best I could with blessings from various spiritual leaders. Two Catholic Masses were performed in our living room and paranormal specialists were called in to "bring the ghosts to the light." My attempts to normalize our home were to no avail. By the time Maribelle introduced us to a Haitian woman known as Ophelia, we were desperate. Ophelia claimed to be a voodoo priestess whose specialty was ghosts.

Ophelia also claimed to be a lawyer and businesswoman. She was a large woman with a loud raucous laugh, aggressive style and intimidating eye. She had many stories—all questionable—about why she was in Manila and more stories about how her American visa expired and why she couldn't return to the States. I never witnessed evidence that she was either a lawyer or a legitimate businesswoman, but I did believe she was a voodoo priestess and wondered if her greatest skill wasn't con artist.

Mike and I were ready to try almost anything that would stop the noisy, disturbing visitations. Our nerves had worn thin. When

Ophelia offered to rid our house of these unwanted occupants, we threw up our hands and said, "Why not?" I probed to learn as much as I could about her approach, but she was vague with her description. Regardless, her confidence won us both over. Mike could no longer deny the paranormal activity that haunted us, and asked to be present during whatever Ophelia had in store.

Worried that negative energy could somehow attach itself to the children during the ritual, I sent the girls to stay with their friends. Our driver, Albert, picked up Ophelia from where she was staying and brought her to our home. She then sent Albert to fetch one live chicken per family member. During his absence Ophelia explained that she would use the chickens to absorb the negative energy in the house. It wasn't long before Albert returned with four squawking, rambunctious chickens in a gunnysack as Ophelia had instructed.

She opened the bag to count the angry hens and to make sure they were healthy. Satisfied, the voodoo lady tied a string tightly around the sack. The chickens clucked noisily in the beginning, but as Ophelia dragged the sack through every corner of our house reciting prayers as she went, the clucking noises subsided. The process took about an hour. When she was finished, Ophelia dumped the pitiful feathered creatures out of the gunnysack onto the floor. They were so sick that they couldn't walk. Only a short time before those same chickens had been kicking and full of energy. Now they lay in a lifeless lump. Ophelia instructed the driver to take them out to the country and dump them.

"What if someone finds them" I objected, "and tries to eat them? Won't they absorb all that negativity?"

"Well, if they do, that's their karma," Ophelia responded dismissively.

At the end of this ritual I felt poorly. There was nothing uplifting about the procedure and nothing positive about the result that I noticed. In some way I felt we had violated the rights, space and sensitivity of our other-dimensional inhabitants. Mike felt the same way. Our Pakistani exorcism with the priest who utilized holy water, incense and prayer had been highly effective. By contrast, the use of chickens—other living beings—struck us as inappropriate. We were trying to rid our lives of negative energy. Applying another negative process to accomplish that objective wasn't logical. In our opinion, Ophelia had committed violations on all counts, especially to the poor chickens that were dragged around in a gunnysack. We were equally culpable, having enlisted her services.

Ophelia departed shortly after she completed the ritual, leaving Mike and me exhausted and uncomfortable, not knowing what to expect next.

The next day, Mike left for work at his usual time, Sonya had already left for school, and Sasha was upstairs with me chatting away while I was getting ready. I had just gotten out of the shower, still wrapped in towels when I heard a strange howling from downstairs. "Whoooooooaaaaaaaaa" came the doleful wails from below.

Sasha stopped talking and said, "Mommy, what was that?"

My ears perked to hear the howling continue. "I don't know what that is, Sasha. It must be the maids singing."

Suddenly, there was an urgent pounding at our bedroom door. It was Dora who was beside herself with fright.

"Ma'am . . . Ma'am! She's crying!" Dora screamed.

"Who's crying?" I responded with equal panic, not knowing why.

"The old lady is crying!" Dora continued with more urgency.

"What old lady are you talking about?"

At that point, I stepped out into the hallway to see the cook pulling the cleaning lady, Mary, from the stairs, and dragging her down to our bedroom. Despite the chaos, I couldn't help but notice that this tiny Filipina woman had the strength to drag a much larger Mary to me . . . for safety!

Mary had been cleaning the bathroom located in the children's playroom downstairs when confronted by the howling cries from the murdered maid's ghost. Mary was so frightened that she collapsed on the spot. The entire staff was beside themselves with fear, waiting for me to do something. Never had they experienced aggressive paranormal communication and they didn't know how to handle it. Neither did I.

This was it. I'd had it. The stress that came with years of trying, learning, understanding, keeping up a good front, staying calm, giving in, and giving up fun while organizing chicken rituals crashed my awareness. I dreamed of garden lunches with friends while listening to beautiful music, like the other ex-patriate wives did. I wanted to visit the rice terraces of Banaue and the Chocolate Hills of Bohol. I wanted to live a normal life without fearing retaliatory ghosts. I was finished. Finished, finished, finished!!!!!!

I had been a good sport for years. This just didn't fall into my job description as wife, mother and trooper. Howling ghosts. Whoever heard of such a thing? This was all over the top.

We dragged Mary to our bed where we revived her with splashes of cold water to her face. I left the maids to console one another, and then threw on a bathrobe before calling Mike. Mercy answered the phone. Mike was in a meeting. I asked her to tell him that I had to leave the house and was taking Sasha with me. I didn't know where I was going, but would let him know when I got there. Sasha and I were ready to leave when the maid reminded me to put on clothes and comb my hair.

"Oh my God, what's happening to me? I've got to collect myself. I have to remain calm."

Taking a second to compose myself, I called Ophelia.

Ophelia couldn't stop laughing. I imagined her bending over her big stomach, mouth open and white teeth glistening. How could anyone think this story was funny? "Calm down," she said, amused by the story. "They are not going to hurt you. They can't hurt you, but they do want you to feel sorry for them." Ophelia said that as a result of our chicken ritual the day before, the ghosts were voicing their displeasure. The old lady ghost maid did so by howling at our cleaning lady.

According to the voodoo expert, these ghosts were outside our house, loitering in the garden and in the trees, wanting to come back in. They were after sympathy. Admittedly, I did feel sorry for them. Good heavens, if I had known this would be the result—an ongoing battle for territorial rights without compromise—I never would have permitted that horrible ceremony. I thought that we were sending the ghosts to the light like you'd see in the movies. Or that they would just go away to their own dimension. To contend with their presence outside the house as opposed to inside the house didn't seem like much of an improvement nor a benefit to anyone.

I told the maids that they did not have to stay in the house; they were free to go home for the rest of the day. I dressed myself as Dora suggested earlier, grabbed Sasha and left with Albert. The gardener/pool man, Mary's husband, offered to stay. He said that he wasn't disturbed by our household drama, and was happy to wait for Mike and explain what had happened.

Sasha, Albert and I picked up Sonya from school so she wouldn't be taken home by bus, then we entertained ourselves at a café before returning to the house later that evening when I was sure Mike would be there.

Mike arrived home to an empty house much earlier than expected. When we finally arrived, Sasha excitedly recounted the bawls she had heard from the downstairs bathroom. She mimicked the howling cries she had heard that morning while raising up her arms as her voice got louder and her eyes got bigger. I told Mike about Flora dragging Mary and about Ophelia who found the entire scenario laughable. It didn't take long before he and Sonya heard all the details.

After some discussion, Mike and I decided that we were going to do things our way from then on. Resorting to the so-called wisdom of priests, priestesses, shamans, masters or any other spiritual notable who professed to know how to handle our extraordinary circumstances was finished. We had to approach this situation logically, the only way we knew how. Mike decided to resign from his job at the same time our housing contract ended in a few months and look for employment back in the States.

Mike and I agreed that during the remaining time we lived in the house we needed to show the ghosts some respect. Up until then, we had treated the ghosts as pests. We denied them their right to exist. If it was true that we inhabited their space, then we needed to rectify this situation. Our plan was to make a pact with them, and communicate our agreement with them telepathically, the same way they communicated with us. The message we sought to convey was that if they would leave us in peace and promise not to harm us, we would leave the house. We apologized again for what we had done, explaining that we had been ignorant and asked for their forgiveness. We committed to them the date we would leave the house if they would in turn agree to leave us alone.

Certainly we didn't know what we were doing with regard to communicating with ghosts, but we did believe they could be reasoned with and that they had received our message.

CHAPTER 90

Life became somewhat peaceful and the ghosts kept their side of the bargain until an evening a few days later while Mike was away on business. The girls and I were watching a movie in the upstairs family room. The air conditioning unit in that room was making a horrible, clanking noise. It was too uncomfortable to watch a movie with the noisy air conditioner on, so we turned it off.

Shortly thereafter, the cook called us for dinner. I got up from my chair and said to the girls, "Let's turn the air conditioner on so the room can cool off while we are eating. When we return, we'll be able to watch the movie more comfortably."

Flippantly I remarked, laughing, "Ha, we'll let the ghosts enjoy the noise while we're downstairs."

We ate our dinner, then returned upstairs to resume watching *Grease*, Sonya's latest favorite movie. We entered the now cooled down room and turned off the noisy air conditioner before getting cozy together. To our surprise and disappointment, there was sound coming from the television, but no picture.

We tried to play at least six different videocassettes, but with each and every one there was only sound. No picture!

"Oh for Heaven's sake!" I lamented, "The ghosts must be angry with me."

Disappointed, we turned the television off and went to bed earlier than we had planned. The next day when the kids got up they asked again to watch the movie.

"Don't you remember?" I reminded Sonya. "It's not working anymore."

"I know, Mommy," Sonya said patiently, "but can't you just try to put it on? Will you just try?"

"Okay," I said, giving in to her optimism.

I went to the TV room with Sonya and Sasha, popped in the cassette, and waited for the picture to return to no avail. "I'm sorry my darling, but I can't get it to work."

"That's okay, Mommy," she said sweetly. "I just like to listen to the music anyway."

Sonya only watched musicals. She had already devoured *The Wizard of Oz* and *Meet Me in Saint Louis,* having memorized Judy Garland's lines. She enjoyed the pouty, tearful deliveries that she mimicked perfectly. Sasha's favorite movie was *Fantasia,* which she could watch three times a day, never tiring of the water pail and snake scenes. If they couldn't see the picture, they were content listening to the music while recalling the images from memory.

Four-year old Sasha was less willing to accept defeat. "Well, Mommy, it's the ghosts! They're angry with you! Why don't you just apologize to them?"

"Sasha, do you really think that will make a difference?"

"Well, Mommy, you can try . . ." she persisted.

I enjoyed her innocence and willingness to communicate with the beings who had been responsible for so many scary dreams. Now that she was not afraid, she accepted communication with them as a possibility.

We stood in the middle of the television room together. I looked upwards at the ceiling; Sonya and Sasha joined me to look expectantly upwards at nothing while I made my apology.

"Ghosts, you know something? I really was just kidding. It was a joke. Where's your sense of humor? They're just kids, for crying out loud, and all they want to do is watch a movie. I really didn't mean to offend you, and I am very sorry if I did."

"Well, Sasha, I apologized." Not holding out much hope, I added, "but I don't know if it's going to work."

I left the room with the girls sitting on the sofa looking at a blank screen, satisfied to hear the enchanting voice of Olivia Newton John singing *Hopelessly Devoted to You* while visualizing the scenes. However, it wasn't necessary. Before I made it to the end of the hallway, Sonya shouted happily, "Mommy, the picture is back!"

Right or wrong, we accepted that our house belonged to the ghosts and we were the intruders. We kept our agreement to them and made our plans to leave.

Mike resigned from his Manila assignment with Barter & Biddle and received a promotion. We left our ghost house on Lapu Lapu Avenue at the end of the contract as promised, spent the few remaining weeks at a hotel in Manila and arrived at Dulles Airport in Virginia in January of 1996.

CHAPTER 91

We moved to our cozy house on Military Road in Arlington, Virginia and stayed there for a little over three years before resuming our international travels. The time in the U.S. came with the space and calm that our family urgently needed to reconnect with sanity, nature, friends, family and what it meant to be an American.

Arlington was a special time to assess, re-evaluate, heal and move on. Sonya was six and Sasha was four. They have always displayed significant differences in their looks and personalities, but as they grew older those differences became even more pronounced. Sonya was a larger, sturdier child who was sultry feminine. She kept the wide, expressive eyes, chestnut colored curly hair and olive colored skin that characterized her Latin side of the family, and she remained the theatrical type who had a flare for drama and style.

Sasha on the other hand was blossoming into a tomboy who wore boy's clothes, had boy playmates, and felt more comfortable building forts than serving cookies in them. She had gorgeous, dark-blonde curly hair until she instructed the beautician to give her one of those hideous mushroom cuts. Her eyelashes grew to be so long that they sometimes got tangled and made her eyes look squinty. Freckles spotted her nose to complete an already impish look. She was a small child with an elfin quality about her, so I always joked that I found her under a leaf!

Victoria became a real sister to them and a regular fun part of their lives. She visited frequently and made efforts to become the big sister that they had heard about for so many years but never had a chance to get to know. She had grown into a gorgeous young woman with dark hair, an hourglass figure, and had a small face with fine, aquiline features between a high forehead and dimpled cheek. I've always found it interesting that she was the physical blend of her younger sisters, exhibiting both the sultry side of Sonya and the impish features of Sasha.

Victoria had worked in real estate since graduating from college. She was originally hired as an apprentice to a successful agent, until she developed skills sufficient to manage on her own. Although she remained the spendthrift of her youth, she was now twenty-six years old. I could finally enjoy her company without assuming any unwanted authoritative role or accountant to her excessive lifestyle.

The girls loved Arlington; they were free to enjoy open spaces encumbered only by shrubs, trees and bushes. This was the first time in their memory that they could open the door and walk outside without fear of what lay beyond brick walls, metal gates and security guards that protected them. Surely this detail escaped them, but I couldn't help but notice the freedom they enjoyed being children and communing with nature. They commented on the smell of clean air and the feel of freshly cut grass between their toes and noticed that the streets were not littered with debris. When they did come across someone's trash thrown carelessly on the street or in the park, they were quick to pick it up, offended that anyone could be so inconsiderate. I enjoyed driving along Military Road during April, where most every yard displayed brilliantly colored azalea bushes and sweet smelling Magnolia trees.

It wasn't unusual for the kids from our cul-de-sac neighborhood to walk to the nearby nature reserve where they spent hours looking for all the curious, slimy creatures that hadn't found a hiding place before their arrival. When the children were finished playing, or it began to rain, they could retreat to the cabin that housed early American artifacts, indigenous birds, insects, snakes, turtles and an active honeycomb where they could watch the queen bee and worker bees behind a glass cover.

Sonya and Sasha could have breakfast in the morning with Cory and Michael, lunch with Liza, Aaron and Adam and dinner at our house with the whole gang, never tiring of their time together. The homes in the cul-de-sac consisted mostly of doting retirees and families with children between the ages of one and twelve, young enough to be innocent, but not old enough to get into too much trouble. The entire cul-de-sac of families enjoyed the playful street activity and neighborhood theatrical productions that all the children participated in.

Sonya and Sasha played soccer and Sonya signed up for ballet classes, which she eventually refused to attend after realizing what it was. "Deux pied, deux pied, that's not real dancing anyway, Mommy," she tearfully lamented until I didn't have the energy to fight her any longer. The controlled, sophisticated ballet steps held no comparison to the bodacious variety that had more moves and she obviously preferred.

Both the girls were good athletes, but Sasha was recognized early on as someone who was athletically gifted. After watching Sasha play soccer at school, the coach offered her a spot on the travel soccer team without a tryout. Parents lined up to get their kids on the team, so I assumed Sasha would be excited when I asked her if she would like to play. Instead, she hesitated before saying, "I have to think about it."

I waited a few days before asking her again.

"Well," she said thoughtfully, "I'm so much smaller than the other girls (who were all older and larger) and I'm afraid I'll get hurt. I don't mind playing during the practices, but I'd rather go fishing on the weekend."

That was that. Sasha played soccer at school but declined her coveted slot on the travel team. She did what she wanted to do most on the weekend, which was to play in the neighborhood and go fishing.

The girls found sanctuary with their friends from the cul-de-sac and in their new home, but school provided more of a challenge. Most of the kids who attend international schools rotate through the system. It's typical for companies to reassign employees and their families every two to three years, so almost all of the kids in the international schools have lived in other countries. Everyone knows what it's like to be the new kid, which is routine. Such is not the case in most American schools where the average family buys a house and lives in it for twenty years or more. Friendships are formed before kindergarten and continue through high school. This makes it difficult for newcomers—especially other American kids who speak with accents and tell strange stories.

Mike's new position required months of travel, usually to Gujarat, India, located in Western India on the Pakistani border. The girls and I missed him during those months, but it is difficult for me to say if he was happy we returned to the States again or not. The international lifestyle suited him. I assumed that he wanted to be a part of the girls' lives, but it occurred to me that his travels came as a relief for him.

CHAPTER 92

When I wasn't busy with the girls or managing our home, I
organized the bits and pieces of notes that I had written over
the years, anxious to make sense of our former lives. I searched
magazines and papers for metaphysical studies and ferretted out
every Feng Shui lecture and seminar in the D.C. area until I found
the name of a Chinese master who taught Feng Shui and BaZi
classes near the University of Maryland. Eventually I took every
class that the Chinese master offered, devouring his every word.

In 1996, interest in Feng Shui had not yet ignited. Classes
in the D.C. area were scarce if not impossible to find. I had been
taking a correspondence course from Manila and coupled that
information with what I learned from Windy and the local Chinese
Master. Sometimes I got confused when trying to reconcile the
various schools of Feng Shui thought so I decided to focus on the
one consistent factor in all of the studies—elemental theory—to
help me put the pieces of our lives together.

Feng Shui is the oldest known existing science. Feng Shui
means "wind and water," and is poetically referred to as the wind
we cannot see and the water we cannot grasp. Each of the five
elements—Fire, Earth, Metal, Water and Wood—has distinctive
characteristics that can be separated into two personalities. One
aspect of each element is positive (Yang) and the other is negative
(Yin), which effectively gives us ten elements instead of five. There
is no judgment, such as "good" for Yang and "bad" for Yin. Positive
and negative refer to an element's polarity and the attributes that
describe them. All elements and conditions can be "good" when in
balance. Likewise, all elements and conditions can be "bad" when
out of balance. The generic male is considered to be Yang while the
generic female is considered Yin. However, it is possible to have a
man with feminine qualities and a female with masculine qualities.
The ideal is to achieve balance where both the Yin and Yang
components work harmoniously with one another.

Elements have qualities that are used to create balance within an environment, or to recreate harmony in the space between Heaven and Earth. Our birth date provides the astrological footprint to our life's potential, a personalized account of these five elements and how they affect us as individuals. The elements are organized by "pillars" according to the Year, Month, Day and Time we are born. The day of one's birth is called the Day Master. This element dictates our primary characteristics, but the location of the other elements relative to the Day Master will determine the *quality* of this element.

To illustrate, think of it as a chess game where the Queen is your Day Master. On her own she has little to no power, but based on her position and relationship relative to the other chess pieces on the board, she exhibits her true strength and potential for power. In other words, the Day Master is our identity, which is influenced by the position of the other elements. It is said that our BaZi chart, Chinese Astrology chart, is a snapshot of our destiny. I humbly revise that observation and say that it is a snapshot of our *potential*—both good and bad! The beauty of Feng Shui, and understanding the elemental influences on one another, is that we can positively affect our lives. Our BaZi astrological chart provides an opportunity to look at our potential, our strengths and our weaknesses so that we can improve ourselves.

Birth charts are not static, but rather appear in a time and space continuum where rotations of the Earth and movements of the stars and planets equally affect us. The Year Cycle, the Luck Cycle and the Season equally affect the health of one's chart.

Finally, I was able to step back from our lives and address the past years from an unemotional perspective. Light began to shine on the complicated dynamic between Victoria, Mike and me. Now I realized that our relationship was about more than the spoiled sixteen-year-old daughter who came to live with her dad and stepmother.

Mike is Yang Bing Fire Day Master, the Sun, who assumes omnipotence. Just as the Sun knows it will rise every day and set every evening, so do Bing Fire Day Masters know they will prevail.

Bing Fire Day Masters inspire growth and project warmth. They possess omniscient qualities, assuming they know more than you ever will. They *need* no one.

Victoria is a Yang Wu Earth Day Master, the Mountain. The Earth element contains four out of the five elements: Earth, Metal, Water and Wood—all of the elements, *except* Fire. Fire produces and nurtures Earth in the production cycle of elements, but the Mountain has always existed. Therefore, Wu Mountain Day Masters *need* no one to produce them. An entire forest fire will not increase the size of a mountain. Wu Earth needs Bing Fire to *enjoy* his warmth when the Sun removes the morning chill from the night.

In the same way that the Sun makes the Mountain feel better, Victoria needed the warmth of her father's attention to feel better about herself. Bing Fire and Wu Mountain are both dominant elements who recognize dominance in the other. Because of this, they fear challenging one another. This attribute helped to explain why Victoria's father did not correct her. Victoria's chart shows that she would challenge anyone who claimed authority over her, including her father who resisted doing so in any case. Bing Fire and Wu Earth are especially dominant when their Yang energy is not countered by their respective controlling elements. Qui Water, Rain Clouds, control Bing Fire, and both Yin Yi Wood and Yang Jia Wood control Wu Earth.

I am a Yin Yi Wood Day Master depicted as flowers, vines, blades of grass, and even weeds. Wood element Day Masters are exactly the opposite of Fire and Earth. Wood needs all of the other elements for survival. Sunlight is required for growth, Earth and Water are required for nurturing and Metal is needed to cut Wood so it can become useful. Wu Mountain Earth is hard earth. Jia Wood, the tree cannot easily grow in hard earth, but Yi Wood, the vine, can silently cover a mountainside. Ji Earth, the soft moist earth of the paddy field, is best for Jia Wood tree to anchor, take root and flourish.

When Mike and Victoria were together, I was overwhelmed by the intensity of their combined elements. Mike has very little Water in his chart, but an overabundance of Fire, Earth and Metal.

Yin Yang Symbol, Tai Chi, Tao

The boundary of these two energies is a line representing man

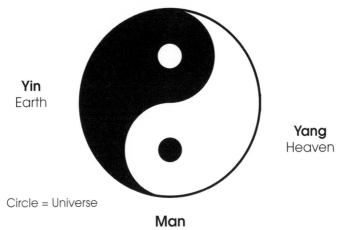

Yin
Earth

Yang
Heaven

Circle = Universe

Man

Heaven and Earth operate within the domain of the Universe

The Yin Yang Symbol is also the symbol of Tai Chi, which is a Chinese word that literally means "ultimate potentiality." Our Tai Chi is our Tao or path.

The Yin Yang symbol is in the shape of a circle and consists of two colors. The black color represents Yin energy, which is Earth. The white color represents Yang energy, which is Heaven. Black and White, Yin and Yang, Heaven and Earth are all opposing qualities of dualism. The boundary of these two energies is the invisible line representing Man. This indicates that man exists between Heaven and Earth, which operate within the domain of the universe.

There is a black dot inside the white part, and a white dot inside the black part, telling us that inside of everything yang there is a bit of yin and inside of everything yin there is a bit of yang. If you tried to walk through the diameter of the circle, you would experience both black and white, or both yin and yang energies. In other words, one does not exist without the other.

Note that the Yin Yang symbol is rounded. This gives a sense of continual movement and interaction between the two energies, and suggests a constant state of change.

Bagua

There are many schools of Feng Shui, which can be confusing. But, the Bagua, a so-called energy map, is the tool that is used consistently in all the various schools. The eight-sided Bagua is based on the oldest book in the world, the I-Ching, which is known as the Book of Changes. Each of the eight sides, which are called guas, represents a compass direction and refers to a different aspect of one's life: Wealth, Career, Fame, Family, Children, Helpful People, Knowledge, and Relationships. In the center of the Bagua is the Tai Chi, or Life Force, also known as the Tao. Each compass direction of the eight-sided Bagua is associated with a different body part, a location of the home, and member of the family. An element—Fire, Earth, Metal, Water, Wood—is associated with the compass direction, including the center. Once you understand how to interpret the Bagua, you can apply the information to create balance and affect change.

Victoria has no Water whatsoever. Wood needs Water to survive. Without Water, their overabundant Fire, Earth and Metal elements were destructive to my Yi Wood. Fire scorched the delicate vine and Wu Earth absorbed my Water.

Yi Wood Day Masters are delicate, but they are also very resilient. Try to cut a vine or a weed. The vine will find a way to sprout up somewhere else. Vines and weeds have an uncanny ability to grow anywhere on almost anything.

Wood dominates Earth. When Mike was away from home during the early years of our marriage, my Yi Wood could manage Victoria's Wu Mountain. But, when the three of us were together there was an elemental imbalance where my Wood nurtured Mike and Mike's Fire nurtured Victoria's Earth. I was without nurturing from either one.

I expanded on the floor plans I had drawn for Windy and analyzed yearly elements alongside our BaZi charts and then factored in the elemental conditions for the areas where we had lived. At that time I didn't know enough about Feng Shui to follow any particular system. I did the best I could with the information that was available.

After examining all these factors, I could now understand why the years we spent in Karachi were so difficult. Sonya and Sasha both have Jia Wood as their Day Master. Jia Wood is the Yang counterpart to Yi Wood. Jia Wood is a big, strong tree like the Red Wood tree or the Oak tree. A Jia Wood tree's roots are as deep underground as the branches are tall above ground. For this reason it is difficult for Jia Wood Day Masters to relocate from one home to the next. They do not enjoy being uprooted in the same way that a tree does not enjoy being uprooted. Jia Wood Day Masters are also somewhat mysterious, exposing only a part of themselves at any time. Both Jia Wood and Yi Wood need Qui Water—Yin Water from the clouds as opposed to Yang Ren Water from the ocean— and nutrient rich Ji Earth, the rice paddy, to survive. Wood also needs sunshine, Bing Fire.

We lived in Karachi during 1990, 1991 and part of 1992. The

predominant elements during those three years were Fire, Earth and Metal, all representing a challenge for our thirsty Wood element.

An over-abundance of Fire in Karachi dried out the Earth. With an average annual rainfall of four inches, there was too little Water to nurture us. I imagined Sonya and Sasha as the trees we saw in a Karachi landscape and remembered how difficult it was for anything to survive there. Their Jia Wood tree had the same difficulty. The absence of Qui Water, rain clouds, allowed the Fire element to gather more strength and scorch our Wood. And, an overabundance of Metal found in the salted Earth chopped at our Wood's roots, working against all three of us. The Fire, Earth and Metal elements were overwhelming, not to mention the Gulf War that presented another version of a Fire and Metal presence. There was no nurturing for our Wood anywhere in the Karachi environment, and the Stars were against us too. Consequently, this imbalance posed a genuine threat to our lives.

CHAPTER 93

With my new understanding of elemental relationships and Yin Yang balance, it was time to reconcile these theories with the elemental mechanics of Black Magic and why my life was plagued by these negative practices.

Black Magic is a Yin art that manipulates energies to create an imbalance intended to harm another. I was made victim of this practice primarily because I attracted it to myself when I let God—Light—a Yang vibration—out of my life, which invited Darkness—a Yin vibration—in. Where there is no Light, there is Darkness. I am a woman, which is yin. My Day Master element is Yi Wood, which is Yin. Black Magic is a Yin practice. The characteristics of the Yin nature are softer, making someone like myself more vulnerable. Yin Yin Yin Yin is an imbalance of Yin energy.

Sasha was an infant and an easy target. It's interesting that the maid chose Sasha's toe on which to put the hair. The placement of the hair on her toe chopped at the roots of her Jia Wood Element, her feet. Fortunately, Sasha has four Yang pillars, which I believe made her less vulnerable to the Black Magic, and helped her to deflect the negative energy. Fortunately, too, I found the hair in time. If I hadn't, she could have been affected not only physically, but energetically as well.

Sonya was vulnerable because of her illnesses, a yin condition, and the medication. More yin energy. She was also a very sensitive, feminine child—all yin qualities. Sonya has two Yang pillars and two Yin pillars. Black Magic ritual intends to create an overabundance of Yin energy. Fortunately, Sonya has a Yang Day Master. Unfortunately she was weakened by the illnesses, medication and lack of Water. She was extremely vulnerable under those conditions. The onslaught of Fire, Earth and Metal elements from the Karachi elements and the heavenly stars while being attacked by Black Magic could have claimed her life.

Yi Wood people, vines, are more resilient than Jia Wood. They can sprout up again, like weeds! Yang Wood—trees—don't have that capability. Once a tree is cut, it's consumed. I suppose one could say that it was only a question of time before the Karachi elements, Fire, Earth and Metal, would have devoured all of us.

The dry, intense heat and arid environment of Karachi did not affect Mike since he is Yang Bing Fire, or the Sun. Nothing can really affect the Sun, except the rain clouds that cover him up. Just like the Sun, Mike got up every morning, regardless of what the day had in store for him. Bing Fire, the Sun, is at the center of his own universe and feels invincible. The Sun is an optimist, usually of strong constitution. The Sun just is. He doesn't offer explanation, seek permission or apologize. The Sun believes in his own benevolence because he bestows his Light, vision, and provides warmth to the other elements. The Sun does not need other elements for survival, but even the all-knowing, all-powerful Sun needs to feel useful. The Sun needs to see growth from his output. Without Wood in the Sun's life, the Sun has no purpose. There is a reciprocal relationship between Fire and Wood elements that is unique among the elements, and aptly describes the special relationship that my Bing Fire husband had with me, and our two daughters.

I was satisfied to understand this account of the elemental relationships that helped explain my attraction to Mike and why I couldn't . . . wouldn't give up on us.

Ghosts or not, our move to Manila was good for all of us. Intuitively we resonated to the nurturing Water and Wood qualities of the tropical climate. I learned something of pearls, crystals, ghosts, Feng Shui and the mysteries of the Universe that I could not have learned any other way.

CHAPTER 94

The Tao and the Bagua are integral symbols for the metaphysical sciences. The Tao, or Yin Yang as it is commonly referred, is located at the heart of the eight-sided Bagua. The Bagua is used as a road map to understand the eight principles of reality considered intrinsic to everyone's life. The Tao, or Dao, means "the Path." The Tao itself is neither a thing nor a religion but a symbol that describes the natural order of the Universe. It is a concept used to provide guidance for harmonizing one's will with nature and in so doing lead a more fulfilling and balanced life. Tao—our path—is unique to the individual. It's easier to *experience* Tao than to define it.

Our Tai Chi, meaning "God's energy," is our Tao or Path. Tai Chi is magnetic, and is the same energy that exists in our DNA. Trees, Earth, Water, Sunshine and Metals all have their own polarity. Tai Chi and our DNA or life force are interrelated in a quantum metaphysical way. In Latin, meta means "change." In Greek, meta means "beyond" and physics refers to the study of matter and its motion through space and time. Our energy changes over time based on our Luck Cycle, and the Year, Month and Day. Our surroundings, our thoughts, our food, our education, our entertainment, our friends, our family and our society, all affect our energy.

The Tao symbolizes the perfection and equanimity in the

Universe. Quite simply, the Tao represents the ever-changing, gently moving, intricate, negative and positive aspects of life as seen in night and day, woman and man, black and white, left and right, Moon and Sun. How could one describe daylight if there were no night, or man if there were no woman? The Tao describes man's position between Heaven and Earth.

There are many metaphysical teachers and Feng Shui masters who are careful to disassociate Feng Shui from anything that may sound religious or spiritual in nature. Although I respect their knowledge of metaphysics, I must be honest with my own beliefs and experience. I agree that the Tao has nothing to do with religion. Having said that, I do believe there is a connection between *spirituality* and science, and that the Tao, located at the heart of the Bagua diagram, is centrally positioned to best emanate energy to the other eight guas. In my opinion, this implies that one's spiritual connection is central to one's harmonious existence and nurtures every other aspect of one's life: Reputation, Relationships, Creativity and Children, Benefactors and Ancestors, Career, Education, Family, and Health and Wealth. Spirituality and science are linked.

Metaphysical principles are not unique to the Chinese. They have always existed. It is the Chinese who have given us the Bagua, the I Ching and other ancient texts that we can study and learn from. These are the tools that provided a structure that I used to help myself, but Chinese wisdom is not the only wisdom available. Indigenous peoples who span seventy countries worldwide practice their own version of Feng Shui. These peoples have retained their knowledge systems and beliefs and possess invaluable knowledge of practices for the sustainable management of natural resources. They have a special relationship and intuitive understanding of their connection to the Earth, natural resources and to the Universe. They, too, understand the position of man in the space between Heaven and Earth, and how changes in their environment and the rotations of the Earth affect their balance and their lives. They *feel* their connection to life.

Most—if not all—religions practice metaphysical principles

in prayer, meditation, and ritual, all methods that have evolved from our indigenous beginnings that have been used to connect to God. Ritualistic practices and activities affect polarity and are, therefore, scientifically related. Think about birthdays, weddings, funerals, graduation ceremonies and any other important events in your life that warrant recognition. Activities surrounding these ceremonies gather energy, which is either Yin or Yang. There is no escaping it. We are all connected to one another and to our surroundings.

Consider for a moment that if we hurt someone else, we inadvertently hurt ourselves. Under the circumstances, it would behoove us to create the best possible environment, and to practice the Golden Rule, "Do unto others as you would have them do unto you."

I believe in spiritual evolution and that religions evolve accordingly. All religions have found a valuable place in time for someone at some time, but *not everyone at the same time, because we are each on our own path.* Today there is a brewing hostility towards religion that I don't share. Religion has a place. I believe that religions have sprung up—with good intention—from those who have made the connection to God and want to help others to do the same. Religions *attempt* to provide a framework of existence to best help man reach his spiritual potential. The problem with religion isn't the religion per se, but interpretations from those who don't understand it, and those who seek to manipulate and abuse it for personal gain. Religion has been good for individuals, societies and cultures, and can continue to be good if we allow one another spiritual freedom. We are each on our own individual path, connected by our thoughts and feelings. Eventually, all paths lead to God, but not necessarily at the same time and in the same way.

It is significant to note that we are in the twenty-first century, analyzing a science that existed four thousand years ago that is relevant today. The only thing that has changed is man, his identity to life and how he describes himself. The description of elements and their polarity remains the constant, until described in context of their relationship to the dynamic movement of the stars. This science, founded on feelings and empirical evidence, doesn't trample on religious beliefs. It simply explains the connection that we have to one another, to the Universe, to God, and to All That Is.

My path was a unique journey that presented opportunities for me to learn the nuances of Yin and Yang energies. I had taken my divine connection as a child for granted. When I let this divine connection, Light (Yang), out of my life, the vacuum was filled with Darkness (Yin). My spiritual balance was tilted to the extent that I was out of step with the Universe and perilous to defend myself against the negativity that I attracted. It was not necessary to take this path. I chose to do so with Free Will. I no longer feel like a victim and don't blame anyone for how difficult those years were. I do not accept that our charts predetermine destiny. Our charts describe our potential. Feng Shui and BaZi are tools to help us gain control of our lives and maximize that potential.

Feng Shui is the science that helps us connect the polarity of our DNA to the polarity of our environment and our placement within the Universe.

CHAPTER 95

During the years in Arlington my life changed. I should say that my life *evolved* into having a fuller, richer meaning. Metaphysical Tools—Feng Shui, BaZi and I Ching—helped me to collect more strength and get better control over my surroundings to assert more influence where I felt it was needed. Understanding relationships from a Feng Shui perspective helped me to detach emotionally and take slights less personally. Life was about balance. Finally, I figured it out. My goal now was to create that balance in my life and in the lives of my family so we could weather the storms ahead without being destroyed in the process.

Arlington was a safe haven, a reprieve of sorts. I accumulated my strength, and felt better about life. I pursued Feng Shui as a student, a practitioner, a presenter and a speaker. For something fun to do, I worked as a Hillary Clinton impersonator after being discovered by a local talent company. It was a blast. "Hillary" attended parties, gave speeches, and handed out chocolate chip cookies with "Bill" and "secret service men" until "Monica" became more popular and eventually gave "Hillary" the rub. I couldn't help but take note of the sobering fact that my fun job as "Hillary" paid significantly more than working as a cytologist who made life-altering decisions.

Time in the States was rehabilitating for all of us. We reacquainted ourselves with family, made new friends, recharged our lives, renewed optimism and found the strength, both spiritual and physical, to continue our journey. I was grateful that the girls could enjoy this American experience while they were young. Arlington provided a wholesome standard the girls could drift back to when they needed to find their own normal. It gave them a sense of personal security to explore the world without fear; just as the farm in Iowa had done for me.

Sonya and Sasha were settled and happy. We had created lives for ourselves and would have been satisfied to stay in Arlington forever. I was totally engrossed with house plans, birth charts and Feng Shui factors that corresponded to the stars and the time we were born, never wanting to leave the lush, green neighborhood on Military Road. Such was not to be. There was much to be learned, and metaphysical sciences were just the beginning.

We lived in the States for about two years before Mike suggested that we take another overseas assignment. Dhaka, Bangladesh would probably not have been my first choice, but it was the opportunity that presented itself. I had regained my strength from the moves, the TB and other illnesses that had taken a toll on my health and could address this suggestion optimistically. The girls were older, too, which made them more resilient and better equipped to communicate their thoughts more clearly to me. Fortunately, there was no war and I was not pregnant.

Before studying Feng Shui and BaZi, I was the proverbial blade of grass blowing in the wind, following my husband as the dutiful wife. Now it was different. I analyzed our four charts to see if we could do well with another move to Southeast Asia. Indicators seemed positive. The description of Dhaka city sounded perilously close to that of Karachi, with the exception of one thing. Dhaka had water. *Lots and lots of water!*

After careful consideration, Sonya, Sasha and I rallied behind Mike's decision to move to Dhaka and enthusiastically threw our support behind his efforts to win the proposal. Bangladesh was supposed to be a moderate Islamic country where we could dress in western clothing. Unfortunately, Dhaka was grossly under developed just like Karachi. Once again we were instructed to take with us a year's supply of specialty items such as clothes, medications, food stuffs, tooth paste, shampoos, canned goods or whatever else we needed.

Part Three

DIVINITY

CHAPTER 96

We arrived in Dhaka on April Fools' Day 1999—an interesting detail that always amused me—and lived there for a little more than three years. By this time I was adamantly firm that the Feng Shui of our house was paramount to our housing selection. We had lived in seven houses during our thirteen-year marriage. By examining our Feng Shui and BaZi details from those years, I had sufficient evidence that our house affected our lives. Mike and I agreed that all housing decisions going forward would be mine.

We must have viewed fifty properties. All had a host of crazy, unsolvable issues—some not even habitable—before finding a lovely four-bedroom apartment. The room proportions were generous, the lay out was comfortable and the finishing was well done. Everything about the apartment was welcoming and pleasant and it was located within a few blocks of the school.

The apartment was on the fourth floor and felt safe. Guards were already provided as part of the building's security staff, which spared us the expense and trouble of hiring one ourselves. The apartment was modern and gorgeous: four thousand square feet of sensible living space that was pretty and charming with lovely details. I particularly liked looking over the tree tops from the balcony windows instead of viewing the squalor at street level. This was all good Feng Shui to me.

Negotiations between the owner, Assif, and the project manager, Bashir, were nail-biting as the price was used as an excuse for them to flex their massive egos. The rental price was well within our budget, but Bashir, who hadn't seen the apartment, determined that it wasn't worth the asking price. He fought relentlessly to extract the last rupiah to prove who was in charge. Bashir behaved far too recklessly at our expense, totally oblivious to the nuances of good housing. He said scary things like, "Don't worry. If this contract falls through, there will always be another."

He really didn't get it. Suitable housing in Dhaka, as far as I was concerned, was a rare find, and "no," there would *not* always be another apartment. The dramatic trophy houses that would have been tough to maintain, furnish, manage and finance didn't interest me. A pleasant home—according to my own criteria—was mandatory. We *lived* in our homes. There was no park to play baseball nor mall to hang out at. There was only a handful of good restaurants. All we had was our home for a retreat. Entertainment of every kind was done in the home, which was truly our sanctuary.

Mike suggested that I write Bashir a letter explaining why this particular choice was important. I did so, addressing Feng Shui nuances as well as the wasted resources spent on electricity to cool and light unusable spaces and curtains to decorate foyers with thirty-foot ceilings and floor to ceiling windows. There was no room in the budget to accommodate this excess nor for the furniture needed to fill the massive, nonsensical rooms that no one would occupy. Bashir would not have understood the "pretty" requirement so I didn't risk mentioning it.

Eventually, the housing contract was negotiated to the satisfaction of all parties and we lived happily in our apartment during the three years we resided in Dhaka. Assif had designed the apartment building according to Vastu principles, the Indian version of Feng Shui. After we got to know one another better, both Bashir and Assif became Feng Shui/BaZi advocates who asked me to do the charts for themselves and their families.

A Westerner's happiness in a third world country is directly attributable to home and staff. By the time we reached Dhaka I was getting the hang of how things worked in third world countries. We were fortunate to have hired three competent and loyal people to work for us during our stay in Dhaka. They helped to make life there enjoyable.

I couldn't help comparing Bangladesh to Pakistan: both had been part of India, both were Islamic, both had low literacy rates, both were impoverished and both were corrupt. Despite those similarities, there were differences, too.

The borders of East and West Pakistan were established in 1947 when Pakistan separated from India to settle religious disputes between the Muslims and the Hindus. Approximately ten million Muslims agreed to uproot their lives to move from India to Pakistan. East Pakistan was separated from West Pakistan—where the national government was based—by 1600 kilometers (1000 miles) of Indian territory, proving to be geographically awkward to govern. Therefore, East Pakistan (Bangladesh) was subjected to political discrimination and economic neglect at the hands of West Pakistan.

In 1970, something like 500,000 people were killed when the devastating Bhola Cyclone hit East Pakistan. Once again West Pakistan dragged its feet in delivering economic relief and medical assistance. This was the last straw. With backing from India and the Soviet Union, a war of liberation was fought. The Bengalis of East Pakistan declared their independence in 1971, and Bangladesh was born.

Culturally speaking, it's understandable to assert that there are many similarities between Pakistan, India and Bangladesh. After having travelled to all three countries and having lived in two of them, I can say that there are also significant, detectable differences between them. One is not like the other as could be supposed.

Bangladesh was a more docile country than Pakistan, and Dhaka city is a more docile city than Karachi city. I attributed this difference to Dhaka's location in the center of the great deltaic region of the Ganges and Brahmaputra Rivers. Bangladesh is surrounded by India and the Bay of Bengal and Dhaka is located in the center of Bangladesh. The Buriganga River is the main river that flows past Dhaka City. With the annual rainfall being approximately seventy-five inches, plus the existence of more rivers, the Balu, Turag, and Shitalakhya, it is no wonder that Bangladesh is plagued with catastrophic floods.

Water impacts people, cities, cultures and societies in a significant way. Bangladesh is example of my observation that impoverished countries with plenty of water are far better off than those without. Struggle for basic, human survival is at the crux of most of Bangladesh's *and* Pakistan's existence. Literacy rates,

corruption, religion and poverty are basically the same in both
countries, but the presence of Water in Bangladesh is a significant
distinction between them. Water seems to lessen desperation
and dissipate anger and frustration. In effect, the abundance of
water douses the "Fire" element, or the intense heat in Dhaka, and
helps to mitigate tension to create a gentler society than what we
experienced in Karachi.

Having said that, street scenes in Dhaka were not pleasant
either. We had heard about the Bangladeshi mafia organizations
that kidnapped children, brutalized them, and then put them on
the streets to beg. Based on what we saw, I believe this was true.
The deformities of the beggars did not appear to be caused by the
usual culprits: thalidomide, nutritional deficiencies, heat exposure,
dehydration and lack of oxygen. These deformities appeared to
be gross, brutal, malevolently inflicted crimes that occurred too
frequently to come from "natural" causes. Arms and legs were
missing or twisted into bizarre shapes, burnt or bludgeoned until
they hung limply. Feet were missing, hands were missing and
faces were scarred. Children carried children through heavy traffic,
weaving through cars for a single poisha (there are one hundred
poisha to a Taka and about eighty Taka equal one U.S. Dollar).

Just as in Karachi, we did not experience one public holiday
celebration or opportunity to participate with the larger group of
Bangladeshi society. Our social life centered around the school and
the American and International Clubs, which had pools, restaurants,
tennis courts and garden spaces with huge walls that provided
security and privacy from the masses. Most entertainment was done
in our homes where we shared cultural experiences with friends,
both western and Bangladeshi.

* * *

Dhaka is where Sasha picked up a tennis racquet and proclaimed,
"I'm going to be a pro player when I grow up." She was only in the
third grade so we wouldn't hold her to it, but we went out of our

way to foster this ambition on the off-chance that she was serious. She amazed me by organizing a work-out schedule for herself. Every free moment she had was spent at the American Club slamming balls against the practice wall until we found a coach to refine her technique.

A friend predicted that Sasha would reinvent herself in Dhaka, which is exactly what happened. She let her hair grow out again and decided to project a more feminine image. Gradually we could see this little girl emerge into her own unique, powerful identity.

While Sasha was finding herself, Sonya struggled with her own sort of growing pains. Sonya is a social person by nature who enjoys being liked. Even though she is a naturally bright child, she chose to dumb herself down. Her family and school work suddenly took a back seat to friends, whom she needed to be with constantly. I liked Sonya's friends, but most of them were given far more freedom than I was comfortable giving a fifth grader, a never-ending source of friction between us. Fortunately, she swam on the school team and became an excellent swimmer. The discipline of practice and swim meets gave Sonya a sense of achievement and provided the structure which helped to reinforce our family values.

After the house and kids were settled, I became an active member of the community where I participated at school board meetings, trying to improve everything from school lunches to academic programs to better behavior. On more than one occasion I stepped into the fray on these issues, particularly the school lunch debate, assuming mistakenly that if parents and educators were better informed about the harmful health effects of sodas and other junk foods, they would remove these items from the school. I was wrong. To my dismay, most of these folks, both parents and educators alike, disagreed with me. They spouted social concerns and choices, not acknowledging that healthy choices must be provided before they can be chosen. My guess is that these educated parents and school authorities either did not believe that these foods were harmful, were ignorant about nutrition or were addicted themselves to the junk and didn't want to be confronted. There was also an economic factor. Soda companies gave large donations to the schools, helping our authorities to turn a blind eye to an obvious problem at our children's expense.

Yi Wood Day Masters may seem placid and agreeable until their principles are challenged. In the old days, before studying BaZi, my Yi Wood tendency would have fought for principles and beliefs in a never-ending quest to do the right thing. I have since learned that people don't have the same principles as mine. The new me was learning to choose my battles, and restrain from taking on those where I wasn't wanted. Weighing my responsibilities to society, family and myself, and acting accordingly, has been a real dilemma for me. It's hard for me to understand how people can justify hurting themselves, their children and society. I always think that they can't be aware, because if they were aware they wouldn't be doing what they were doing and mistakenly assumed they needed me or someone like me to educate them. After several failed attempts to explain the harmful effects of soda at school board meetings, I recognized that the only real influence I had was on my own family, and focused on doing the best I could for them instead.

CHAPTER 97

Bangladesh provided the perfect opportunity for me to pursue my varied interests more fervently. I lectured on pearls to various women's clubs and international groups, but Feng Shui and BaZi remained my primary passion. I organized the study materials I had collected from various masters over the years to develop a very basic course on Yin and Yang theory. The course discussed universal connectivity, the state of constant change, and how balance is achieved by using the five elements: Fire, Earth, Metal, Water and Wood.

Mike had become a Feng Shui enthusiast by this time, anxious to delve deeper into the mechanics of Feng Shui beliefs. He compared the Yin Yang concept to a binary system that uses two symbols, as in the I Ching, another metaphysical science. In this case it would be Yin, referring to the negative, and Yang, referring to the positive. Balanced energy would be represented as yin yang yin yang yin yang yin yang, or negative positive negative positive negative positive negative positive.

Working with Feng Shui helped me to balance myself and improve it in our lives. I ran a continuous yin yang analysis through my mind of what was occurring around me and why, viewing every person, encounter and situation through a Feng Shui lens. It was during this period that I had the focus to address the monumental significance of the Yin Yang symbol, the Tao, and how it very simply and succinctly describes every aspect of life.

The classes I taught were small, about six to eight students. Our personal BaZi charts were used as case studies, and the charts of their family members were used to explain how one's elemental composition affects another's. We examined linkages between the various elements, how they affected the strength or weakness of a chart, and how the chart of one family member is related to the chart of another family member. Until one studies these comparisons at a personal level, it's difficult to make the connections.

I explained how every object, person and place has an energy field and how we are all connected through this energy. We are connected not only physically, but also through our thoughts and behavior—both for the good and the bad. Even when we are sitting alone on a mountaintop this universal energy grid connects us. Every aspect of our well-being is impacted by our unique elemental composition and its relationship to the change and flow that comes from our position within the space between Heaven and Earth at any given time. In one way or another we are all "linked." As a collective energy we affect our family, our community, our state, our country, our planet, and our universe. We are all connected. We are literally part of one another.

Depression among the ex-pats was commonplace in Dhaka. My students wanted to know why. I used the blind beggar who stood at our gate as an example of the chain reaction caused by thoughts.

He was a good-looking young man who was always neatly groomed. Despite his handicap he remained pleasant. Concave dips took the place of the slight roundness that normally appears when one has eyeballs. Flaps of skin—which did not open or close—covered his sockets. After some months of speculating on his condition, I asked Abdallah, our driver, what had happened to his eyes. Obligingly, Abdallah posed the question to the blind man who responded by pulling a newspaper clipping from his pocket, and then asked Abdallah to read it to me. It was the story of how he lost his sight.

According to the article, a father had promised a young man a rickshaw as dowry if he would marry his daughter. The young man agreed, but after two years of marriage the son-in-law still had not received his rickshaw. He confronted his father-in-law, asking him to honor their agreement, but the older man refused. That night, the father arranged to have his daughter out of the house so he and his son—the bride's brother—could pay a visit to the young husband. They broke into the house where the couple lived and while the son-in-law was sleeping, his wife's brother held him down while her father spooned out her husband's eyes.

Every day as the blind man walked to the street to beg, he was reminded of the incident that took his sight. This negative, yin thought is sent out through his energy field. Everyone who sees him and feels badly for him projects another Yin thought which is sent out and travels further. Imagine those thousands of Yin thought particles bumping into one another and increasing exponentially as one travels around Dhaka and sees one atrocity after another. There is mostly Yin Yin Yin Yin Yin Yin, when it should be Yin Yang Yin Yang Yin Yang. As we pick up those negative thought molecules from the energy fields around us, we become depressed.

"How can we change this or protect ourselves from being affected by the negative energy?" the students asked.

Initially we reviewed elemental relationships. I offered suggestions as to how each one could strengthen their own energy field by enhancing their "critical" element, the element that they needed the most to bring balance to their chart.

By this time I was combining spiritual suggestions with technical solutions to affect the energy vibration that was needed.

"We can lift a vibration by offering a prayer for the affirmed, asking that the energy from a negative experience is commuted to positive."

Another suggestion was to "change your thought about the person's circumstances offering compassion instead of pity. In other words, respect the path—the Tao—that the person has chosen." This doesn't preclude offering help to those who seek it. On the contrary. Compassionate thoughts show empathy and give grace and can help another to rise up from their plight as opposed to condemning them for it.

As a practical and general precaution I suggested that my students remove their shoes before entering a house to avoid bringing negative energy from the streets to inside their home.

CHAPTER 98

There is an eleven hour time difference between New York and Dhaka. When it is morning in the U.S., it is evening in Dhaka. On September 11, 2001, Mike was watching TV in the family room while I finished getting ready to go out to a party. Suddenly Mike shouted, "Germaine, oh my God, come look at this!"

I rushed to the family room. There was a news clip that showed smoke pouring from the World Trade Center. Mike and I looked at one another trying to figure out if this was real or some sort of crazy enactment. The TV news announcers came back with more bad news. The second tower had also been hit. We watched in total disbelief as a plane flew straight into the second tower. Could this possibly be true?

We no longer wanted to attend the party. The events were startling and confusing. We preferred to stay in with Sonya and Sasha. When I called to cancel, our hosts—who were American and Bangladeshi—encouraged us to attend, arguing that there was nothing we could do about the tragedy. The European Union ambassador would be there, which could be interesting.

About fifty people, who hailed from all over the world, had already arrived. Surprisingly, the general mood of the guests wasn't different from any other party we had attended in Dhaka. The United States had been attacked. Thousands of people had just been killed and no one seemed to be alarmed or even concerned. I was preoccupied by the broader terms of the attack, anxious to speak to the ambassador for his perspective. He expressed sorrow about the attack in New York City, but thought that the U.S. was vulnerable because of our foreign policy in the Middle East and we should have expected retaliation much sooner. Of course, I knew that he referred to the relationship the U.S. had with Israel vs. the Islamic world and knew, too, that the U.S. was resented by many allies for its unbalanced consumption of oil relative to the rest of the world, which further complicated a delicate political balance. The U.S. was accused of being at the center of political conflict in the Middle East in order to insure that our consumption could be perpetuated. Association implicated our allies by our greed and waste. They resented us and they resented what they considered to be our disregard for natural resources. Politically the situation was very complex, and I wouldn't engage in that debate. I am not saying that this wasn't a valid point, but the attack represented something greater than the debate on the consumption of natural resources and politics. To me, the attack on the New York City World Trade Center triggered a shift in course for humanity as we knew it.

We left the party with the EU first deputy and his wife. The elevator ride to the ground floor was painful. To make small talk in the cramped confines of the lift I said, "I wonder if school will be closed tomorrow."

"School closed?" the first deputy—who was from Belgium—sniffed, anxious to be confrontational with an American. "Why should school be closed? What does it matter?"

I was so taken aback by his callousness that I had no immediate response. Fortunately the elevator ride ended before I had a rebuttal.

Rumors regarding the attack began to emerge; a popular one being that Israel was behind them. It was less than twenty-four hours since the Twin Towers had been struck. There was no investigation that warranted these claims, only perceptions of who the culprit really was. No national nor international leader stood up to dissuade or contradict these beliefs, which further fueled the rumors.

Our driver, along with the other Muslim drivers in our apartment complex, also had an interesting reaction. They became more aggressive, on the verge of being rude. Before, they had always been very polite and respectful. When it became known that Osama bin Laden was behind the attacks, they were proud of him, feeling camaraderie and vindicated by the assault. Vindicated from whom was unclear. The U.S. was a generic representation of whomever it was who made them feel weak and oppressed. Centuries of feudal subjugation left them feeling helpless, angry and frustrated. They wanted to be just like America, but despised us at the same time. It was easier to blame an unapproachable giant than their elected leaders or themselves for their problems or the troubles in their society. No one was about to point fingers at their own corrupt government or an entire system of corruption that grew out of it.

Quickly it became frightening to live in Dhaka. Thousands of angry men congregated in mosques on Friday, their day of prayer, got a dose of vitriol and then marched en masse down the streets shouting hateful anti-American sentiments. Parents rushed to the international clubs to collect their children, fearing the mobs would arrive before they did.

One of the most frightening incidents occurred on a Friday after October 7, 2001, when the U.S., U.K., Australian and Afghan United Front militaries attacked Afghanistan in retaliation for the Taliban strike on the World Trade Center. I was upstairs in a beauty salon in Gulshan having a rather personal feminine treatment, clad only in the most minimal clothing and a sheet. A popular mosque was located directly across the street. Without warning, the technician bolted out of the room and down the stairs, frantically running to help the other technicians to lock the gates before the mob arrived. I looked out the window from my room to see throngs of men holding placards with hateful slogans, screaming and shouting and waving their fists. From my vantage point, which was a small round window above the treatment bed, I would have estimated two to three thousand men, but according to the newspaper estimate the next day, there were ten thousand protesters.

My point of reference for the word on the street was usually my driver. It's safe to say that his opinions reflected those of at least ninety-five percent of the other drivers in Dhaka and extended to the opinions of the guards and staff too. Abdallah didn't think it was right that the U.S. attacked Afghanistan. He believed that since we were the superpower we should behave in a more benevolent and forgiving manner, suggesting that the U.S. should dismiss the attack on September 11. It was an interesting shift of attitude from the days when he felt more potent.

CHAPTER 99

After having lived in Dhaka for about three and a half years, we moved in June 2002 to our next assignment, Bangkok, Thailand. The family was excited to move again, particularly to Thailand, where we had enjoyed several memorable vacations. Thailand represented a completely different way of life for us, a welcome change. Bangkok is a modern, highly developed city with modern amenities. There was no need to hire a large staff of household help nor shop for a year's worth of basic necessities. Bangkok is part of the twenty-first century, with every convenience that you would expect from a bustling, modern society. Thailand is a Buddhist country tolerant of an individual's personal style and self-expression. This significant religious difference translated into more freedom to dress, play and travel the way we liked.

Sonya was a freshman in high school and Sasha was entering seventh grade. They wanted to wear western clothes without me nagging them constantly about their shorts and spaghetti strap tops. Finally they could dress in the current styles without feeling disrespectful or culturally out of place.

The International School Bangkok (ISB), where the girls would attend classes, had a great reputation. It was strong academically and ranked high for both swimming and tennis within the Interscholastic Association for Southeast Asian Schools, IASAS, ISB's international conference.

Our new life in Bangkok was exciting, except that for weeks I hadn't been feeling well. I had already visited the British Embassy doctor before leaving Dhaka—the American Embassy clinic serviced only U.S. State Department personnel—but he couldn't find anything wrong with me.

Upon arriving in Bangkok I went to the Bumrungrad Hospital for tests and was diagnosed with pneumonia, which had been spreading like wildfire through the ex-pat community in Dhaka before we left. The doctors couldn't find anything else wrong with me. Still, there was this nagging pain in my right side, weakness, and light-headedness.

The pneumonia presented an inconvenience while we were house hunting, but I couldn't allow it to deter me from what needed to be done. Our household shipment was sent to the States before Mike accepted the assignment in Bangkok. We arrived in Thailand with only our clothes and no promise that our furniture would follow.

Under the circumstances, we looked for furnished housing in Nichida Thani, the community outside Bangkok where ISB is located. Personally, I preferred our apartment life-style, which was easier for me in many ways. The beautiful complex on the lake was enticing but the girls were tired of living in an apartment, desperate to enjoy once again a house with a yard. They also had an ulterior motive. They believed we would get a dog if we had a garden with immediate access to the outdoors. Against my better judgment we acquiesced to their begging and rented a house instead of the apartment. However, we did *not* get them a dog.

The house was very nice and located not too far from the school, but the Feng Shui was all wrong. There were two toilets and a stairwell in the center of the house. Our bedroom was located in the SW corner, which did not bode well for my health. Sasha worried that the career corner, an aspect of the eight-sided Bagua, would affect her tennis opportunities when she grew up. I voiced my concerns about the Feng Shui issues, but the girls begged me to fix them. I did the best I could to remediate the problems—which were way over my head.

My health condition worsened. The pain on my right side became excruciating and felt better only if I lay absolutely flat. I couldn't walk. Mike took me to the emergency room for x-rays to find that my colon had twisted into a knot. That wasn't all. Lo and behold, I had an extra three feet of colon! The surgeons wanted to operate immediately, but couldn't until the pneumonia cleared. Regardless, there was no way I could have surgery until we organized ourselves into our house. I needed to purchase bed linen and pillows, bicycles, dishes and pots and pans. The few pieces of furniture already in the house would have to suffice. I needed to hire a maid, buy groceries and register the girls for school. Without a car, I also needed to organize transportation.

I delayed surgery for two months, hoping to recover from the pneumonia, regain some strength and get our lives more settled. My doctors did not want me to risk flying back to the States for surgery in case I had another gut-knotting episode on the plane, so I agreed to have surgery at the Bumrungrad Hospital in Bangkok.

All sorts of frightening scenarios raced through my mind as I calculated the possibility of something going awry while I was unconscious. I was frightened for myself, but more frightened for my children, who I was leaving during a time when they needed me. Who would take care of them? No one knew us in Bangkok and no one knew how much I loved them. Yes, Mike was there to raise them, but they needed a fully functioning mother . . .

The doctors were impressive—all with lofty credentials. There wasn't anything I could do but ask God to be with me. I was a nervous wreck, wanting desperately to feel close to Mike before I was put under. Surely the pressure of his new job, my surgery, and financial concerns weighed on him. Even with the smorgasbord of issues to choose from, I still couldn't understand why Mike seemed so angry. For months he had been more preoccupied than usual, and became upset with the smallest things. Now I needed him to be sweet with me, to leave behind whatever was bothering him until after my operation and recovery.

The excess three feet of colon was removed, along with my appendix, during a surgery that lasted several hours. Surgeons in Asia are practical, and come from a less litigious society. They figured that since they were in the vicinity and able to remove my appendix easily, they would do so without permission—as a favor to me. It was fortunate that they did. The pathology report revealed a carcinoid tumor, an explanation for the mysterious symptoms that I'd had since Dhaka. Left unchecked, the result would have been fatal within six months.

It's interesting how life works out. Sometimes we must trust that things really do happen for a reason . . . a good reason. I reflected on the chances of such bizarre health conditions all at the same time, and circumstances that forced me to have surgery in Bangkok instead of the States or Dhaka. I recounted the countless nights of prayers when I begged God to help me live in order to raise my children. If I had returned to the States for surgery, most likely the surgeons would *not* have removed my appendix and I would *not* be writing this story. Also, if my gut had not been twisted into a knot, the appendix problem would have gone unnoticed.

I remained in the hospital for several weeks before I was sent home, but returned to the Bumrungrad a few weeks later after developing a blood clot in my leg. This stay was much easier than the first since I was able to visualize my family in a comfortable setting with mealtimes, friends and homework schedules. By this time I had met their teachers and their friends' mothers and I was feeling more secure with their happiness.

CHAPTER 100

Sonya and Sasha loved school. Sonya made both the swim team
and the soccer team, which kept her busy every minute with a bevy
of beautiful, international, well-grounded, sweet, overachievers who
had been living in Bangkok for many years. They took Sonya under
their wing and introduced her to a side of life that didn't exist in
Dhaka. There was something refreshing about the freedom to walk
from one friend's house to the next along wide streets lined with
towering palm trees without the leering gaze from a depraved male
society. The Thai environment brought the best out of Sonya, who
once again enjoyed working hard and becoming more independent.
Whatever she lost in Dhaka, she made up for in spades in Bangkok.

During the summer of her sophomore year, Sonya decided that
she did not want to be on the swim team any longer. She wanted to
dance. The school had an outstanding reputation in IASAS dance,
but it would be almost impossible for Sonya to make the varsity
team without having had years of formal training. Sonya was a
dancer at heart. She resonated to every beat, lost in her movements
as though she became the music. To me, it was natural that she
should *want* to become a dancer, but it is different to dance on stage
with a choreographed team than to dance for your adoring parents.
The coveted positions on the varsity team were met with fierce
competition from girls who had been training since kindergarten.

The summer of 2004, Sonya chose to remain in Bangkok,
filling the months with dance classes, instead of vacationing in the
States with Mike, Sasha and me. She pushed herself by organizing
a schedule that kept her practicing seven days a week. When school
resumed in the fall, she added her name to the list of girls who
confidently filled the roster.

Sonya's performance was an unexpected surprise.
The teacher—who had prepared both Sonya and me for
disappointment—was taken aback. She made her evaluations, but
for fairness, she asked each girl to write down the name of one
person, other than herself, who they felt deserved a position on the

varsity team. All of the girls—one hundred percent—wrote down Sonya's name. She made the final cut.

CHAPTER 101

Sasha and Abby found one another. The likelihood of that happening was zero to none as I couldn't imagine another person quite like Sasha. She remained petite and adorable, and might have looked feminine, but the tomboy in her is what guided her.

I have never seen two girls have so much fun together. They played endlessly, trolling creeks and abandoned buildings looking for geckos, birds' nests, snails, tadpoles, frogs, turtles . . . whatever they could find. They developed their own language— which drove me nuts—had the same sense of weird humor, imitated *Stuart* and his mother from Mad TV, and laughed at the same stupid jokes. They went fishing, hung out at the Nichada Club where we lived and rode their bicycles from one side of the community to the other. For a few days while Abby's bicycle was being repaired, Sasha gave Abby a ride home from school. Abby—who sat behind the seat— "helped" Sasha by taking one peddle. Together they pumped in rhythmic, synchronized movements shouting "cabbages" for the one peddle and "condoms" for the other, enjoying the provocative name of a popular restaurant in Bangkok, *Cabbages and Condoms*, which promoted safe sex.

Sasha continued playing tennis, developing into a worthy opponent. We hired a coach for her, Brett, an Australian fellow who had lived in Thailand for many years and spoke Thai fluently. He was familiar with the complexities of Thai society and how it related to the life of a tennis player, navigating us through the maze that allowed her to play competitively. She never lost sight of her goal to play professionally. Brett set out to take her there, relentlessly expecting one hundred percent devotion in one hundred degree heat.

Sasha continued to flourish. She had an identity as a tennis player, a purpose in life, and a best friend, Abby.

Mike threw himself into his work. He travelled to the Banks & Biddle office in downtown Bangkok, which meant a one hour commute from our house in easy traffic. He seemed to enjoy Bangkok and his colleagues, but showed little interest in socializing or getting to know the community beyond watching Sasha play tennis.

Mike's second hip began to bother him quite badly while we were living in Dhaka, but now the pain was excruciating. Thai doctors confirmed that his joints were bone on bone and that he needed a hip replacement soon. He planned to have the surgery in Bangkok instead of returning to the States, but his health insurance prohibited surgery outside of the United States. Mike's pain became intolerable; plans for his surgery were expedited. He'd have the hip replacement in Northern Virginia where he could stay with Victoria during his two months of recovery, and telecommute to work from her home.

Mike was worried that his position with Banks & Biddle was vulnerable since the company was laying people off. Even though he had been with the company for fifteen years he was concerned about taking extended leave, feeling as expendable as the next person.

Mike left for the States at the beginning of February for preliminary tests and to meet with doctors. I flew to Virginia on February 11, 2003 to be with him. Shamefully, the insurance company allowed only a one night stay in the hospital for hip replacement surgery, but the North American Blizzard of 2003 saved us. The blizzard spanned February 14th to February 19th, dropping thirty-six inches of snow in the D.C. area. The historic and record breaking conditions compelled the state authorities to issue a request for emergency driving only, which in turn pressured the insurance company to allow Mike a full week in the hospital until the roads were cleared. Victoria's SUV made trips to the hospital possible.

My poor darling. He was a strong man with robust health who relied on no one, generally upbeat with a positive attitude that moved mountains on the sheer faith that he could. It was difficult to see him like this, helpless in his silence after surgery. He held my hand, wanting nothing more than to have me sit with him while he slept.

Every day that followed I could see more improvement, and in no time at all he was working with the physical therapy nurses. His goal was to be released from the hospital as soon as possible so he could get back to work.

I left Sonya and Sasha in Thailand with the maid during my two week stay in the States, and made arrangements with friends to look in on them. I also made sure that their passports were easily accessible if they were needed. The second Bush Administration was threatening to strike Iraq, which made me apprehensive about being away. After our previous experiences in Pakistan and Dhaka, I worried about leaving the girls in a foreign country without parents, not being able to predict how the Thai population would respond to an attack on Iraq. Muslims are a minority in Thailand. Normally there were not radical Islamic uprisings, but I did not feel comfortable being away from the girls just the same.

I stayed with Mike for several days after he was released from the hospital so I could feel assured he could get around adequately with crutches and take a shower without my help. The physical therapy nurse made regular visits to the house, which made me feel more comfortable. Mike had already lifted his spirits and resumed his positive attitude, eager to show his boss that he had not slowed down. As much as I hated to leave Mike, I felt comfortable that Victoria would take excellent care of her Dad. I needed to get back to Thailand and the younger girls.

I left for the airport to catch a flight to Bangkok, fondly remembering Mike in his bedroom. He worked from his laptop computer, which was perched on a small, round, bedside table. My heart swelled with love and adoration for this man who, despite his surgery, worked tirelessly for his family to make our lives possible.

CHAPTER 102

More guests visited us in Bangkok during the first year of our stay then during our previous ten years in Asia. Finally, our friends and family felt comfortable visiting us. They had read about the beaches, the restaurants, the *wats* or temples and the mythical historic architecture that decorated the city like ornaments on a Christmas tree.

There was so much to do that it was hard to know where to begin. After the initial tours to the palace and the Jim Thompson museum, I introduced them to treasure hunting, an art form that is unsurpassed in Thailand. The difference between shopping and treasure hunting is that shopping is for things that one needs and expects to find, or that someone can pick up for you. Treasure hunting, however, requires a skilled and creative eye that knows how to convert a rusty canister into an exquisite table piece. Hunters and huntresses who embark on treasure hunting must have the physical stamina to endure the intense heat and crush of people and the negotiating savvy to get their price or walk away. Treasure hunting is a finely-tuned art form, not for the faint of heart. A successful huntress is an archaeologist who brushes dirt off abandoned artifacts and an artist who can design the perfect frame for that "crazy thing, the wall hanging!" They see gems in broken chards that become necklaces and dented copper rice bowls that become decorative pots.

We had lived in Bangkok for nearly a year, but with so much going on in our personal lives I hadn't recovered sufficiently nor did I have the time to explore the extraordinary antique shops, art galleries and beautiful Thai silk outlets that offered luxurious treasures for a pittance of what it cost in the States, normally available only through designers. There were wood carvers, designers and artists. There was celadon, blue and white pottery, green and white pottery and blue and white pottery with gold accents. There was benjaron, a fine, ornate ceramic that was typically Thai, and there were crystal glasses.

My favorite place to treasure hunt was at the Chatuchak

market, acres and acres of open air stalls and kiosks located near
Nichada Thani. The Chatuchak market offered every conceivable
thing under the sun. It is advertised as being open only on the
weekends, but the ladies of Nichada Thani preferred to go on Friday,
the same day that the locals went. The weekends were so crowded
that it was difficult to move from one stall to the next.

With our furniture back in the States, I was presented with
the perfect opportunity to practice treasure hunting.

CHAPTER 103

We loved Bangkok and we loved Nichada Thani. It could not be
denied, however, that our house had a problem. After having lived
in many houses during a relatively short period of time, we had
all become sensitized to unbalanced energy and felt "it," whatever
"it" was, and knew that the problem needed to be corrected. I was
confident that there were spiritualists in Bangkok who would be
able to help.

Our real estate agent was a seasoned professional with a list of
service providers for whatever was needed. Wan was a Thai woman
married to an ex-pat, who had lived overseas herself. Her life was
about as complex as ours. There was nothing that she found absurd
or unusual. After having worked with expatriates her entire career,
she became the go-to person for resourcing all sorts of specialists,
including spiritual specialists. Wan put us in contact with Chali who
had had success with a monk with "extraordinary gifts."

Chali was a Thai/French/English translator with a pearl fetish,
married to a Frenchman. She was infatuated with pearls just like me,
and designed exquisite South Sea pearl necklaces, earrings and rings.
Chali was a spiritual woman, in contact with a variety of spiritual
people for different reasons. After listening to my description of
the energy problem in our house, Chali contacted a monk who had
helped her in the past. He agreed to help us too, but first he needed
our birthdates and the address of our house.

Without ever having met us, the monk told Chali that our maid had performed black magic on us. "Oh brother, here we go again," I thought to myself. Then the monk said something interesting, "There is a statue located behind the house. It's buried deep in the ground and it wants to come out!"

"Wow, that was definitive," I thought excitedly, hoping that the monk had planned on producing a statue.

I wasn't in the least bit surprised to hear about the maid and her black magic, a phenomenon that has become the story of my life, literally! It was like having the Angela Lansbury, "Murder, She Wrote," syndrome. Everywhere she went a murder was committed. Everywhere I went, black magic was committed. The difference this time was that I now recognized black magic as a phantom fear. I had found God again and maintained His presence by filling my heart with His Light. This latest encounter was an opportunity to reject black magic, an empowering position to be in. The statue that "wanted to come out," however, was quite interesting.

A date was set when the monk would come to our house to remove the black magic and dig up the buried statue.

At this point we were neither overwhelmed nor frightened by the monk's diagnosis, just curious and hopeful that he would fix whatever was wrong. He described our maid and her circumstances in detail, down to the description of her brother who supposedly helped her with the deed. The monk said that her daughter was staying in the maid's quarters too. This was all true. We knew the maid had a brother but we had never met him. We also suspected that the maid's grown daughter and sometimes the daughter's boyfriend had been living in her quarters—which we didn't allow— but we were never able to catch them. And, a considerable amount of food was missing; too much to close a blind eye. I would have fired her much earlier if it hadn't been for my illnesses.

Coincidentally, our friends from Karachi, Joe and Rosella, were visiting us from Egypt. Joe was an avid amateur photographer who had chronicled the countries they had lived in over the years. They were with us now to film the episode with the monk, too.

They'd been with us through most of our paranormal experiences, but Joe remained a naysayer, wanting physical proof of all this other-world activity, if indeed there was any.

The monk had requested that incense, flowers, candles, fresh water and a sterling silver bowl be prepared for him. We gathered the items and anxiously awaited his arrival. I allowed Sasha to take the day off from school to witness this event, which I believed would be noteworthy, even if a statue wasn't produced.

Finally Wan and the monk arrived. The monk was a small, humble man with a round, happy face who wore street clothes. I had expected him to wear the traditional orange robe; Buddhist men typically become monks by the time they reach twenty, whether they remain a monk or not. But this monk had performed his monastic service in a monastery, then left for a civilian position in the government. He continued to practice this spirit specialty for which he was trained.

Wan translated the monk's instructions. First the silver bowl was filled with pure, spring water—not tap water. The monk lit the incense, organized the flowers on the table in front of him and kept some aside. He then lit the candles and said some prayers. After his prayers, he picked up a lit candle and dropped wax onto the water in the silver bowl. The wax collected on the water in a way that showed him the location of the buried statue. With many false starts because the candle kept burning out, he finally determined the exact location where he should look for the statue.

Before going to the garden the monk wanted to cleanse Mike and me of the maid's curse. He asked us to lie on the floor. Without fanfare, and with large, sweeping movements he said some prayers over us. In a few minutes he was finished. We proceeded to the garden.

The monk sent me to find someone to dig a hole. I ran from one house to the next looking for a gardener who could help until I found two gardeners who returned home with me, not knowing how big this hole was going to be and how much help we needed. We followed the monk to the back of the house, stopping abruptly when he did. Wan carried the remaining flowers and water with her. The monk dipped his fingers into the silver bowl with water and sprinkled the site that was to be dug up.

I checked the earth's condition, suspicious to know if we were being set up in some way. No, the ground did not have freshly turned soil. The earth was hard. Grass grew on top. There was no evidence whatsoever that it had been previously disturbed. The monk instructed the gardeners to start digging.

The ground came up one shovel at a time as we waited in anticipation. Deeper and deeper the hole became until it was about three feet in depth and three feet wide. The monk looked into the hole, but didn't see anything. He seemed puzzled. Then, he pulled out what looked like a pocketknife and held it to his ear. He continued to hold this object to his ear while looking upwards towards the sky as if he was consulting with someone from above. After receiving a message, the monk instructed the gardeners to dig deeper until he shouted, "Stop!"

At this point the monk looked into the hole again. He sprinkled a bit more of the blessed water into the deepening cavity and had further communication with his pocketknife and the sky. The message this time was, "the statue has already come out. It is located in the clumps of ground. Look carefully for it."

We all fell to the ground frantically, sifting through the clumps of turned earth until the gardener found one clump that did not crumble. We watched expectantly as he broke away the black soil that clung to an object, and were as surprised as anyone when he uncovered a perfectly formed gold statue. I was expecting something equivocal, and would have been satisfied, but there was nothing equivocal about this statue. It was perfectly detailed, and perfectly preserved.

"Where had the statue come from and why was it there?" we asked.

Presumably, the statue had come from a spirit house. Most Thai homes have a spirit house, sitting on a pedestal in their garden. The spirits in these little houses are provided fresh fruits and daily

Monk using candles and water to determine the location of the statue.

Monk at the site in the backyard where the statue was buried.

Golden statue that was found.

offerings of incense and flowers. Thais believe that if the gods are neglected, they will become angry and remove their protection from the home.

The spirit house on our property had been abandoned and bulldozed underground when the Nichada community was developed. Now the spirit's statue wanted to come out.

The monk tossed the remaining flowers in the hole before the gardeners returned the dirt, and then wrapped the statue in a silk cloth to take with him. The statue was not ours to keep and could have been problematic for us if we had done so. The monk took the statue so it could be placed in a wat, or temple, where the spirit could be on its way.

Joe was satisfied, finally, with his tangible "proof."

There was a physical relief when the statue was released. It was like a cloud had been lifted. In retrospect, I believe that the spirit knew I was sensitive to inter-dimensional activity and would somehow find a way to have it released. Strange as it may sound, I believe that this spirit interceded with contract negotiations on our behalf, insuring that our offer on this house was accepted over another, which was stronger than ours.

The spirit may have been released, but the Feng Shui of the house remained an issue. There was no way to correct the internal, structural issues without renovation so we made plans to move at the end of the rental term.

CHAPTER 104

Mike's company sold the contract management side of their business, and Mike's position became one of the casualties along with many others. Fortunately, the Singapore office hired him, thwarting what could have been a devastating financial blow. We remained in Bangkok where Mike telecommuted when necessary with Singapore, but usually he worked from the local office in Bangkok.

It was our good fortune that an apartment on the tenth floor of the Lakeshore apartment building was available when the rental contract on our house ended. This was the same building Mike and I wanted to move into a year earlier, before giving in to the wishes of Sonya and Sasha. The apartment was one of only two apartments that had a 1500 square foot garden wrapped around the entire length of the unit. There were two wings to the building that jutted out onto Nichada Thani Lake, and there was only one apartment on each floor of each wing. The living room, dining room and master bedroom had wall to wall sliding glass doors that opened onto the balcony where huge planters with fully grown trees graced our view. A lovely walkway from the elevator to our unit grew exotic plantings.

The kitchen and large family room became the meeting place for all the girls' friends. They gathered in the evening to bake chocolate chip cookies while watching *Friends* and doing their homework. Many nights the dance team showed up to practice routines in the dining room.

Our first year in Bangkok was a struggle with surgeries and illness. Now I looked forward to settling-in and making this gorgeous home on the tenth floor even more exquisite.

This was the best time of our overseas travels. We each developed our unique interests wrapped in the comfort of loveliness, safety and security.

Our belongings were eventually shipped from the States and we could enjoy all our things under one roof for the first time in our lives. There were now two shipping containers. One container had been in storage since we left Arlington in 1999 and a second container that had been sent to the States from Dhaka a year earlier. This was our opportunity to refurbish sofas, reframe paintings and assess what was worth keeping or what could be thrown away.

Our shipment arrived shortly before Christmas. I enjoyed seeing the old relics and treasures from our past, and integrating the various colors and styles we collected over the years into an harmonious look that flowed from one room to the next. By this time I had learned my way around the markets and artisans and realized that there wasn't anything that couldn't be created with a little imagination. This was Bangkok, after all, where everything was possible. Little by little our home was transformed into our own private paradise high above the treetops, overlooking water that reflected lights from the surrounding community.

CHAPTER 105

On December 26, 2004, the day after Christmas, we were enjoying our holiday together at home. Sonya had originally planned to vacation with her friend's family on their boat in Phuket, but the trip was cancelled when they received unexpected house guests.

And then it struck, a force so powerful that waves reverberated in the lake below us. The club pool reacted to the same force, spilling water into the businesses that surrounded it and sending tables and chairs crashing into one another.

It wasn't long before we heard news of the tsunami that hit Phuket, swallowing people, buildings, trees and islands. In horror we contacted everyone we knew who was vacationing in the islands over Christmas break, counting our blessings that Sonya was with us. Responses drizzled in one by one until our inventory of friends had been accounted for. In an attempt to be helpful, Sonya, Sasha and I went to a relief organization to offer assistance.

The Thais were completely organized. They had the necessary merchandise, phone trees, administrative systems and volunteers in place without skipping a beat. Quite honestly, we were in their way, but they were too polite to say so. We didn't speak the language and it was obvious to me that we were slowing them down. After an hour or two of letting us pack food stuffs and medical supplies and letting us feel good about ourselves we were thanked for our help.

Sumon, a friend of ours from Dhaka, made his way to Bangkok after the tsunami. He had been staying in Phuket with his friends for the holiday when on the morning of December 26 they went to the beach. As Sumon describes it, "the sand was so hot that we couldn't lie on it." They decided instead to take mopeds into town to get out of the heat and returned to their hotel room to get wallets and passports in order to rent the cycles. They left town minutes before the tsunami hit, scrambling to stay in front of the waves that chased them. When the tidal wave subsided, Sumon and his friends returned to their hotel only to find that the ocean had swallowed the seaside village where they had been staying. Fortunately, Sumon had his passport and wallet and was able to catch a flight to Bangkok to visit us while it was still possible. He told his story of horror, reflecting on the chance that his life had been spared. Hundreds of thousands of people had died that day Why not he?

CHAPTER 106

Our time in Bangkok ended far too abruptly when Mike was offered—and accepted—a five year assignment in Jakarta, Indonesia, which we hoped would end our nomadic lifestyle for a while and create stability until Sonya graduated from college. Unfortunately, the contract began during the second semester of Sonya's junior year in high school. It was heartbreaking news for Sonya but there was little that could be done. We weighed the possibility of keeping her in Thailand with friends versus taking her with us to Jakarta, but no real solution emerged that would have been acceptable.

Sonya excelled at ISB and was devastated by the prospect of moving again, especially now. She desperately tried to reason with us, "I created a life for myself here. I am somebody."

It was true. Sonya had become a brilliant dance performer and 4.0 student while taking a demanding IB (International Baccalaureate) curriculum. She was named All-Tournament and Most Valuable Player during their IASAS soccer finals and was one of the dance team's most alluring talents. She grieved at the thought of leaving her friends and starting over again during her senior year, anticipating senior parties and graduation trips without them. "No one will even know me in Jakarta," she cried, and there would be no historical memory in the yearbook with classmates who scribbled "most likely to succeed," or "best dressed," or "most beautiful." She saw all her hard earned work to "leave her mark" evaporate in front of her.

Personally, I did not want to leave Bangkok either. I knew how Sonya felt and my heart broke for her. It wasn't easy to ask her to leave a home and friends that she loved, but I did believe that it was in Sonya's best interests to live with us in Jakarta as opposed to leaving her with friends in Bangkok. I hoped she would appreciate this decision over time.

Sasha would begin school in Jakarta as a sophomore and was fine with moving. She was sad about leaving friends, particularly Abby, but was not as social as Sonya. She preferred being at home with me when she wasn't digging for worms, catching lizards or playing tennis. The move for her was not as traumatic.

The school tennis team in Bangkok was excellent, but the one in Jakarta was just as good. Sasha's international life would not be affected. She could make new friends and still visit old friends at the IASAS tournaments before graduating in three years from an academically outstanding school. The girls finished their semester in Bangkok. Our move was set for mid-June, shortly after the school year ended.

Indonesia was completely different from the other Islamic countries where we had lived. It was considered to be a moderate *and* progressive Islamic country. Jakarta was clean and modern and claimed a high literacy rate. There was no grotesque poverty like in Pakistan and Bangladesh and the city was charming and lovely with wide boulevards and beautiful flowers.

Culturally speaking, the country is unique and fascinating, a delicious, tropical paradise that consists of approximately eighteen thousand islands. There are about three hundred ethnic groups who speak over five hundred languages and dialects. Indonesia is the biggest Islamic nation in the world, claiming that ninety percent of its occupants are Muslim. The island of Bali is predominantly Hindu, however, and the Indonesian constitution—which does not claim an official state religion—allows other religions to practice freely.

Mike stayed in a hotel in Jakarta while the girls finished the school year in Thailand. He loved Jakarta and didn't seem to mind being there alone. He was in his element and feeling more confident, relaxed and in control of his life. After many years of moving around, Mike anticipated financial consistency while the girls finished high school and Sonya would have completed four years of university. Finally he could relax a bit.

I visited Mike in Jakarta several times during those months, both to see him and to find suitable housing for us. Finally we found "the" house. I loved the iron gate with the flowered trellis in the driveway. More flowered trellises separated the front of the house from the back, where the pool and flower garden were located. The main level had a beautiful, modern kitchen with an oven large enough to roast a turkey and all the rooms were generously proportioned with ample closet space.

The floor plan was exquisite: balanced and tasteful, and "pretty" doesn't begin to describe it. I couldn't believe that we would actually live in this gorgeous house. There were Feng Shui glitches, but I hoped that the overall balance of the house would compensate for them. If it didn't, better houses were not to be found, which made it easy to justify this choice.

We signed a lease and scheduled our move-in date for the beginning of May. I flew to Jakarta the day our shipment arrived, only to be detained at the airport for six hours. When I finally arrived at our new home, I was astounded to see that the shipment boxes had already been inventoried. Somehow Mike had managed to avoid every other move-in and move-out day during our entire marriage, so I was surprised that he was managing quite well without me, and actually enjoying the opportunity to take charge of this move.

My goal was to have everything unpacked, arranged and set up before summer vacation, when I hoped to console Sonya with a beautiful bedroom and invitation to her friends to visit during IASAS events. Jakarta International School, JIS, was in the same conference as ISB so there were many opportunties for the girls to see their friends. They wanted a house. This was it.

I worked non-stop to finish organizing our new home, determined to create an inviting space so the girls could enjoy their summer without being involved in the unpacking mess where boxes are everywhere and it takes days, if not weeks to sort everything out. At this point we had made four moves in four years, not including temporary housing. It was important to me that this move be as easy as possible for the girls so they could jump right in and enjoy their new home and make friends without anxiety.

I hired workers to help me hang paintings in the foyer over the weekend. Mike was home, but remained in the bedroom to read and nap while the workers were there. It wasn't unusual for him to avoid this process.

It was quiet for the longest time. After an hour or so I could hear the low, mellow strains of Barry White, one of our favorite singers, coming from the bedroom. I was so excited to hear the pulsating rhythms that I got down from the ladder and went to the bedroom to listen to the music with him. To my total surprise, I opened the door to see Mike dancing by himself. Certainly this *was* out of character. Oh well, I danced with him.

Little did I know that this would be our last dance together.

I returned to Bangkok satisfied that our new home in Jakarta was set up beautifully for our girls' arrival. Indeed, it was a sad farewell to Thailand. We had been accepted by this sweet country openly; free to explore her beaches, indulge in her art, eat her delicious food, and visit the historic treasures that were carved from the inner warmth and generosity of her people. We were not just saying good-bye to friends. We were saying good-bye to a country where we felt at home.

CHAPTER 107

Sonya, Sasha and I arrived in Jakarta to find Mike waiting for us.

Sonya was sullen and teary eyed, still angry that we pulled her away from her happiness. The new house and life that awaited her were small consolation for what she left behind, but she perked up slightly upon seeing her room with the brightly colored bougainvillea that spilled over her balcony railing, and the upstairs lounge area that she, too, imagined would become every bit as memorable as the kitchen in Bangkok. Maybe there was hope to console her after all.

The next day we visited Jakarta International School where Sonya and Sasha were introduced to their counselors and met some of their classmates. It came as no surprise that they knew some JIS classmates through IASAS tournaments in soccer, tennis, swimming and dance, already familiar with a large international crowd of students from all over Asia.

Sonya's senior year, which should have been easy for her academically, became a nightmare. In theory, the IB program is synchronized so that students who travel through the international system can leave one school and pick up at the next school without disruption. This was not the reality. Sonya had the burden of making up three semesters of IB Math—along with her regular curriculum—in one semester to complete the necessary credits for graduation.

Another disappointment: the dance program at JIS was very much inferior to the training at ISB. Sonya mourned the abrupt end to her dancing career, but bravely pulled herself together. Instead of dance, Sonya shifted her interest to the JIS drama program, which was outstanding. Although she did not join the dance team, she did choreograph the dance routines for the school musical, *Bye Bye Birdie*, and played a small, but significant role as Gloria Rasputin to the absolute delight of those who watched her. Despite her many challenges, Sonya set out once again to "make her mark."

It was easier for Sasha to adjust. She only needed a tennis court and someone to play with. If she couldn't find a partner, the wall would suffice. The rest would fall into place.

CHAPTER 108

Eventually Sonya made new friends and Sasha found a club where she could play tennis. Sasha made new friends, too, but nothing could fill her longing for a pet. She begged for a pet. Again I resisted, remembering the many painful experiences with pets that had all been heart-wrenching disasters. I simply couldn't commit to bringing another pet into our unpredictable lives under any circumstances.

Sasha whined all the way to her tennis practice, "Why can't we just have a cat?" she pleaded.

We had tried every pet imaginable including birds, dogs, turtles, geckoes, fish and even snails, but one after the other they died hideous, unspeakable deaths. I vowed to never have a pet again.

But there she was, snoozing contentedly under our car in the driveway. She was an orange and yellow tabby, presumably a street cat, who felt comfortable with people just the same. She was the seductress of the neighborhood, and certainly a beauty, who had a male following drooling after her. The girls decided to call her "Mrs. Cooper" after the TV character in the program called Orange County.

Mrs. Cooper was a lovely cat with a sweet temperament. We promised one another that she would remain an outdoor cat and we would not take her out of Jakarta. Agreed. We would feed her, love her, take care of her, but we would not allow her to sleep in the house or to live with us. Agreed.

It wasn't long after meeting Mrs. Cooper that she gave birth to five absolutely beautiful kittens. She delivered them in the garden where we had the pleasure of watching her from the window as she stealthily moved them from one hiding place to the next. It was so interesting to see her do cat things, witnessing her strategies and imagining what must have been going through her mind as she did them.

At two months old we gave the kittens away. Mrs. Cooper showed signs of fatigue, anxious for her kittens to become independent. Just the same, she seemed to be aware of their absence, which made me sad and doubt what I had done.

Our intent was to have Mrs. Cooper spayed before she could get pregnant again, but we were too late. By the time we took her to the vet, she was already weeks along. The vet refused to do surgery.

A month later Mrs. Cooper was bulging; her pleasant disposition was wearing thin. She usually stayed in the staff quarters off the kitchen—an open air space—where we kept food for her. Her whines became incessant and she paced anxiously back and forth. It was pretty obvious that she was getting ready to deliver.

The whole experience brought back memories of Dhaka and our precious dog, Lily, who gave birth to six puppies in our bedroom closet. She was less than a year old herself when the puppies were born, but developed Parvovirus before the pups were two months old. There was no medicine available in Dhaka to treat her, and the numerous IV drips she endured after losing most of her blood and body fluids did not help her to recover. The vet advised us to put her down, hoping to spare the pups from catching the virus too.

Sonya and I took Lily to the vet in Dhaka to receive the lethal injection; one of the saddest days of my life. Lily had faced her previous experiences with needles and syringes without flinching and without a whimper. She was an obedient dog who didn't need us to keep her still, but we held her in our arms just the same, to comfort ourselves as much as to comfort her. Lily looked at us with big sad eyes while licking the tears that streamed down our faces. The doctor inserted the final injection. Sonya and I repeated to Lily over and over that we loved her and asked her to forgive us. She looked at us innocently while licking our tears, doing her best to make us feel better until her body went limp.

The pain was coming back to me now as Mrs. Cooper's pleas for help persisted. She begged to come inside, looking at me as if she expected me to understand and come to her assistance.

"If Mrs. Cooper delivered inside, she and the kittens would become domesticated," I feared. "After that there was no way they would be able to fend for themselves on the street. If we keep them, they'll die."

Her crying became more aggressive. She was intent on coming into the house, pleading to do so. Finally, I gave in to her cries, bringing her to the family room next to the master bedroom. She was still not content. Now she wanted to go inside our bedroom. This is where I drew the line. I was not going to have another litter of anything born in our bedroom.

The girls and I made a bed for her outside our family room door with crates and laid towels for coziness. We hoped she would be satisfied but she wasn't. After waiting several hours for her to deliver, this was the best I could offer.

In the morning, Mrs. Cooper had indeed given birth to another litter, but this was not a happy delivery like it was the first time. It had rained in the middle of the night. Mrs. Cooper was very sad. The bed we provided would have protected her from the rain, but that wasn't it. After we went inside, she moved to a nest she had made in the bushes. She and her babies had become drenched. Mrs. Cooper had asked for our help, and we abandoned her. She had come to count on us. She entrusted us with her love, putting herself and her babies in our hands. She had expectations created from our actions. Mrs. Cooper believed the love she felt was mutual and never could have believed we would send her out during her hour of need.

After that night, Mrs. Cooper was never the same. She seemed to have lost her mind, bitter from emotional rejection. She never again displayed the sweet disposition she had had when we found her under our car. She hung around the house for food, but never again came to us for snuggling or to wrap herself around our ankles. Our relationship had been forever broken. She lost her trust in us and had given up on hope. Mrs. Cooper no longer had the strength or mind to care for her baby kittens like she had for the first litter. Eventually the kittens all died, and after that she neglected herself too, allowing her golden coat to become matted and dirty.

I deeply regret the choice I made that night. Mrs. Cooper reminded me of the power of love, and how the absence of love from someone you've come to expect reciprocation is soul destroying. I was reminded, too, that love makes all the difference in a life, whether that life is a human, a plant or a cat.

CHAPTER 109

I started writing this story in 1996, and had planned to end it with our return from Manila. Sasha begged me to finish, asking me repeatedly why I couldn't bring it to an end. I wasn't looking for an excuse, but always had one. Either we were moving and I had the settling in and packing out chores to focus on—which was true—or we had switched computers and I couldn't get my material from one computer to the next—which was also true. To eliminate that particular obstacle, Sasha very sweetly took that chore onto herself by transferring my manuscript from the old computer onto the new one. I hated to disappoint her with the writer's block that paralyzed my thoughts. Finally I realized the problem. I didn't know how the story ended. What was this elusive caravan and how would I identify it if I found it?

I thought the story was about Feng Shui and the peace I discovered when I could understand and explain how balance could be achieved by harmonizing the five elements of Fire, Earth, Metal, Water and Wood and how *the polarity of this energy connected to the polarity of our DNA, and that this was the connection between all things.* I was relieved to discover a tool that could help me balance my own energy and get more control of my life. I understood that it was I who had created the spiritual vacuum where darkness entered when I denounced God out of intellectual arrogance, and I was responsible for the spiritual imbalance that set in motion other energy imbalances.

As we moved from one Asian country to the next the story got longer with the new experiences. My perspective changed with more maturity after I had the occasion to live out metaphysical and spiritual theories that I had read about. Somewhere in all of this I became aware that the real story lies within the life that is created as a result of recognizing an imbalance, whether it be body, mind or soul, and then taking steps towards creating something new.

For many years I felt that Mike and I valued our marriage differently. Since we came to live in Indonesia, that disparity was hurled at me. It's interesting how children and the rigors of life can distract one from reality long enough to help us plow through the demands of living. Then the children become adults and the life that was created as husband and wife stares you down. Mike and I were finally at a place in our lives where we could coast. Life could have been easier.

For many months Mike had been irritable and had become more aggressive in the way he dealt with me. He went out of his way to make problems my "fault," pushing me away. Suddenly there were problems where there need not be one. Mike didn't ask me for a divorce formally. I believe his strategy was to make life miserable enough so that ultimately I would decide to leave. He "forgot" our twentieth wedding anniversary and my birthday and asked me not to attend his birthday celebration at the office; one that I had arranged.

Actions do speak louder than words. Somewhere in all of those years together he decided to wrap it up. Finish it off. Somehow our life together became over. Was he tired of being married? Was he bored? Was he restless? Was there someone else? Our broken marriage was nothing new except that it was *my* broken marriage, *my* life, and the pain was unique to me.

There were many long absences in our marriage that presented *me* with loneliness as much as it did him. I preserved the vows we took to love, honor and respect one another. Now I asked myself, were the thousands of kisses we shared real? If only I remembered them, did they really exist? After knowing Mike for twenty-five years, my heart still leapt with excitement when I heard his voice on the phone. What did he feel?

If the love and effort I brought to our twenty-year marriage didn't matter, did the life we created as husband and wife? What did it say about our children?

Notre Dame's Theodore Hesburgh says it best: "The most important thing a father can do for his children is to love their mother."

I couldn't help ask myself, "if I wasn't loved, were our children? What value was placed on them?"

The signs were there but I ignored them. Mike had never been able to defend our marriage to himself nor to his mother and daughter. A style of operating was to put other people, places, work or circumstances between us, escaping from any possibility of emotional intimacy. What was there to fear? Getting to know the deepest part of me would have exposed only deeper love that I had for him. Was he trying to keep me from knowing him?

How does a person assess his own worth against the worth of many? How and why does one arrive at life-altering decisions that affect everything that is held near and dear? I was at a loss to understand and at a loss to help myself.

CHAPTER 110

My friend, Nicole, listened quietly to my marital woes. We had become friends in Bangkok, but Nicole and her family left Thailand suddenly after her husband had miraculously survived a brain aneurism. I thought quite sadly that I had lost touch with her. It was a wonderful surprise the day we re-discovered one another at school. Nicole and her family had recently moved to Jakarta, too, where her husband, Dean, had been appointed general manager of an international company.

Nicole gave me a book, *Remembering Wholeness*, by Carol Tuttle, which helped me through this difficult part of my life. I loved the way Tuttle practiced metaphysics, remembering Christ as our teacher. Tuttle explains spirituality in a way that is beautiful and useful without being dogmatic. Her book celebrates spirituality as the dynamic life force intrinsic to who we are, and teaches us how to anchor this life force to help us affect change.

One of Tuttle's techniques is the "Energy Circle", where you draw an imaginary circle on the floor and take hands full of imaginary self-esteem, new car or whatever it is that you want to attract, and throw it into the circle. (*Remembering Wholeness*, p. 321)

When it was clear to me that Mike had already left our marriage emotionally I was beside myself with grief. Weakness overpowered me, making it difficult to throw imaginary anything into an energy circle. Instead, I visualized the process until I got my strength back and could stand up while performing the technique. I did my best to clear my head and focus on myself as opposed to anger, blame and self-doubt. I recognized that I needed to heal first before making any life altering decisions that would affect the entire family.

I did my best to analyze the various aspects of my potential future without Mike and what the outcome could possibly be. Was there any hope of saving this marriage? I drifted into fantasies where I was back in Mike's heart, melted deep inside of him, feeding him long, lingering kisses. Then I saw my reflection in the mirror.

I was fifty-five years old, and intimately familiar with the aging process. I had already given the best of myself to Mike and it wasn't enough. Would I ever meet a man to sincerely love me? It isn't that I was physically unattractive, especially for someone in my age group, but it was hard to believe in myself or see myself as attractive after having given one hundred percent of my life . . . my love . . . for over twenty years and then have it rejected. It's interesting how marriage—or at least love—suspends age. You can live with someone for decades and not notice that your spouse has grown older. Somehow love is timeless and we become ageless to one another—and even to ourselves—if there is love.

The magical wonder of my love had been shattered. Any delusions I may have had about myself and about our marriage came to a screeching halt. Reality screamed at me, *"I don't love you anymore!!"*

I read Tuttle's Chapter 48, *It's About Healing Families, Not*

Breaking Them Up, over and over again and took to heart every word she wrote. I agreed with her and believed that marriages were sacred and the family unit should be preserved at all cost. Unfortunately, it takes two to make a marriage and it isn't possible to force another person to love you. How could I stay in a marriage that had become soul-destroying from neglect, criticism and rejection? Where would I get the energy to bless myself?

CHAPTER 111

I reached out to Patricia, a spiritualist who had become my friend. Victoria introduced me to Patricia in 1996 when she was moving into the D.C. area from New York City and was looking for an apartment. Victoria was her real estate agent. I was drawn to Patricia's peace and serenity. She was a beautiful, unpretentious woman who was wiser than anyone I had ever met. Patricia was the one who had suggested that Sasha would re-invent herself in Dhaka and who told me that Feng Shui would become my life's purpose. She also said that I would eventually return to real estate. In 1999, before leaving Virginia for Dhaka, she told me that I would write books, "but that will come." She wasn't surprised to hear from me, nor to hear about my sadness, knowing that this day would come, too. She had tried to prepare me for it over the years by encouraging me to start various businesses—which she did once again—anticipating that I would need a new career. I had sourced several interesting product lines from the countries where we had lived. Now she advised me to organize meetings with department stores and suppliers before leaving Jakarta, so I could visit them over summer vacation and begin an import/export business.

"Take your mind off of Mike and put it on yourself. You need your energy," she admonished. "Take one step at a time, Germaine."

It was the end of May. All four of us would be returning to the States shortly for the summer. There was so much to do before we left.

CHAPTER 112

I bought books on relationships and marriages, hoping that Mike would show some interest in them. It was no use. I wished I could let it go, and hoped that Mike would come to his senses and make a sincere attempt at reconciliation.

If I left Jakarta, I would have nowhere to live. No car. No career. No retirement. Our furniture was all in Jakarta. How could I care for Sasha who would still be in high school? Except for the three year stint in Arlington, we had not lived in the States for seventeen years. The world had changed completely since then. I didn't know how to navigate the new electronic skill set and gadgets that replaced the work place environment that I had come from. I had become functionally obsolete and had no clue what kind of job I could possibly get. The prospect of starting over at my age was physically, mentally and emotionally overwhelming.

Sonya graduated from Jakarta International School that May, presumably unaware of the drama that was unfolding in her home. I decided not to say anything to her until college applications, boyfriend problems and a permanent move to the States were behind her.

She labored under the realization that she would never again live in Asia, her home for seventeen years. Soon she would be returning to the United States as an American citizen, frightened for the first time in her life that she would not be accepted. She had no friends in Washington, D.C., no driver's license, no car and she didn't understand the transportation system. There was no apparent avenue to pursue her dream to become an actress. She was impatient to become an actress *now*, completely stressed by not knowing how to make that happen.

Sonya completed high school with honors and had made her mark on the school in Jakarta in the same way she did in Bangkok. She was well-liked and successful academically, and as an athlete, dancer and actress. She decided to stay out of college for her first semester until she could get her bearings in the States. She sought to become independent and decided to work first while she learned her way around.

Sonya considered the possibilities of giving dancing or swimming lessons to make some income, like she did in Bangkok and Jakarta, but instead she accepted a job as a cashier at Balducci's grocery store, where she found out that she knew nothing about food other than that she enjoyed eating it. She was embarrassed not to know the names of common American produce like endives, or how to process a credit card. She might have been born in the United States, but was an awkward American who didn't know popular culture references and didn't understand the American sense of humor. Because she was an American there were expectations that she know Americana and have an intimate familiarity with nuance.

Culturally speaking, this move was the most difficult for her.

CHAPTER 113

After a brief summer vacation in Minnesota with my family, Mike and Sasha returned to Jakarta. Mike resumed work and Sasha started school, which began mid-August. Sonya and I stayed with Victoria during this time so that I could help Sonya get settled, visit my mother in Iowa, and begin my marketing endeavors as Patricia had suggested.

I called Patricia from Iowa to update her on my pathetic saga, anxious for her comfort and advice. She firmly and adamantly commanded, "Germaine, you move back to the States, *now!*"

"But Patricia," I objected, "I'm so tired. I don't know where I'll get the energy."

I had never known Patricia as an aggressive person, but I was such a slobbering mess of emotion that she needed to take a firm position so that I would hear the message. "Germaine, you find the energy, and get back to the States, _now_!!" she repeated emphatically.

We had only been in Jakarta for a year. Another move. I had put so much effort into that house. Sasha had already begun school.

Where would I go? What would I do?

"Oh God, my God, please help me. Please God, I beg you. Please help me. Please present circumstances under which I can return to the States easily."

The next morning there was a call from Mike. The U.S. Government was looking for money to finance their war effort. His contract had been cancelled. We had one month to vacate our house and move our things to the States.

The answer to my prayer was quick and conclusive. Was I imagining things? For a brief moment I indulged in "what if" scenarios, but quickly gave them up. I had no idea how this was all going to turn out, but had no doubt that this news came as a direct response to my prayer from the night before. God would not present this gift if there was not a plan. Patricia's soothing words floated around me, "Take one step at a time, Germaine."

Back and forth discussions with both Mike and Sasha yielded a definitive decision. Mike thought he could get work on other contracts in Jakarta until he found something permanent. Sasha, ever the pragmatic, felt that this would be a good time for her to return to the States for her tennis. She did not have a U.S. national ranking, and felt she needed to be stateside if she were to either get a college scholarship or go pro. She was ready to return.

Things moved quickly. I got Sasha enrolled into a Virginia high school before it started in September and found housing for us before returning to Jakarta to pack up our house. Once again, Victoria graciously extended her home to Sonya and Sasha during this two week period.

Sasha started her junior year for a second time without blinking an eye. She seemed completely oblivious to having given up half her summer for a few extra weeks of school in Jakarta before taking a flight to the States on her sixteenth birthday, only to start the school year all over again.

Our routine started immediately once I returned from Jakarta and we moved into our house. Sasha began school at seven o'clock in the morning. I picked her up from school in the afternoon with a meal in the car so that she could eat it on the way to the metro station, catch a train where she travelled one and a half hours to Maryland to practice tennis for three hours, and then make the return trip home. Sometimes I'd pick her up from the train at nine o'clock in the evening in freezing temperatures. She did as much of her homework on the train that she could, but most nights she was up until the wee hours to finish. The next day we'd do it all again.

CHAPTER 114

Mike returned from Asia shortly before Christmas 2006. The house was completely arranged and Christmas decorations were up. We found a nice, cozy townhouse; not the gorgeous home we left in Jakarta, but it was special in its own way. I was anxious to have everything set up beautifully for Mike and to have the family back together. Now that we were in the States, I hoped things would be different for Mike and me.

Our cozy Christmas setting ended sooner than anticipated when Mike accepted a nine month assignment in Jakarta. I knew that he would have taken work anywhere in order to meet his financial obligations to the family. I was grateful to him for that, but he would be in Jakarta without us for nine months. What hope would there be to reunite as husband and wife?

During those months I simmered in misery, unable to get beyond my hurt and anger. In my loneliness I relived every disappointment, pain and slight that had been dealt me over the past twenty-five years. Had I offered too many opinions that irritated him? Had I become too assertive or was I making too many decisions without his consult? The months we spent apart during our marriage were as lonely for me as they were for him, but I kept the memory of his touch alive and longed for his return. Had he not done the same? Did he not find me attractive any longer?

During most of our marriage I was kept busy organizing, nursing and struggling. I did my best to make life comfortable for my family. I was the facilitator, the one who made things pretty. I did my best to make our transitions easy; that didn't mean that our moves and our circumstances *were* easy. I worked hard at what I did while trying to remain pleasant. I loved my "job" because I loved my family and shouldered our emotional lives because I was cast in that position, not because I wanted to be there alone.

Good old Germaine. Always there to be counted on. Always the nice person. Mike didn't have any real complaint against me except that he didn't love me anymore. I felt like a worn out, beaten down shaggy old family pet, loveable and pathetic at the same time.

What about this life we created as husband and wife? Did this life just disappear? Did it evaporate into the ether from whence it came? What was real about our marriage? Was it so meaningless that it should be given up and forgotten? I felt discredited, minimized and undervalued as a wife, woman and mother.

The nine months that Mike was away provided invaluable time for assessing myself critically and examining my life realistically. Mike was the wage earner, I was everything else. My job was to hold every other aspect of our lives together, including our relationship. I finally realized that Mike had been pushing us apart since the day we were married, and I kept holding us together. There had always been a cool detachment that prevented intimacy between us, and a perceived disinterest in our lives. Always an excuse. Usually work. I let it go, doubling up my efforts with the girls so they wouldn't notice his lack of involvement. At this point I was too exhausted to fight any longer. All my energy went to him and our kids, making sure their lives continued as seamlessly as possible amidst the chaos. It wasn't just a role that I assumed for myself, it was expected of me. I gave of myself whole-heartedly and wouldn't have given less under any circumstances. Regardless, I didn't expect this contribution to be taken for granted.

At some point I realized that no matter what I did, it would never be enough. Certainly I wasn't a perfect wife, but I gave a hundred percent despite my imperfections. Over the years I had become an expert on Michael Avila, excited to know every detail about his existence. While I was enamored with the man who filled my most intimate thoughts, he kept me at a distance.

Yes, it was time to let him go. It was time to end the emotional disparity between us. There was no use hanging on any longer. For what? To be reminded that I wasn't worthy of his love? Years of fighting for recognition and self-worth had taken its toll. Every time I felt the need to justify myself I was stripped of just a little bit more of the energy that kept me whole.

"What is love?" I forced myself to ask.

"It's a noun, it's a verb and it's an adjective. It's an emotion, it's an action and it's a qualifier."

"Fine, but what *is* love?" I asked myself again.

Love is a vibration, it is energy. Love is healing. We become prettier, more lovely and happier when we are in love. Love is strength, kindness, vulnerability and generosity. There are actions, considerations and expectations that are associated with love which in one way or another we have all experienced. Love is nurturing. Love can come from a parent, a relative, a friend, a romantic interest, a plant, the garden, sunshine, a person who says "thank you" or smiles at you, the water or a pet. I think it is safe to say that everyone feels better when in the presence of love. In the absence of love, we become less of ourselves.

Love carries a frequency that is nourishing. Love is food for the soul. A simple, loving thought can raise one's energy and one's vibration. If I was going to heal, I needed to change my thoughts about Mike and our relationship. I needed to overcome the anger and bitterness that dragged me down.

I learned that negative, Yin, vibrations that come from sadness can be heightened to a Yang state by giving thanks so that a positive outcome can result. This is what I tried to focus on, realizing that I would never be able to heal from the bitterness unless I raised my vibration to get beyond the debilitating feelings that I held against my husband. The slights and pain I felt were real, but I had a choice. I could *choose* to remember the hurts, or I could *choose* to remember the things for which I was grateful.

In the beginning—and in my anger—I didn't want to remember anything good about Mike. I wanted to hold him responsible for the negative parts of our lives without giving him credit for the good. As I practiced giving thanks, however, it got easier.

With a practiced, steady resolve I first offered gratitude for our children. They were awesome, making me proud as a mother and humble as the privileged person who raised them. Whether I wanted to admit it or not, they were Mike's children, too, and together we shared the gene pool that contributed to their talents. He was also an advocate of their further study and advancement, and supported their achievements. Without his dedicated hard work and financial support, their classes and coaches would not have been possible.

Then I was grateful for the house we lived in. "He owed it to us," I held onto resentfully, but was willing to concede that "he provided it whether he owed it to us or not." Next, I listed all the things the house provided: shelter, proximity to school, heat, electricity, toilet, even the stove that heated our meals.

I was catching onto this technique, beginning to feel much better about things. I lay there with my eyes closed, going over our twenty some years together as if it were a life review. We had opportunities to do and see things that most people will only read about. I gave thanks for those things too, even the bad experiences. I learned from those experiences and they enriched me personally.

Slowly I perked up from the depression that clouded my soul and draped every moment of my life with gratitude. When I got into the car, filled it up with gas, put on my coat, bought a coffee, it was always *thank you, thank you, thank you.* I even thanked Mike for the time he was away because it gave me an opportunity to pull myself together again. Expressing gratitude helped me to find my way back to love.

When the girls became upset with our changed family dynamic, I asked them to be grateful for the interesting life they led and all the wonderful qualities about their father so they, too, could experience and remember the healing power of gratitude and lift their vibrations in the process.

Expressing thanks was the process that forced me to see things from another perspective. Counting the things I was grateful for brought balance to the equation. When this balance was asserted it became easier to forgive him and to forgive myself. The process helped me to rise above the bitterness and commute the pain into a loving feeling, which is both a divine and scientific phenomenon.

As Alexander Pope said, "To err is human and to forgive divine."

Gratitude and forgiveness literally raise one's frequency, which in turn raises our physical vibration. By shifting our emotions to a higher frequency, we can see things more clearly, feel more empowered, heal the pain and attract a more positive outcome to ourselves. We can literally shift a Yin condition of sadness, anger and depression to a Yang condition of Love, all by expressing gratitude.

Suddenly I saw Mike differently. He was the same man he always had been, the same man I fell in love with. "If only I could have relived the difficult moments from this perspective," I thought sadly. At some point I realized that our broken marriage wasn't about me. It was about him and whatever—however—he needed to proceed with his future.

At a cosmic level, Mike provided opportunities to help me learn about myself. There was no better person than he to father my children and provide the international experiences that helped me discover Feng Shui, Balance, and the power of Good over Evil. Our experiences helped me to find God again.

There was no better person than Mike to help me balance my energy. He provided the perfect storm that forced me to fight for myself –for us – to make myself stronger, to assert to the Universe that I was worthy. He provoked me to find the courage I needed to stand up and defend myself against selfish patterns of behavior that denounce a woman's right—the family's right—to worthiness, and he gave me the opportunity to be a self-respecting role model for our children in the same way my mother was for me. Positive thinking is really about seeing the positive—the opportunity—in a negative situation as opposed to deluding oneself that something is positive when it isn't. Positive thinking has a Yang vibration.

Some spiritualists believe that we design our next life ourselves in the Cosmic space between dimensions and lifetimes. In this space we are filled with God's love and can choose our parents, spouses, siblings, children, relatives, friends and enemies without fear or judgment. In this space we assign these dear ones the roles they will play to help us learn the lessons we need to raise our vibration in this lifetime and we choose the experiences that will provide opportunities for spiritual growth. In other words, the people who commit the most grievous offenses against us on Earth are the souls we most trust and love in the spiritual realm. We agree to have these trusted souls partner with us in these reincarnations and play the painful roles because spiritually they act out of love. They are in service.

It was difficult to consider this perspective in the beginning, but now I believe it to be true.

CHAPTER 115

I did not want to leave the marriage as enemies and throw away the most cherished love of my life. I prayed non-stop, begging God to mend our hearts, enable us to negotiate our settlement amicably and continue our lives thinking fondly of one another. We owed it to ourselves and to our children to treat one another with respect, and to pass on the highest vibration possible to them.

Spiritually, I offered my forgiveness and asked for his. God was with us during this time, applying salve to the wounds between us and helping us to work together to forge an amicable and healing relationship during the divorce proceedings.

The reality of love is allowance. Its application is surrender. Allowing the "is"—what is to be. It was time for me to let Mike go, to surrender to him and set him free. Finally I was able to let him go because I loved him, not because of malice.

The last verses of Begin the Beguine wafted around me:

> *What moments divine, what rapture serene,*
> *Till clouds came along to disperse the joys we had tasted.*
> *And now when I hear people curse the chance that was wasted,*
> *I know but too well what they mean;*
>
> *So don't let them begin the beguine*
> *Let the love that was once a fire remain an ember;*
> *Let it sleep like the dead desire I only remember*
> *When they begin the beguine.*
>
> *Oh yes, let them begin the beguine, make them play*
> *Till the stars that were there before return above you,*
> *Till you whisper to me once more,*
> *Darling, I love you!*
> *And we suddenly know what Heaven we're in,*
> *When they begin the beguine!*
> *When they begin the beguine!*

Had the song that accompanied our first dance together as husband and wife also foretold the end of our marriage?

CHAPTER 116

What I had overlooked in this process is self-love. Once I had let Mike go, I could look at myself without the oppressive feelings of anger and bitterness that trapped me into a lower vibration. It was one thing to climb back from bitterness and let Mike go from a position of love, but the real test to my spiritual resolve was to love myself *despite* twenty years of thoughts, kisses, tenderness, dreams and effort that had been rejected.

It's difficult to be self-loving in the face of rejection, but somehow I had to find a way back to the embrace of my own love. It was much easier to do this after forgiving Mike, and making peace within myself.

Self-love cannot be taken away or denied. It isn't exclusive to being rich, poor, black, white, tall or short. Self-love springs equality. Self-love is empowerment. It stems from a thought about how you feel about yourself. Self-love is an entitlement. It is your birth-rite because you come from God who is pure love.

Of course, it's easier to love yourself when affirmed by another, but what if that doesn't happen? It doesn't mean that we are less entitled to receive love. It doesn't mean that we are less deserving of love.

I had been the beneficiary of many forms of love in my lifetime, beginning with my mother and a nurturing life on the farm in Iowa. This was the womb, the nutritive sac that fed my vibration for all those years. When I set out in search of the caravan, I rejected my mother's love, sunshine, fields of corn and simplicity. I had forsaken my true wealth for that of science, sophistication and people I held in a higher regard, and in the process I lost sight of my spiritual connection and self-worth. I allowed the precious foundation I had inherited to dwindle to "rock bottom" because of the choices I had made. I didn't have to do things the way I did. If I had been more mature, I could have left home to seek my fame and fortune without hurting my mother—without taking her energy—if I had done so in love.

There are many reflections and pieces of my life that have since come together. My mother, the epitome of love and generosity, chose to remain with her husband because of the love and commitment she had for her family. Certainly she spent days and nights praying to her angelic beings for help in the same way that I did, and certainly she received strength from them. As a child, I questioned her choices, which I had no right to do. My mother was on her own path, her Tao. Christ teaches, "Judge not, lest you be judged yourself." Her choices were different from mine because of her limited education and eleven children.

It took courage to remain secluded on a farm in a relationship with my father who did not show her the care and consideration she deserved. My mother did not choose the path of least resistance when she evaluated her options. I don't think she said, "What is best for me?" I believe she said, "What is best for my children?" She believed in the sanctity of marriage and family. She valued the connection she had to her eleven children and believed our lives would be better for us if she held the marriage together. She weighed our lives more strongly against the neglect, pain and loneliness she endured on the farm. She allowed her love to transcend the hardships, and in so doing she preserved the higher vibration for her children and their children. This is her legacy.

Love is a Yang vibration. Love is organic to our existence. Love is alkaline. It is a natural feeling; a state of being that life naturally seeks. Love is balance. Love is achievable with a single thought. Love is Divine.

Finally, the caravan I had been searching had a face and a name and it was called *Self-Love,* the kind of love that comes from a spiritual link to God, the link that connects us to one another. It's that resource that comes from understanding that we must assume our worthiness *because* we come from God's love.

CHAPTER 117

The last time I spoke to Patricia she said that she was taking her family to their country home where she could be alone with her children for a while and "take care of family business." She was somewhat hurried, about to walk out the door, and suggested that I call her in a few months. What seemed to be an eternity passed before I tried to call her again. I was anxious to speak to my dear friend, eager to thank her for helping me through an excruciating time of my life.

I dialed her number, expecting either her voice or the

answering machine. Instead, there was the voice of another woman providing the details for her memorial service that was to be held the following week.

I was Patricia's last phone call before she secluded herself with her family and succumbed to her final battle against breast cancer. She had given me her precious, vital energy to find my own, showing me that indeed I was stronger than I thought.

How does one repay the love and generosity of that action? How can I thank her, except to do my best to emulate her selfless example?

My search for the caravan has ended. I am grateful for the opportunities and experiences that helped me to discover Feng Shui and BaZi, and how I can best use these sciences to help me align my DNA with Earth's magnetic energy, to one another, and to All That Is. I am most grateful for my mother who was my original imprint of Love; the imprint that connects me to the God within.

I have come to realize that the *simple* answer to every question is always Balance and the *simple* cure to every imbalance is always Love.

Why did the tsunami happen? Because the collective energy of humanity had become out of balance with Earth's energy. Why did 9/11 happen? Because civilization is out of balance. Why did our marriage run amok? Because our feelings for one another were out of balance.

What is the *simple* solution to every one of these issues? Raise the vibration, which is done by projecting Love onto the problem.

CHAPTER 118

As this story ends and the next one begins, I am filled with optimism and excitement. I am sixty-two years old as I write the final pages of this story. I have had the opportunity to express my heart-felt, loving sentiments to my mother, and I remain close to my siblings. I have glorious children, wonderful friends, and abundant opportunities. My current BaZi cycle is filled with Water and my spiritual guides are with me, pointing me towards an exciting new career and rewarding adventures.

In closing, I thank you for taking me into your home and sharing my journey, and I offer you my blessing:

May your life be nurtured with parents who keep your feet warm and stomach full and who fill a reservoir with grace for you and your children. May your journey be invigorated with wind in your sails and water to carry you. May your Divinity spread into the ethers of the Universe and guide your experiences to dreams fulfilled and best wishes from others.

Let us lift the vibration of the planet by committing our connection to loving one another. Let our connection—our Divine Light—be a beacon of strength and hope for one another and for our children. Let this be our legacy.

Love, *Balance* and Divinity always ~

Germaine

Afterword

Sonya and Sasha have received the spiritual tools to help them process their experiences and their parents' divorce, and to help them develop and understand their spiritual lives.

Sonya graduated from a film and theatre conservatory in New York City where she works as an actress, waiting to land the role where she will once again "make her mark."

Sasha graduated from high school in Virginia and went on to play college tennis. After graduation she hit the pro-circuit as she had planned.

Victoria is the mother of two beautiful children and has a successful real estate practice in the D.C. area.

Mike continues his international travels with his work and has become a role model for fathers and ex-husbands. He has been a steadfast support to our children and me, and someone whose counsel I continue to admire and respect.

I work as a real estate agent in the D.C. area, where I contribute my passion and knowledge of housing to people who are buying or selling their home. I practice Feng Shui and BaZi by helping others create their sacred space. My Yi Wood energy is well nurtured in the lush environment of the D.C. area and ready to demonstrate that the world would be a better place to live if designers, architects, builders and homebuyers practiced Feng Shui principles. I advocate green technologies, and strive to maintain balance with high quality, unprocessed organic foods, practicing metaphysical sciences and reaffirming my connection to you, to God and to the Universe.

Works Cited

Melody. "P." *Love Is in the Earth: A Kaleidoscope of Crystals.*
Wheatridge: Earth-Love House, 1991. 308. Print.

Tuttle, Carol. *Remembering Wholeness: A Personal Handbook for
Thriving in the 21st Century.* Seattle, WA: Elton-Wolf Pub., 2002.
Print.

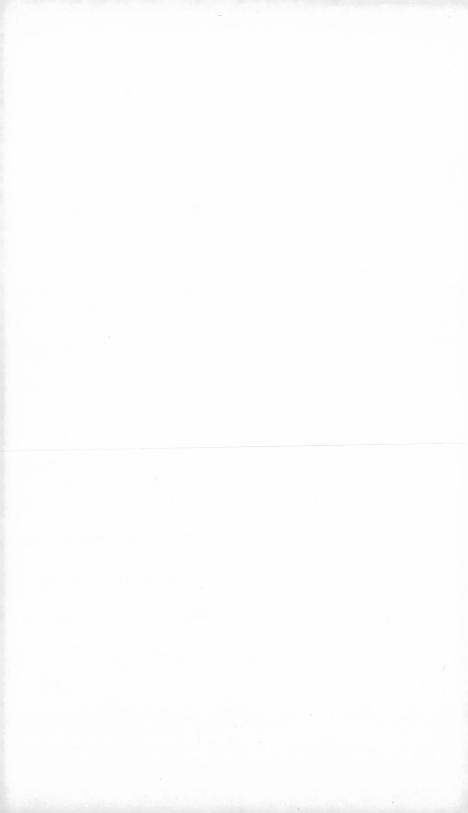